KLEIN'S LAST QUARTERLY ECONOMETRIC MODEL OF THE UNITED STATES

Wharton Quarterly Econometric Model:
Mark 10

ECONOMETRICS IN THE INFORMATION AGE: THEORY AND PRACTICE OF MEASUREMENT

ISSN: 2010-1236

Series Editors: Lawrence Klein & Kanta Marwah

This series of publication focuses on frontier econometric methods and applications with special reference to the analysis of modern economic and social problems and phenomena. Development of global financial markets, use of longitudinal data to study household consumption behavior and health-care management, evaluation of policy effectiveness, macro-econometric modeling and big-data analysis are important topics that fit well in this series. Research that blends new statistical techniques with conventional and large economic data will be given priority.

Published

Vol. 6 *Klein's Last Quarterly Econometric Model of the United States: Wharton Quarterly Econometric Model: Mark 10*
by Lawrence R Klein
edited by Shinichi Ichimura, Soshichi Kinoshita & Mitsuo Yamada

Vol. 5 *Econometric Modeling of Japan and Asia-Pacific Economies*
edited by Soshichi Kinoshita

Vol. 4 *Macroeconometric Modeling of Japan*
edited by Shinichi Ichimura & Lawrence R Klein

Vol. 3 *Econometric Modeling of China*
edited by Lawrence R Klein & Shinichi Ichimura

Vol. 2 *Interregional Input-output Analysis of the Chinese Economy*
edited by Shinichi Ichimura & Hui-Jiong Wang

Vol. 1 *Selected Papers of Lawrence R Klein: Theoretical Reflections and Econometric Applications*
edited by Kanta Marwah

Econometrics in the Information Age:
Theory and Practice of Measurement – Vol. 6

Series Editors: Lawrence Klein & Kanta Marwah

KLEIN'S LAST QUARTERLY ECONOMETRIC MODEL OF THE UNITED STATES

Wharton Quarterly Econometric Model: Mark 10

Editors

Shinichi Ichimura
Kyoto University, Japan

Soshichi Kinoshita
Nagoya University, Japan

Mitsuo Yamada
Chukyo University, Japan

World Scientific

NEW JERSEY • LONDON • SINGAPORE • BEIJING • SHANGHAI • HONG KONG • TAIPEI • CHENNAI

Published by

World Scientific Publishing Co. Pte. Ltd.
5 Toh Tuck Link, Singapore 596224
USA office: 27 Warren Street, Suite 401-402, Hackensack, NJ 07601
UK office: 57 Shelton Street, Covent Garden, London WC2H 9HE

Library of Congress Cataloging-in-Publication Data
Names: Klein, Lawrence R. (Lawrence Robert), 1920-2013, author. |
Ichimura, Shinichi, 1925– , editors.
Title: Klein's last quarterly econometric model of the United States : Wharton Quarterly Econometric Model: Mark 10 / Lawrence R. Klein ; edited by Shinichi Ichimura [and two others].
Description: New Jersey : World Scientific, [2018] | Series: Econometrics in the information age: theory and practice of measurement ; Volume 6
Identifiers: LCCN 2017043812 | ISBN 9789813229938 (hc : alk. paper)
Subjects: LCSH: United States--Economic conditions--Econometric models.
Classification: LCC HC106.8 .K595 2018 | DDC 330.973001/5195--dc23
LC record available at https://lccn.loc.gov/2017043812

British Library Cataloguing-in-Publication Data
A catalogue record for this book is available from the British Library.

For any available supplementary material, please visit
http://www.worldscientific.com/worldscibooks/10.1142/10708#t=suppl

Desk Editors: Herbert Moses/Lum Pui Yee

Typeset by Stallion Press
Email: enquiries@stallionpress.com

Printed in Singapore

Preface

This book presents Professor Lawrence R. Klein and his group's last quarterly econometric model of the United States economy that they have produced at the University of Pennsylvania. It was widely used as the *WEFA Econometric Model Mark 10*, which we adopted as the subtitle of the book. This is, however, the edited version of the original documents. We wish to explain why and how we prepared this book as Klein's Last Quarterly Econometric Model.

When Prof L. R. Klein passed away in October, 2013, he was actively engaged in several research projects such as "current quarter models" with high frequency data, global LINK modeling, and the quarterly econometric modeling of the US economy, while advising many private and government econometricians in the US and abroad. This book focuses on the last field of his research. He was based at the Wharton School or the Department of Economics, the University of Pennsylvania, where he not only taught but also trained many outstanding econometricians in modeling among graduate students and visiting scholars from all over the world. His typical way of guiding them year after year was to get them improve an already available core model of the US economy for better analysis, forecast and policy prescription under the contemporary conditions.

Since 1961, an economic research unit (ERU) for that purpose had been set up at the Wharton School. It was reorganized in 1969 as the Wharton Econometric Forecasting Association Inc. (WEFA) in order to offer the application services of modeling to the outside client companies. The core models were called WEFA Model and successively named as Mark III, IV, etc. It reached Mark 9 in the late 1980s and Mark 10 in 1992.

In the 1970s and 1980s, there were several attempts to merge the WEFA, DRI (Data Resource Inc.) initially established by Harvard Professor Otto Eckstein (1927–1981) and several others to create a large information-consulting company. In 1987, WEFA and Chase Econometrics were merged, keeping the name WEFA. In 2001, WEFA and DRI were merged with a wider scope and renamed Global Insight. In 2008, it was acquired by IHS (Information Handling Service Inc.). Hence, the copyright of all WEFA models belongs to IHS now. We are told that their experts continued updating the WEFA type forecast up to 2007, but IHS no longer relies on WEFA models.

In March 2014, Ichimura took an initiative to bring together several economists in Tokyo and talked on the way of leaving the footprints of Prof. L. R. Klein for econometric modeling in some form of publication. This group constituted Prof. Shuntaro Shishido (International University of Japan), Prof. Soshichi Kinoshita (Nagoya University), Prof. Yoshihisa Inada (Konan University), Prof. Hidehiko Ichimura (University of Tokyo), and Dr. Yuzo Kumasaka (IT Economy Co., New York). They discussed their experiences and observations on the circumstances mentioned above and tried to find the best way to achieve the objectives. It was agreed that the ideal would be to identify and publish the latest WEFA model when Prof. Klein's leadership was clear. As all agreed, Mark 10 would perhaps be the one crystallizing many contributions of participating students and visitors yet containing predominantly Klein's ideas, advices, and suggestions.

Ichimura thereafter started contacting many of Klein's former students and friends. The target was to find the complete reports or documents of WEFA Model Mark 10. Soon, many working papers of earlier WEFA models and McCarthy report reached us, but Mark 10 report was not found even at the University of Pennsylvania library. What rescued us from disappointment was an email from Dr. Belabush Nariman of IHS notifying his discovery of a document of Mark 10. After Kinoshita's close examination, however, it missed an overview section containing some flowcharts and other materials of the model. We immediately asked B. Nariman and others further to search some missing parts. Despite their efforts, none was found. Ichimura asked Lawrie Klein's younger students again for further efforts. About 6 months later, Dr. Michael G. Papaioannou at IMF found the missing sections at home in Greece during his 2015 summer vacation. It was exactly the missing link to complete the whole document of Mark 10. We were so happy to start our editorial work.

First of all, we requested Dr. B. Nariman of IHS to take steps to use their copyright to produce a book: *Klein's Last quarterly Econometric model of the US economy*, by L. R. Klein as the author and edited by S. Ichimura, S. Kinoshita, and M. Yamada. After a while, Ichimura received an approval by email from IHS with the provision that their copyright is clearly mentioned somewhere in the book.

The original document of Mark 10 needed a fair amount of reediting for the general reader because it was basically a manual for the experts ready to operate the model by computers. Besides, it did not repeat some expositions given in earlier reports. Needless to say, the reader of this book would have no chance to read old reports or some important research findings on older WEFA models. That is why we quoted in Chapter 6 as an example, some multiplier simulation results with Mark 9. Thus, the whole parts of the original reports had to be majorly reorganized. It took us about 2 years after the first Tokyo meeting to reach the stage of completing the first draft of reedited WEFA Model Mark 10.

Soon after completing it, however, Kinoshita discovered that the WEFA published in 1998 a newer version Mark 11: "The WEFA U.S. macro model with chain-weighted GDP" by Daniel Bachman, Peter Jaquette, Kurt Karl, and Pasquale Rocco in the *Journal of Economic and Social Measurement*, vol. 24, no. 2 (pp. 143–154). We examined carefully the contents of the article and discussed, among editors and friends who were at the University of Pennsylvania in the mid-90s, how to deal with it. Our conclusion was that Mark 10 would still be Klein's Last Quarterly Model with his clear leadership so that we need not change the substance up to Chapter 6. We decided, however, to ask Dr. Bachman, chief of four authors to write an addendum as Appendices and explain what kind of new problems WEFA tackled. The most serious problem was the change of US National Income and Product Account (NIPA) by BEA. The second was their use of "the Error Correction Method" rather than Almon type of polynomial equation methods for estimation.

Our sincere hope is, as all Prof. Klein's students wish, for this book to remain as his imperishable footprints for 70 some years of academic career and also a token of our common memories of WEFA modeling efforts at the University of Pennsylvania. The book will certainly record the footprints of many of Klein's disciples when they were young.

We wish to thank many friends in the United States, Japan and others for their advice and cooperation in making this publication possible. We hope that this book will please not only old students and colleagues but also younger students who have heard so much of Klein models but have not yet seen the latest in complete and printed form. We wholeheartedly admire the WEFA Model Mark 10 as a monumental achievement of American econometricians along with Prof. L. R. Klein.

A telephone call on May 14 informed us suddenly that Soshichi Kinoshita passed away. We deeply regret that we could not share the happy day of seeing the completed Klein's Last Model book with him. It was indeed he who prepared the first draft of this book out of the many miscellaneous working documents. Very soon, however, we will see the last Klein model will become available to all econometricians all over the world. How pleased Kinoshita will be!

Shinichi Ichimura
Soshichi Kinoshita
Mitsuo Yamada
April 25, 2017

About Lawrence R. Klein (1920–2013)

In 1930, the Econometrics Society was founded to create and establish *Econometrics* as a new genre in economics. Despite significant contributions by leading professionals such as Ragner Frisch, Jan Tinbergen and others, no real breakthrough had taken place until in 1939 when a group of selected economists assembled at the Cowles Commission at the University of Chicago and began working intensively to develop new statistical methods and mathematical models. It was this group that in 1944 young Lawrence R. Klein was thrown into by his teacher Paul A. Samuelson right after receiving his PhD from MIT at the age of 24.

He was the youngest member, but played a key role among this group of great economists, especially on the empirical side. After some years, he succeeded in combining Keynesian macrotheoretical models with the Timbergen type of simultaneously estimated equations. For further details, see [1] below. By wisely using this model, he correctly predicted the postwar boom, rather than recession, and thus earned his reputation.

Elaborating this model further, he completed, in 1955, a Klein type of macroeconometric model [2]. This model laid the foundation of an empirical example of econometric studies for any national economy in the world. There is no need to further explain his contributions to econometric research, education and applications. He was awarded the Nobel Prize in 1980.

Prof. L. R. Klein was born in Omaha, Nebraska and passed away at home in Pennsylvania on October 23, 2013. His qualifications include: 1942: BA, Economics, University of California, Berkeley; 1944: PhD in Economics, MIT; 1944–1947: Cowls Commission, University of Chicago; From 1947, he visited several Western European universities: 1948–1950: NBER and Institute of Consumers' Survey, University of Michigan;

1950–1954: Dept. of Economics, University of Michigan; 1954–1958: Institute of Statistics, University of Oxford; 1958–2005: Prof., University of Pennsylvania. 2005: Prof. Emeritus.

Major honors include: 1960: President, the Econometric Society; 1968: The Benjamin Franklin Prof Economics and Finance (University of Pennsylvania); 1977: President, American Economic Ass.; 1980: Nobel Memorial Prize. His main works are as follows:

[1] Klein, L. R. (1950). *Economic Fluctuations of the U.S., 1921–1941,* Chicago.
[2] ——, 1955 (with Goldberger, A.). *An Econometric Model of the United States, 1929–1952*, North-Holland, Amsterdam.
[3] ——, 1961 (with Ball, R.J., Hazlewood, A. and Vandome, P.). *An Econometric Model of the U.K.*, Basil-Blackwell, Oxford.
[4] ——, 1967 (with Evans, M.). *The Wharton Econometric Forecasting Model,* University of Pennsylvania.
[5] ——, 1975 (with Fromm, G. *et al.*). *The Brookings Quarterly Model of the US,* McNally.
[6] ——, 1995 (ed. M. Dutta). *Economics, Econometrics and the LINK,* North Holland.
[7] ——, 1997 (ed. K. Marwah). *Selected Papers of L. R. Klein*, WSPC.
[8] ——, 1998 (ed. B. Hickman). LINK Proceedings, 1991–1992, WSPC.
[9] ——, 2003 (ed. S. Ichimura). *Econometric Modeling of China*, WSPC.

About the Editors

Shinichi Ichimura
Professor Emeritus, Kyoto University

He is a Japanese economist who is well known all over the world. In 2005, he retired from all official positions, but still actively writes academic books and essays as Professor Emeritus of Kyoto University.

He was born in Kyoto City, Japan in 1925 and graduated from Kyoto University in 1949 and obtained PhD in 1953 from MIT, US — the first postwar Japanese PhD in economics. His professional article in English appeared early in 1951 in the *Review of Economic Studies,* and since then he had published many articles in *Econometrica*, *The Review of Economics and Statistics* and others. He was elected as a fellow of the Econometric Society in 1961 and served the Society as a council member from 1971 to 1982.

He earnestly participated in the Japanese government's compilation of first Inter-industrial Tables for 1951 and applied it to the policy issues of the Japanese Economy then, publishing the results in 1957 [1]. Later, in cooperation with L. R. Klein, visiting Osaka University in 1960, Ichimura succeeded in constructing the Osaka University Macroeconometric Model of the Japanese Economy in 1967, while he was a visiting professor at the University of Pennsylvania [2].

In 1968, however, he moved to Kyoto University to head the newly established Center for Southeast Asian Studies and guided its formation and area research. He and his colleagues not only published many articles in their own journal, *South East Asian Studies*, but also founded a new professional association — the East Asian Economic Association — with many members in Japan and East and Southeast Asia. He was the first editor of its journal, *Asian Economic Journal*, from 1988 to 2000 and was then elected as the President during the period 1992–1998. He still serves as an honorary adviser to the EAEA.

He retired from Kyoto University in 1988 and became the Vice President of the private, newly established Osaka International University and again moved in 1995 to hold the directorship of the International Center for the Study of East Asian Development (ICSEAD) established by Kitakyushu City affiliated with the University of Pennsylvania. Throughout these 17 years, his research on Asia continued and expanded into China. His main contributions have been collected in the book *Japan and Asia*, published in 2015 [8]. Its introduction describes a history of his working on Asian development, and its appendix offers a complete list of all 78 books and 284 articles published by him so far. His main works in econometrics are as follows:

[1] Ichimura, S. (1957). *The Structure of the Japanese Economy*, Sobunsha, Tokyo (J).
[2] ——, (1974) (with Klein, Koizumi, Sato). *An Econometric Analysis of the Japanese Economy,* The Association for Asian Studies, Kyoto.
[3] ——, (1985) (with M. Ezaki). *Econometric Models of Asian LINK*, Springer Verlag, Berlin-Tokyo.
[4] ——, (1991) (coed. Y. Matsumoto). *Econometric Models of Asia Pacific Countries*, Springer-Verlag, Berlin-Tokyo.
[5] ——, (1998). *Political Economy of Japanese and Asian Development*, Springer-Verlag.
[6] ——, (1998) (coed. H. J. Wang). *Interregional I-O Analysis of the Chinese Economy*, WSPC, Singapore-London.
[7] ——, (2008) (coed. L. Klein). *Macroeconometric Modeling of Japan*, WSPC, Singapore-London.
[8] ——, (2015). *JAPAN and ASIA*: *Economic Development and Nation-Building*, WSPC, Singapore-London.

Soshichi Kinoshita (1935–2017)

The teaching and training of econometric modeling in Japan has been limited to a few outstanding universities until recently, mainly because of the shortage of well-trained econometricians. Nagoya University was one of a few exceptional ones. The reason was that Hiroya Ueno (S. Kinoshita's teacher) participated in a seminar conducted by Prof. Klein, who visited Osaka University Institute of Social and Economic Research in the summer of 1960 for a few months. Ueno was a good friend of Ichimura's and keenly interested in newly developing econometric modeling. He taught econometrics at Nagoya University and trained Kinoshita and many others. Prof. Kinoshita succeeded his chair and trained Prof. Yamada and others.

S. Kinoshita was born at Toyokawa city, Aichi-Ken in 1935 and passed away at home in Nagoya, May 14, 2017. His qualifications inlucde: 1958: BA, Economics; 1968: PhD, Economics; 1964–1965: Nagoya University. He held the following important positions: 1966–1967: Research Associate; 1968–1983: Lecturer; 1983–1999: Assoc. Prof.; 1999: Prof., Nagoya University; 1999: Prof. Emeritus; 1999–2008: Prof., Sugiyama Jogakuen University; 2007–2016: Director, Sugiyama School Corporation. His representative works are as follows:

[1] Kinoshita, S. (1968) (with Ueno, H.). A simulation experiment for growth with a long-term model of Japan, *International Economic Review* **9**(1), pp. 14–48.

[2] ——, (1971) (with Watanabe, T.). An econometric study of the Japanese steel industry, in Klein, L. R. (ed.), *Essays in Industrial Econometrics*, Vol. III., University of Pennsylvania.

[3] ——, (1991). Linked International Model for the Pacific-basin Economy, in Ichimura [3].

[4] ——, (2012) (ed.) *Econometric Modeling of Japan and Asia-Pacific Economies*. WSPC, Singapore-London.

Mitsuo Yamada
Professor of Economics, Chukyo University

Born at Kakamigahara, Gifu-Ken in 1952, Prof. M. Yamada's qualifications include: 1975: BA Economics; 1976: MA; 1979: finished Dr. course; 1998: PhD; 1979: Nagoya University. He held the following positions: 1980: Research Associate, Nagoya University; 1987: Assoc. Prof., F. of Econ., Saga University; 1992: Assoc. Prof.; 2000: Prof., F. of Humanities and Social Sciences, Mie University; 2015: Prof. of Econ., Chukyo University (jointly thereafter); Director, Chubu Region Institute for Social and Economic Research. He was honored in 2012–2015 as President, the Pan-Pacific Association of I-O Studies. His main works are as follows:

[1] Yamada, M. (1988) (with T. Mizoguchi). An econometric analysis of the Japanese empire before the second WW: Database and its application, *Asian Economic Journal* **2**(2), pp. 53–99.

[2] ——, (1992). An econometric analysis of technological change in Japan, the US and the FRG, in Ayres, R.U. *et al.* (ed.), *Computer Integrated Manufacturing*, Vol.4: *Economic and Social Impacts*, Chapman & Hall.

[3] ——, (2002). Overseas production of Japanese firms and Japan–US Interdependence. *Journal of Applied I-O Analysis* **8**, pp. 15–36.

[4] ——, (2007). Interdependence among economy, energy, and environment in China: 2000–2020, *The Journal of Econometric Study of Northeast Asia* **6**, pp. 29–56.
[5] ——, (2014). Input-output analysis of the interdependence between Japan and China through Japanese overseas production, *Journal of Economic Structures* **3**(3), pp. 1–28.

Contents

List of Figures and Tables

Chapter 1

A Brief History of Evolving Wharton Models 1961–2000

1. Introduction

Lawrence R. Klein initiated econometric modeling of the US economy at the Wharton School around 1961. Since then, as new ideas in modeling came forth, the existing model had been revised and updated by the members of the Wharton team with L. R. Klein for forecasting and analyzing the US economy until around 2000. Each version of the revised models was distinguished from the preceding one by numbering it successively like Wharton Mark III Quarterly Econometric Model or more briefly Mark III, Mark IV, etc. The last one was Mark 10.

In retrospect, the first of Klein's quarterly models to be called Mark 1 was presented at the NBER conference and published in *Model of Income Determination* 1964 [1]. This model was expanded and updated by Michael K. Evans and Michael D. McCarthy at the Economic Research Unit of Wharton School under the supervision of Klein. The first stage of Wharton quarterly models was published by M. Evans and L. Klein [2], and then by M. McCarthy [3]. McCarthy named his version Wharton Mark III. Since Wharton Econometric Forecasting Associates (WEFA) was founded in 1969, Econometric modeling work was not only continued by the WEFA group but also used more widely outside the Wharton school. Mark IV was presented at the Joint Economic Committee, the 95th US Congress [4] along with other similar quarterly models by DRI and Chase Econometrics. The number of variables, for instance, in each model was DRI 800, Chase 455, and Wharton 669. R. Jeffrey Green reported that when he was the director of WEFA in 1979–1981, he was engaged in the construction of Mark VI. Soon he moved to the Business School, Indiana University.

Thus, WEFA model had grown increasingly larger in size and more complex. Mark III had already about 320 variables, of which 60 were stochastic and 105 were exogenous. Mark IV contained 669 variables and Mark 9 had about 750 variables. Mark 10 had about 970 variables, of which 320 were stochastic and 170 were exogenous. The expansion of the model was unavoidable by more detailed specification of consumer behavior and sectorial disaggregation of price and demographic variables.

2. Characteristics of the WEFA Mark 10 Model

Mark 10 is a quarterly, econometric model of the US economy built and maintained by the WEFA Group under the supervision of Prof. Klein. It has been used at WEFA to generate both the short-term and long-term US economic outlooks. WEFA economists used it in a variety of consulting projects. A large number of WEFA clients used Mark 10 in their own planning, forecasting, and risk-analysis activities.

It consists really of two models: a core macroeconometric model and an industry model. The former model is broken into three blocks:

(1) predetermined block of demographic detail,
(2) a simultaneous block of the main economic indicators and final demand categories, and
(3) a post-determined block of variables which do not feed back into the second block. The latter (industry model) is a "satellite model" of the core model. Its results depend on, but do not affect, results from the core model (see Figure 1.1).

Prof. Klein himself never called any models Klein models, but the article he and F. G. Adams wrote [5] and subsequent use of Mark 10 at WEFA show that he regarded it as his group's model.

3. Characteristics of the Core Macroeconometric Model

Since Mark 10 is used in both short- and long-run simulations, it is designed to exhibit characteristic short-run behavior of the US economy and also have stable long-run properties. As is the tradition at the WEFA Group, dating back to the original short-run forecasting model built under the guidance of L. R. Klein in the 1960s, Mark 10 is a Keynesian model.

To achieve long-run stability, many supply-side features have been incorporated. The key feature of the supply-side is potential gross

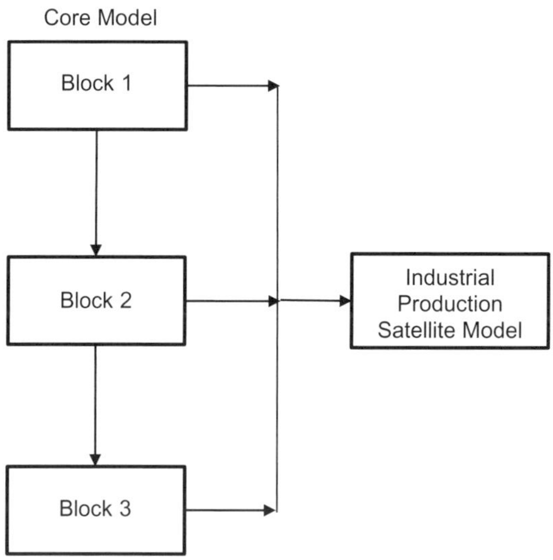

Figure 1.1. Block Structure of the Mark 10 Model

domestic product (GDP). Potential GDP is the output of the economy when all available capital and labor are employed. Hence, the gap between potential and actual GDP gives a good indication of excess supply/demand conditions. If demand (actual GDP) is close to supply capacity (potential GDP), then prices will reflect these conditions by moving upward.

In Mark 10, potential GDP is based on an estimated constant elasticity of substitution (CES) production function of the US economy. The elasticity of substitution between capital and labor, which is constant over time, was estimated to be 0.65, i.e., a 10% rise in the price of capital relative to labor induces a 6.5% decrease in the capital–labor ratio to produce the same output. As shown in Figure 1.2, the potential GDP supply constraint located in the "Wages, Prices and Supply Constraints" box is central to the model; it affects, and is affected by, all other major sectors of the model.

Another important supply-side feature is the Phillips curve for determining wages. When the demand for labor pushes down the unemployment rate, wage inflation accelerates. This increases the demand for capital relative to labor through an increase in the optimal capital stock. The optimal capital stock, determined by the same CES production function mentioned above, rises when the price of labor to capital rises.

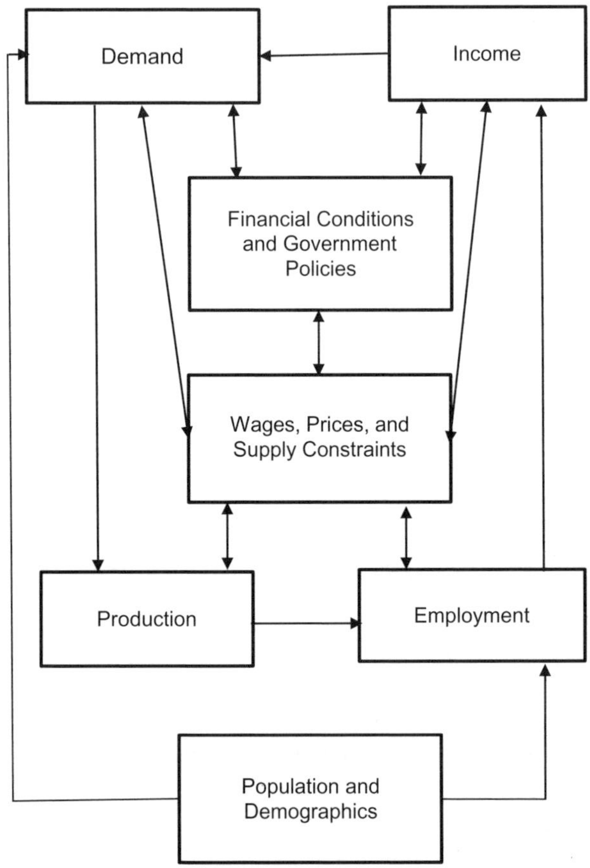

Figure 1.2. Simplified Flow of the Mark 10 Model

Increase in the optimal capital stock stimulate investment, dampening demand for labor.

The labor supply and demand section of the model uses a great amount of demographic detail for labor supply and a small input–output (I/O) model for demand. There is a great amount of demographic detail determining the labor supply. Population by age and sex is exogenous and the labor force participation rates are also exogenous, making labor supply essentially exogenous as well. The I/O model in Mark 10 is small, with details only for one-digit Standard Industrial Classification Industries, such as mining and construction. The I/O model uses the vector of final demand categories in Mark 10 to determine the required output to produce all the goods demanded. It is simply a truncated version of **the Industry Model** detailed in Chapter 3. The output calculated in this manner, along with the level of capital stock, then determines the demand for labor.

References

[1] Klein, L. R. (1964). A Postwar Quarterly Model: Description and Application, in *Models of Income Determination*, eds. by Conference on Research in Income and Wealth, NBER.

[2] Evans, M. K. and L. R. Klein (1968). The Wharton Econometric Forecasting Model, ERU, Department of Economics, Wharton School of Finance and Commerce, University of Pennsylvania.

[3] McCarthy, M. D. (1972). The Wharton Quarterly Econometric Forecasting Model, Mark III ERU, Department of Economics, Wharton School, University of Pennsylvania.

[4] Lee, L. D. (1978). A Comparison of Econometric Models: A Study, US Congress, Joint Economic Committee, Washington: U.S. Govt. Print. Off.

[5] Adams, F. G. and L. R. Klein (1991). Performance of Quarterly Econometric Models of the United States: A New Round of Model Comparisons, in L. R. Klein, eds. (1991), *Comparative Performance of US Econometric Models*, Oxford University Press, New York, relied on Mark 9, but WEFA continued its activity and used Mark 10 throughout the 90s.

Chapter 2

Outline of the Core Model

The core model of WEFA Mark 10 in this book constructs the US Economy model by subdividing the whole system into the following 10 different sectors *plus* one miscellaneous sector: (1) Final demand, (2) Income determination, (3) Labor market, (4) Price and costs, (5) Government revenue and expenditure, (6) Production and sectoral demand, (7) Population and demographics, (8) Money and finance, (9) Auto and petroleum market, (10) International sector, and (11) Miscellaneous.

This chapter describes the basic way of thinking in our core model, following the exposition given in Chapter 1, and the detailed equations are provided in Chapter 5.

1. Final Demand Sectors and Income Determination

The national income and product accounts measures the outcomes of central circular flow of economic activities in three sectors (consumer households, businesses and governments) of domestic spending, income from abroad and tax policy in this model. If the rest of the model were frozen, these blocks would produce a Keynesian system similar to the model pioneered by Tinbergen and Klein. This Mark 10, however, has imbedded the additional price factors in the investment and other primary demand equations. Some expositions are given in the following sections.

1.1. *Consumer spending on durable, nondurable goods and services*

They are distinguished as follows. Durable goods are divided into six categories: furniture and household equipment; new cars; used cars;

truck, recreation vehicle; tire, tube, accessories and parts; other durable goods. Nondurable goods are divided into six categories: two food and beverage categories; clothing and shoes; gasoline and oil; fuel oil and coal; other nondurable goods. Services are divided into seven categories: three household operations; two transportation services; medical care; other services.

Main determinants of consumption are income, relative prices, and demographics. In addition, the consumer sentiments index, which is monitored by the University of Michigan, *Survey of Consumer Sentiment*, is used, where appropriate, to capture the cyclical behavior of some consumption categories. Short- and long-run effects have been separated by using polynomial lag distributions, especially in those cases where relative price appears important.

1.2. *Business investment*

This includes 14 investment categories: four durable equipments, six business constructions, and four inventories. Nonresidential investment is determined, based on the neo-classical formulation as outlined by Hall and Jorgenson and others [1]. Output variable (usually GNP), user cost of capital, defined on the basis of Dale Jorgenson's work, and corporate cash flow, which reflects the cost of financing investment projects. User cost of capital is used directly in some investment categories or affects investment through the optimal capital stock. Of note, also, is the time rate of lagged response of investment realization to the more important determining factors. Simple polynomials are used for the lagged pattern, and the appropriate length of lag and degree of polynomial is determined by the search method.

1.3. *Residential investment*

Residential investment sector includes two housing starts (single and multi-family unit starts) and three housing sale categories (new and existing single family units for sale and new single family units for sale). Housing starts and sales, in turn, drive investment demand in three GDP account categories: new housing single unit structure, new housing multi-unit structure, and other residential structures. Thus, residential investment is determined primarily through housing starts (single and multi-unit) and sales of existing single unit house, and they are determined by demographic factors, mortgage costs, and income. The sales of existing single unit home are determined by the following variables: credit rationing, share of household head 25–44, Michigan index of sentiment, average disposable income per capita, employment, and housing sale price adjusted for mortgage rate.

1.4. *Inventory investment*

This is divided into four categories: auto dealer; manufacturing; nonfarm, nonmanufacturing excluding auto dealer and farm plus commodity credit corporation (CCC) purchases. Inventories except farm are determined by the relevant components of aggregate demand. Inventory changes in stock of farm plus CCC purchase are exogenous.

2. Population and Demographics, and Labor Market

2.1. *Population*

Mark 10 has a great amount of demographic information. Total population is available by sex and 5-year age groups, while civilian noninstitutional population is available by sex and 10-year age groups. Households are available by 10-year age groups.

2.2. *Labor market*

Labor supply is exogenous through exogenous population and participation rates. Labor demand, or employment, is determined through the I/O structure of the model and Cobb–Douglas production functions. The Cobb–Douglas production functions take into account the capital stock. In the industry, if investment has been particularly strong, thereby raising the capital stock, fewer employees are needed to produce the output indicated by the I/O structure of the model. Of course, if output for the industry is high, due to increased demand, more workers will be employed to produce the demanded output.

3. Government Sector

The government sector is largely exogenous. A switch variable (DUMGEF) can be used to change the exogenous determination from nominal to real expenditures for the federal government. The deflators and wage rates are endogenous, reflecting movements in prices due to changing economic conditions.

3.1. *Government policy*

Mark 10 has a great amount of government policy detail. Purchases are divided into two categories: defense and nondefense. Each category is divided into purchases of goods and pay. The pay portion is determined by exogenous employment and endogenous wage rates.

3.2. *Government revenues*

Federal corporate, indirect business, social insurance, and personal taxes are included. In addition, investment tax credits and tax lives affect the cost of capital and corporate tax revenues. Personal transfer payments and grants in aid to state and local governments are also available.

There is less detail for the state and local governments. Purchases are again split between pay and exclusive of pay. Revenue detail includes collections for corporate, indirect business, social insurance, and personal taxes. There is only one category of transfer payments to persons.

4. Price and Costs

4.1. *The key supply equation for prices*

This is the capacity utilization of manufacturing. The gap between actual and potential GDP determines the capacity utilization rate. As actual GDP gets closer to potential GDP, the capacity utilization rate rises. The capacity utilization rate then begins to push up producer prices. In addition, it affects the key implicit price deflator for nonfarm business gross domestic product. This deflator is determined by capacity utilization, import prices, and unit labor costs. It affects many of the final demand deflators for consumption and investment.

The export deflators are determined mostly by producer prices, the capacity utilization rate, and the nonfarm business GDP deflator. Government purchases of goods are determined by producer prices. Basically, capacity utilization, unit labor costs, indirect business taxes, and exogenous prices, such as the oil price, determine producer prices.

Producer prices, along with the nonfarm business GDP deflator, determine the implicit deflators for final demand, excluding imports. Import prices are determined by the exogenous rest-of-world producer prices divided by the nominal exchange rate. Consumer price indexes are then determined from the implicit final demand deflators for consumption.

4.2. *The Phillips curve*

The employment cost index for private nonfarm wages and salaries is simply called wage here. The key wage equation is a *Phillips curve* specification. Consumer prices and productivity determine wages in the long run, but in the short run, the unemployment rate also affects wages. This equation helps determine the demand for labor. As the labor supply tightens, the unemployment rate falls, pushing up wages. Higher wages tend to make capital goods relatively more attractive and the optimal capital stock rises, stimulating investment. Through the Cobb–Douglas production functions, this reduces the demand for labor. Thus, if wages rise relative to the cost of capital, employment will be adversely affected.

5. International Sector

5.1. *The nominal exchange rate as endogenous*

This model treats the nominal exchange rate as endogenous, while real GDP and producer price index of the rest of world are exogenous. The nominal exchange rate is specified according to purchasing power parity theory. That is, over time, the nominal exchange rate will reflect price differences between the US and the rest of the world. If the US inflation rate outpaces rest-of-world inflation, the dollar will depreciate. Relative interest rates are not included in the exchange rate determination because it is not easy to model movements of foreign interest rates within a US macro model.

5.2. *Exports and imports*

Exports are determined by rest-of-world GDP and the domestic price relative to the exchange-rate-adjusted foreign price. Imports are determined by appropriate domestic demand variables and exchange-rate-adjusted relative prices.

Eight categories of goods and one service are modeled separately for both exports and imports, with one additional goods category for grain exports and petroleum imports. Grain exports are exogenous in the model.

6. Money and Finance

6.1. *The federal funds rate*

This is the key interest rate in Mark 10. It is endogenous. As inflation and/or GDP growth rises, so will the Fed funds rate. Monetary policy is determined through the Fed funds rate, which determines the three-month Treasury bill. The three-month T-bill, over time, affects the five-year Treasury note and the 30-year Treasury bond. The yield curve is affected through these three interest rates, the three-month T-bill, the five-year note, and the 30-year T-bond. They, in turn, affect all other interest rates in the model.

6.2. *Federal deficit relative to nominal GDP*

The five-year T-note and the 30-year T-bond are also affected by the size of the federal deficit relative to nominal GDP. Excessive federal government borrowing pushes up these interest rates and, consequently, all other long-term interest rates.

Reference

[1] Jorgenson, D. and R. E. Hall. (1967). Tax policy and investment behavior, *American Economic Review* **57**(3), pp. 391–414.

Chapter 3

Overview of Industry Model

1. Introduction

The US Quarterly Industrial Production Model covers industrial activity for 125 manufacturing, mining, and utilities sectors, as measured by the Federal Reserve Board's indexes of industrial production. Output is estimated on the basis of industry demand, calculated using a version of input–output analysis, from components of macroeconomic demand forecast by the Mark 10 core model.

All two-digit manufacturing industries are modeled, as are many three-digit sectors. Two-digit detail for mining and an overall index for utilities are also included. All major industry aggregates are estimated by the model, using identity published by the Federal Reserve.

Most macroeconomic scenarios will result in changes in industrial production indexes. Fiscal policy, monetary policy, international trade, and energy supply and price assumptions all can produce changes in final expenditures, and those effects can be traced through to final demand, total demand, and production for industrial segments. For example, an increase in defense spending can be traced back to increased output in aircraft and parts (SIC 372), communication equipment (SIC 366), and electronic components (SIC 367), among other industries.

2. Industrial Demand

The WEFA Group's fully detailed model of industrial activity forecasts sectorial demand on the basis of input–output tables that map out final and intermediate demands by industry. In order to keep the simulation properties of the PC industrial production model as close as possible to those of the large model and to impose a consistent framework for channeling macroeconomic demand into industrial demand, the most important elements of the input–output tables are used to generate estimates of final demand and total demand by industry (Figure 3.1).

Standard input–output analysis is carried out in two steps. First, the expenditure vector from the macroeconomic model is converted into a vector of industrial deliveries to final demand. This conversion is

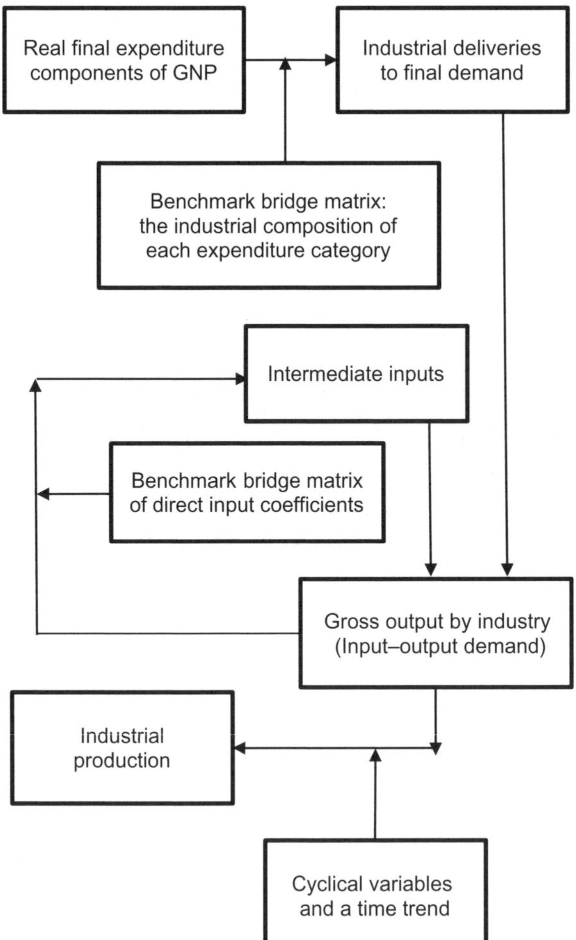

Figure 3.1. A Simplified Flow of the Industry Model

represented for any single time period as follows:

$F = H * G$, where
$F = (n \times 1)$ vector of industrial deliveries to final demand,
$H = (n \times m)$ benchmark bridge matrix recording the industrial composition of each expenditure category,
$G = (m \times 1)$ vector of real final expenditure components of GNP.

Since time-series data on the industrial composition of the final expenditure categories are not available, a fixed bridge matrix, constructed from the 1977 I/O table, is used in this conversion.

Once the final demand vector, F, has been calculated, standard input–output techniques are used to derive estimates of the industrial output required to produce the bill of goods for final use. According to the basic input–output model, intermediate inputs, industrial deliveries to final demand, and gross output are related as follows:

$$A * X + F = X,$$

where

$A = (n \times n)$ matrix of direct input coefficients describing the delivery of sector i's required per unit of sector j's output,
$X = (n \times 1)$ vector of gross outputs by industry.

This equation can be considered as the equilibrium condition in which total demand equals total supply. The product $A * X$ is equal to intermediate demand, and F is equal to final demand. The sum of the two is total demand and is equal to total production. Following standard input–output conventions, it is assumed that the technology of production, as reflected by the matrix of direct input coefficients, A, remains relatively stable over time. In addition, production processes are assumed to exhibit constant returns to scale with no possibility for substitution among inputs.

The basic input–output equation is then solved for output:

$$X = (1 - A)^{-1} * F = H * F.$$

This equation describes the relationship between final demand and the industrial output levels.

The full input–output model, as described above, is embedded in the WEFA Group's large model of industrial activity. In a PC environment, however, it is much more efficient to reduce some of the complexities of the operations, and it is possible to do so without much loss of information. Many elements of the bridge matrix, H, and the matrix of direct input coefficients, A, are zero, and a very large proportion of the total input–output effect can be estimated using only the three or four largest flows in each step of the calculations.

For each of the disaggregate industries included in the satellite model, elements of final demand and total demand are ranked and the largest flows are used. Rankings are calculated for the 1977 flows across elements of G to estimate the major components of final demand for industry, and the elements of F to estimate the major industries contributing to total demand for each industry. For example,

$$\begin{aligned}\text{fio353} = {} & 0.07814 * (\text{ipe87} - \text{ipeinf87}) \\ & + 0.13212 * \text{excapoh87} \\ & - 0.06327 * \text{imcapxmvp870}\end{aligned}$$

or final demand for construction and mining equipment is equal to the weighted sum of investment for equipment, exports of capital goods, imports of capital goods, state and local government purchases, defense purchases, and other exports. These six components account for a very large proportion of final demand from the full input–output system, and

$$\begin{aligned}\text{xio353} = {} & 1.07924 * \text{fio353} + 0.00760 * \text{fiocc} \\ & + 0.00099 * \text{fiosv} + 0.00457 * \text{fio371au} \\ & + 0.00736 * \text{fio491} + 0.05976 * \text{fiolc} \\ & + 0.00057 * \text{fiogv}\end{aligned}$$

or total demand (or input–output demand) for construction and mining equipment is equal to a weighted average of final demand for construction and mining equipments (which carry a large coefficient), contract construction (which is weighted much more lightly) services, automobiles, electrical utilities, local and government. Once again, these components make up most of the total demand flow from the full input–output model.

3. Modeling Industrial Production

Industrial production indexes for disaggregate industries are estimated as a function of total demand from the input–output analysis, cyclical variables, and a time trend. The functional form used imposes a unitary elasticity on the demand term, which embodies most of the explanatory power in the equations.

Additionally, nondemand terms are added to the equations to explain the patterns not well accounted for by input–output demand terms, cyclicality and technological change.

Macroeconomic variables feed down into the industry output equations through demand, but these weighted demand terms are in most cases less cyclical than the Federal Reserve Board's indexes of industrial production. Therefore, cyclical variables, such as capacity utilization or the consumer sentiment index, are included in most equations. Cyclical variables were chosen with care to reflect the appropriate business cycle for each industry.

The 1977 input–output tables in the construction of final demand and total demand series become less realistic as estimates move further from the base year. This is because shifts in relative prices for inputs, as well as various other factors, can, in the long run, change the technological processes used to manufacture goods. To account for this slowly increasing divergence between input–output demand variables and industrial production indexes, a simple time trend is included in most equations. The standard equation specification for industrial production indexes is

$$\text{LOG(JIP\#/XIO\#)} = \text{F (LOG(TREND), LOG(CYCUCAL VARIABLE))},$$

where JIP# = Industrial production index; XIO# = total I–O demand, Trend = dummy for time trend.

This equation describes the relationship between final demand and the industrial output levels.

Chapter 4

Some Estimation Methods

This chapter describes some technical issues on specification and the estimation methods employed in Mark 10. Following are the four methods: (1) PDL estimate, (2) user cost of capital, (3) estimation of short-run employment and (4) CES production function. (1) to (3) are drawn primarily from Klein (1967) [3], Cohen (1968) [2], Preston (1972) [6] and McCarthy (1972) [5], and (4) refers to Arrow *et al.* (1961) [1] and Kmenta (1967) [4].

1. Polynomial Distribution Lag (PDL) Estimate

Consider the case where the dependent variable is influenced by current and lagged values of a single independent variable.

$$y = \gamma + \sum_{i=1}^{n-1} p(i)x_{-i+1} + u. \tag{1}$$

Assume that the weights $p(i)$ follow the simple polynomial

$$p(i) = a_0 + a_1 i + a_2 i^2 + a_3 i^3, \tag{2}$$

and that $p(0) = 0$ and $p(n) = 0$. Equation (2) then reduces to

$$p(i) = a_2(i - n)i + a_3(i^2 - n^2)i. \tag{3}$$

Substitution into (1) gives

$$y = \gamma + \sum_{i=1}^{n-1} [a_2(i - n)i + a_3(i^2 - n^2)i]x_{-i+1} + u, \tag{4}$$

that is,

$$y = \gamma + a_2 \sum_{i=1}^{n-1} (i - n) i x_{-i+1} + a_3 \sum_{i=1}^{n-1} (i^2 - n^2) i x_{-i+1} + u. \quad (5)$$

After making the appropriate transformation which results in the constructed variables, $\sum_{i=1}^{n-1} (i - n) i x_{-i+1}$ and $\sum_{i=1}^{n-1} (i^2 - n^2) i x_{-i+1}$, ordinary least squares techniques are applied and estimates of γ, a_2 and a_3 are obtained. These estimates are then used in (3) to derive estimates of weights $p(i)$.

2. User Cost of Capital

The derivation of user cost or implicit rental price of capital follows the general formulation of Coen [2]. Let g be the unit price of the product and δ the rate of economic depreciation of capital goods per period. The important factors to consider in determining whether capital stock should be increased by unit include the following:

Initial outlay g,
Replacement expenditures in the future period δg,
Additional revenues $(\partial Q/\partial K)p$,
Corporate tax rate μ,
Increase in depreciation charges for tax purposes in period i D_i
Interest rate r.

Net revenue in any future period is then

$$(\partial Q/\partial K)p - \delta g - \mu((\partial Q/\partial K)p - D_i), \quad (6)$$

and discounted net revenue is

$$[(1 - \mu)(\partial Q/\partial K) - \delta g]r^{-1} + \mu \sum_{i=1}^{\infty} D_i (1 + r)^{-i}. \quad (7)$$

If $B = \mu \sum_{i=1}^{\infty} d_i (1 + r)^{-i}$ equals the discounted value of depreciation charges resulting from a current dollar's worth of capital spending (where d_i is the tax depreciation permitted on the investment on one dollar i

periods after the investment in made), then

$$\sum_{i=1}^{\infty} D_i(1+r)^{-i} = gB + \delta g B \sum_{i=1}^{\infty}(1+r)^{-i}. \tag{8}$$

Substituting (8) into (7) gives

$$[(1-\mu)(\partial Q/\partial K)p - \delta g]r^{-1} + \mu g B + \mu\delta g B r^{-1} > g. \tag{9}$$

This implies

$$(\partial Q/\partial K)p > [g(r+\delta)(1-\mu B)(1-\mu)^{-1}] = c, \tag{10}$$

where $(\partial Q/\partial K)p$ is the marginal revenue and c the user cost of capital. The implicit rental price depends on the purchase price of the capital goods g, depreciation method of the interest rate r, the rate of economic depreciation δ, corporate tax rate t, and the depreciation method used, B.

3. Estimate of Labor Requirement

Assuming a Cobb–Douglas production function, output is related technically to capital and labor in the following form:

$$X = Ae^{\gamma t} L^{\alpha} K^{\beta} u, \tag{11}$$

where X is output, L is labor input, K is capital stock, and γ is technical progress over time.

By transforming (11) into logarithms, and solving for L, the short-run labor requirement L^* is derived as follows:

$$\begin{aligned} \log L^* = & -\alpha^{-1}\log A + \alpha^{-1}\log X - \beta\alpha^{-1}\log K \\ & + \alpha^{-1}\gamma(t) + \alpha^{-1}\log u. \end{aligned} \tag{12}$$

Actual labor input is determined to fill the gap between L^* and L under the partial adjustment mechanism of the form,

$$\mathrm{d}\log L = \lambda(\log L^* - \log L_{-1}), \tag{13}$$

where λ is a partial adjustment coefficient.

Inserting (12) into (13), actual labor input can be rewritten as

$$\mathrm{d}\log L = -\lambda\alpha^{-1}\log A + \lambda\alpha^{-1}\log X - \lambda[\log L_{-1} + \beta\alpha^{-1}\log K] + \lambda\alpha^{-1}\gamma(t) + \lambda\alpha^{-1}\log u.$$

Because of a problem with the sign on the capital stock in (13), $\beta\alpha^{-1}$ is estimated from the factor share data as

$$\beta\alpha^{-1} = \sum_{i=1}^{T}[(\text{income} - \text{wage income})/\text{wage income}]\frac{1}{T}.$$

The combined variable $[\log L_{-1} + \beta\alpha^{-1}\log K]$ is formed, and the remaining parameters of (13) are then estimated.

4. Estimate of CES Production Function

Potential GDP is derived from the production function of the whole economy. Assuming the CES production function of capital and labor, output is determined in the logarithmic form as

$$\log X = -\frac{1}{\rho}[\log A + \gamma t + \log(\delta L^{-\rho} + (1-\delta)K^{-\rho})] + u, \qquad (14)$$

where variable L is labor input (manhour), K is utilized capital, X is output (GDP), and parameters δ, γ, ρ, and A are distribution parameter, technical progress parameter, substitution parameter, and initial level of technology, respectively. Applying the equilibrium condition of factor market (marginal product of factor input equals to real factor price), capital labor ratio is determined by factor price ratio as

$$\log\left(\frac{L}{K}\right) = -\sigma\log\left(\frac{1-\delta}{\delta}\right) - \sigma\log\left(\frac{w}{r}\right), \qquad (15)$$

where r is capital cost, w is labor cost, and σ is the elasticity of substitution, which is related to the substitution parameter as

$$\sigma = 1/(1+\rho). \qquad (16)$$

Parameters of CES production function are estimated in two steps: the first step is to estimate δ and σ (and ρ) by applying the Least Square Method to (15), and then in the second step, the remaining parameters are estimated from the estimates of (14).

References

[1] Arrow, K. J., H. B. Chenery, B. S. Minhas, and R. M. Solow (1961). Capital-labor substitution and economic efficiency, *The Review of Economics and Statistics* **43**(3), pp. 225–250.

[2] Cohen, R. M. (1968). Effects of tax policy on investment in manufacturing, *American Economic Review, Papers and Proceedings* **58**(2), pp. 200–211.

[3] Klein, L. R. (1967). Some new results in the measurement of capacity utilization, *The American Economic Review* **57**(1), pp. 34–58.

[4] Kmenta, J. (1967). On estimation of the CES production function, *International Economic Review* **8**(2), pp. 180–189.

[5] McCarthy, M. D. (1972). *The Wharton Quarterly Econometric Forecasting Model, Mark III*, Economic Research Unit, Dept. of Economics, University of Pennsylvania.

[6] Preston, R. S. (1972). *The Wharton Annual and Industry Forecasting Model*, ERU, Dept. of Economics, Wharton School, University of Pennsylvania.

Chapter 5

Estimated Equations of the Core Model

I. How to Read WEFA Estimated Equations

This chapter gives a comprehensive list of the estimated equations and identities of Model Mark 10. To understand their implications, the reader must know the notations for variables and other abbreviated symbols. They are explained in Tables 5.1 and 5.2 of Section III together with their sources and reference guide to save the page space.

An example below displays the equation and additional conventions:

[006] CEDFHE87 (ST, Blk 2) Consumption Expenditures, Furniture & Household Equipment

log(cedfhe87/nhhdcsu)=
  − 0.00598 * spike(80,2)
  + 0.95024 * log(ydpperm87/nhhdcsu)
  + 0.96105 * log((ydpxmed87/ydpperm87)/nhhdcsu)
  + 0.0757 * from0 to3 degree1 far
    log(jcs)
  + 0.1553 * from0 to8 degree2 near far
    log(ir87)
  − 1.3809 * from0 to3 degree1 far
    log(pdicedfhe/pdice)
  + 0.32355

The first line gives, in parentheses, the type of variable (stochastic or identity) and the block in which this equation is solved: and then describes the variable by adding a line if needed.

Since our model is a quarterly model, all variables must be made quarterly even though the original source data may be of a different period, by some adjustment conventions such as: seasonally adjusted; not seasonally adjusted; annual rate; and quarterly rate, etc.

The units of measure the sources (government agencies or private source) of historical data are summarized in Section III.

The equation part displays the transformation of the variable used in the estimation process. For identity and often for stochastic equations, this will simply be an echo of the variable name. In many cases, however, the equations were estimated for transformations of the referenced variable. In the example above, real consumption of furniture and household equipment (CEDFHE87) is first divided by the number of households (NHHDCSU) to put it on a per household basis. The natural log of this transformed series is the dependent variable in the equation. Please note that in the equations part, all variables are expressed, not in capital letters but in lower letters.

In the estimated equations, each independent variable or term is listed along with its estimated coefficient on a separate line. (*Note*: Terms are not divided in this manner for Identity.)

Y.N	=	Y lagged N periods
Y[−N]	=	Y lagged N periods
diff(Y)	=	simple difference, Y − Y[−I]
log(Y)	=	natural logarithm of Y
dlog(Y)	=	logarithmic difference, log(Y) log(Y[−1])
pch(Y)	=	percent change, ((Y − Y[−I]) / Y[−I])•100
pchyay(Y)	=	percent change from prior year, ((Y − Y[−4]) / Y[−4])•100
spike(M, N)	=	1 in year M, period N 0 in all other periods
step(M, N)	=	1 in year M, period N, and beyond 0 before year M, period N
switch(X,Y, Z)	=	Y if X is negative, Z otherwise

Many of the equations in the model contain polynomially distributed lags. Only the sum of the PDL coefficients is displayed in this abbreviated listing of the equations for users' convenience. Additionally, the length, degree, and constraints (NEAR and/or FAR or no constraint) of the PDL are displayed in the example above. Many of the independent terms are included as a PDL. For the log (jcs), the sum of the coefficients on this term is 0.0757, the lags extend from the current period to three lagged periods, the degree of the polynomial is 1, and it was constrained at the far end.

In addition, some mnemonics conventions are introduced to assist the reader in locating variables forecast each month by the U.S. Macro Service. The mnemonic structure underlying the database represents our best attempt to achieve the goals of logic, consistency, and ease of use. We used the following conventions:

87: constant 1987 dollar Indicator (suffix)
U: Data are not seasonally adjusted (suffix)
X: Less:,
SF: seasonal factor (suffix),
    i.e., GPFNXCCC = Federal Govt nondefense purchases
    less CCC payments

II. A System of Estimated Equations

1. Final Demand

1.1. *Consumption spending: Durable, non-durable and services*

Main determinants of consumption are income, relative prices, and demographics. In addition, Mark 10 takes into account the consumer sentiments index which University of Michigan Survey monitors, where appropriate, to capture the cyclical behavior of some consumption goods. Short- and long-run effects have been separated by using polynomial lag distributions, especially in those cases where relative price appears important.

[001] CE (ID, Blk 2) Consumption Expenditures, Total

$$ce = ced + cen + ces$$

[002] CE87 (ID, Blk 2) Consumption Expenditures, Total

ce87 =
    ced87 + cen87 + ces87

1.1.1. *Consumption expenditure on durable goods*

[003] CED (ID, Blk 2) Consumption Expenditures, Durable Goods

ced =
    (cedmvp87 * pdicedmvp+cedfhe87 * pdicedfhe+cedoth87 * pdicedoth)/100

[004] CED87 (ID, Blk 2) Consumption Expenditures, Durable Goods

ced87=
    cedmvp87 + cedfhe87 + cedoth87

[005] CEDFHE (ID, Blk 3) Consumption Expenditures, Furniture & Household Equipment

cedfhe =
    cedfhe87 * pdicedfhe *.01

[006] CEDFHE87 (ST, Blk 2) Consumption Expenditures, Furniture & Household Equipment

```
log(cedfhe87/nhhdcsu) =
    – 0.00598 * spike(80,2)
    + 0.95024 * log(ydpperm87/nhhdcsu)
    + 0.96105 * log((ydpxmed87/ydpperm87)/nhhdcsu)
    + 0.0757 * from0 to3 degree1 far
        log(jcs)
    + 0.1553 * from0 to8 degree2 near far
        log(ir87)
    – 1.3809 * from0 to3 degree1 far
        log(pdicedfhe/pdice)
    + 0.32355
```

[007] CEDMNC (ID, Blk 3) Consumption Expenditures, New Cars

```
cedmnc =
    cedmnc87 * pdicedmnc*.01
```

[008] CEDMNC87 (ST, Blk 2) Consumption Expenditures, New Cars

```
log(cedmnc87) =
    - 0.00247 * ttrend
    + 1.07021 * log(puvcar87)
    + 1.12228 * log(uscar)
    - 0.51526
```

[009] CEDMTP (ID, Blk 3) Consumption Expenditures, Tires, Tubes, Accessories & Parts

```
cedmtp =
    cedmtp87 * pdicedmtp*.01
```

[010] CEDMTP87 (ST, Blk 2) Consumption Expenditures, Tires, Tubes, Accessories & Parts

```
log(cedmtp87/np16a) =
      0.01365 * (1-step(73,4)) * ttrend
    + 1.47225 * (step(73,4)-step(79,4))
    - 0.0007 * (step(73,4)-step(79,4)) * ttrend
    + 1.35204 * step(79,4)
    - 0.00102 * step(79,4) *ttrend
    - 0.7594 * from0 to3 degree1 far
          log(pdicedmtp/pdice)
    - 3.42501
```

[011] CEDMTR (ID, Blk 3) Consumption Expenditures, New & Used Trucks, Recreational Vehicles

```
cedmtr =
    cedmtr87 * pdicedmtr*.01
```

[012] CEDMTR87 (ST, Blk 2) Consumption Expenditures, New & Used Trucks, Recreational Vehicles

log(cedmtr87) =
0.00318 * ttrend
+ 1.0907 * log(utrkle3)
+ 0.3671 * from0 to7 degree1 far
log(puvcar87)
+ 0.64741

[013] CEDMUC (ID, Blk 3) Consumption Expenditures, Net Purchases of Used Cars

cedmuc =
cedmuc87 * pdicedmuc *.01

[014] CEDMUC87 (ST, Blk 2) Consumption Expenditures, Net Purchases of Used Cars

log(cedmuc87) =
+ 0.8925 * from0 to7 degree1 far
log(ydpxmed87)
− 0.1750 * from0 to3 degree1 far
log(pdicedmuc/pdice)
− 3.85814

[015] CEDMVP (ID, Blk 2) Consumption Expenditures, Motor Vehicles & Parts

cedmvp =
(cedmnc87 * pdicedmnc+cedmuc87 * pdicedmuc+cedmtr87 * pdicedmtr+cedmtp87 * +pdicedmtp)/100

[016] CEDMVP87 (ID, Blk 2) Consumption Expenditures, Motor Vehicles & Parts

cedmvp87 =
cedmnc87 + cedmuc87 + cedmtr87 + cedmtp87

[017] CEDOTH (ID, Blk 3) Consumption Expenditures, Other Durable Goods

```
cedoth =
    cedoth87 * pdicedoth*.01
```

[018] CEDOTH87 (ST, Blk 2) Consumption Expenditures, Other Durable Goods

```
log(cedoth87/np) =
       0.98648 * log(ydpperm87/np)
    − 1.0420 * from0 to6 degree2 near far
          log(pdicedoth/pdice)
    −3.71395
```

1.1.2. *Consumption spending on nondurable goods*

[019] CEN (ID, Blk 2) Consumption Expenditures, Nondurable Goods

```
cen =
    (cenfab87 * pdicenfab+cencas87 * pdicencas+cenene87 *
    pdicenene+cenoth87 * pdicenoth)/100
```

[020] CEN87 (ID, Blk 2) Consumption Expenditures, Nondurable Goods

```
cen87 =
    cenfab87 + cencas87 + cenene87 + cenoth87
```

[021] CENCAS (ID, Blk 2) Consumption Expenditures, Clothing & Shoes

```
cencas =
    cencas87 * pdicencas*.01
```

[022] CENCAS87 (ST, Blk 2) Consumption Expenditures, Clothing & Shoes

```
log(cencas87/np) =
       0.00346 * spike(80,2)
    + 1.21174 * log(ydpperm87/np)
    + 0.26115 * log((ydpxmed87/ydpperm87)/np)
    + 0.1340 * from0 to3 degree1 far
          log(jcs)
```

```
    – 0.4608 * from0 to3 degree1 far
        log(pdicencas/pdice)
    – 2.60029
```

[023] CENENE (ID, Blk 2) Consumption Expenditures, Energy

```
cenene =
    (cengas87 * pdicengas+cenfoc87 * pdicenfoc)/100
```

[024] CENENE87 (ID, Blk 2) Consumption Expenditures, Energy

```
cenene87 =
    cenfoc87 + cengas87
```

[025] CENFAB (ID, Blk 2) Consumption Expenditures, Food & Beverages

```
cenfab =
    (cenfmb87 * pdicenfmb+cenfah87 * pdicenfah)/100
```

[026] CENFAB87 (ID, Blk 2) Consumption Expenditures, Food & Beverages

```
cenfab87 =
    cenfmb87 + cenfah87
```

[027] CENFAH (ID, Blk 3) Consumption Expenditures, Food & Beverages at Home

```
cenfah =
    cenfah87 * pdicenfah*.01
```

[028] CENFAH87 (ST, Blk 2) Consumption Expenditures, Food & Beverages at Home

```
log(cenfah87/np) =
      0.31818 * log(ydpperm87/np)
    + 0.52169* log((ydpxmed87/ydpperm87)/np)
    – 0.2181 * from0 to3 degree1 far
        log(pdicenfah/pdice)
    + 2.39284
```

[029] CENFMB (ID, Blk 3) Consumption Expenditures, Purchased Meals & Beverages

cenfmb =
    cenfmb87 * pdicenfmb*.01

[030] CENFMB87 (ST, Blk 2) Consumption Expenditures, Purchased Meals & Beverages

log(cenfmb87/np) =
    + 1.0438 * from0 to3 degree1 far
        log(ydpxmed87/np)
    − 0.1248 * from0 to3 degree1 far
        log(pdicenfmb/pdicenfah)
    − 3.1224

[031] CENFOC (ID, Blk 3) Consumption Expenditures, Fuel Oil & Coal

cenfoc =
    cenfoc87 * pdicenfoc*.01

[032] CENFOC87 (ST, Blk 2) Consumption Expenditures, Fuel Oil & Coal

log(cenfoc87/np) =
    − 1.60372 * log(ttrend)
    + 0.24304 * spike(76,4)+spike(77,1)
    + 0.92784 * log(ydpperm87/np)
    − 0.3461 * from0 to 24 degree1 far
        log(pdicenfoc/pdice)
    + 2.80556

[033] CENGAS (ID, Blk 3) Consumption Expenditures, Gasoline & Oil

cengas =
    cengas87 * pdicengas*.01

[034] CENGAS87 (ST, Blk 2) Consumption Expenditures, Gasoline & Oil

log(cengas87/kucarnew) =
    − 0.11372 * spike(74,1)

− 0.00399 * ttrend
+ 0.70202 * movavg(2,log(ydpxmed87/np16a))
− 0.0729 * from0 to24 degree1 far
log(pdicengas/pdice)
− 1.72097

[035] CENOTH (ID, Blk 2) Consumption Expenditures, Other Nondurable Goods

cenoth =
cenoth87 * pdicenoth*.01

[036] CENOTH87 (ST, Blk 2) Consumption Expenditures, Other Nondurable Goods

log(cenoth87/np) =
0.07626 * log(jcs)
− 0.48941 * log(pdicenoth/pdice)
+ 1.13476 * log(ydpperm87/np)
− 3.25866

1.1.3. *Consumption spending on services*

[037] CES (ID, Blk 2) Consumption Expenditures, Services

ces =
(ceshou87 * pdiceshou+ceshho87 * pdiceshho+cestrn87 * pdicestrn+cesmao87 * pdicesmao)/100

[038] CES87 (ID, Blk 2) Consumption Expenditures, Services

ces87 =
ceshou87 + ceshho87 + cestrn87 + cesmao87

[039] CESHHO (ID, Blk 2) Consumption Expenditures, Household Operation, Total

ceshho =
(ceshhoele87 * pdiceshhoele + ceshhogas87 * pdiceshhogas + ceshhooth87 * pdiceshhooth)/100

[040] CESHHO87 (ID, Blk 2) Consumption Expenditures, Household Operation, Total

```
ceshho87 =
    ceshhoele87 + ceshhogas87 + ceshhooth87
```

[041] CESHHOELE (ID, Blk 3) Consumption Expenditures, Household Operation, Electricity

```
ceshhoele =
    ceshhoele87 * pdiceshhoele*.01
```

[042] CESHHOELE87 (ST, Blk 2) Consumption Expenditures, Household Operation, Electricity

```
log(ceshhoele87/np) =
      1.33435 * log(ydpperm87/np)
    + 0.2694 * log((ydpxmed87/ydpperm87)/np)
    + 0.09   * spike(83,3)
    − 0.1328 * from0 to16 degree1 far
         log(pdiceshhoele/pdicenfoc)
    − 3.29173
```

[043] CESHHOGAS (ID, Blk 3) Consumption Expenditures, Household Operation, Gas

```
ceshhogas =
    ceshhogas87 * pdiceshhogas*.01
```

[044] CESHHOGAS87 (ST, Blk 2) Consumption Expenditures, Household Operation, Gas

```
log(ceshhogas87/np) =
      0.00126 * ttrend
    − 0.0185 * dqtr1
    − 0.01508 * dqtr2
    − 0.001 * dqtr3
    + 0.13012 * spike(76,4)
    + 1.26989 * log((ydpxmed87/ydpperm87)/np)
    − 0.2458 * from0 to4 degree1 far
         log(pdiceshhogas/(pdiceshhoele+pdicenfoc)/2)
    + 4.19692
```

[045] CESHHOOTH (ID, Blk 3) Consumption Expenditures, Household Operation, Other

```
ceshhooth =
    ceshhooth87 * pdiceshhooth*.01
```

[046] CESHHOOTH87 (ST, Blk 2) Consumption Expenditures, Household Operation, Other

```
log(ceshhooth87/nhhdcsu) =
        0.01768 * log(jcs)
    + 1.0511 * from0 to3 degree1 far
            log(ydpxmed87/nhhdcsu)
    – 0.6221 * from0 to3 degree1 far
            log(pdiceshhooth/pdice)
    – 3.71877
```

[047] CESHOU (ID, Blk 2) Consumption Expenditures, Housing Services

```
ceshou =
    ceshou87 * pdiceshou*.01
```

[048] CESHOU87 (ST, Blk 2) Consumption Expenditures, Housing Services

```
log(ceshou87) =
        1.00748 * log(krnet87)
    – 0.00005 * step(81,1) * ttrend
    – 2.2308
```

[049] CESMAO (ID, Blk 2) Consumption Expenditures, Medical & Other Services

```
cesmao =
    (cesmed87 * pdicesmed + cesoth87 * pdicesoth)/100
```

[050] CESMAO87 (ID, Blk 2) Consumption Expenditures, Medical & Other Services

```
cesmao87 =
    cesmed87 + cesoth87
```

[051] CESMED (ID, Blk 2) Consumption Expenditures, Medical Care

cesmed =
    cesmed87 * pdicesmed*.01

[052] CESMED87 (ST, Blk 2) Consumption Expenditures, Medical Care

log((cesmed87-((trpgfhi+trpgnmedcai+trpgfvetmed+trpgfhea)/pdicesmed*100))/np) =
    0.79 * log((ydpxmed87/ydpperm87)/np)
  + 1.43545 * .33 * log((nptf6569+nptm6569+nptf7074+nptm7074)/np)+.67 * log((nptf7579+nptf8084+nptf85a+nptm7579+nptm8084+nptm85a)/np)
  + 1.0523 * from0 to6 degree2 far log((ydpperm87-ceshou87)/np)
  − 0.4031 * from0 to3 degree2 near far log(pdicesmed/pdice)
  + 5.97068

[053] CESOTH (ID, Blk 2) Consumption Expenditures, Other Services

cesoth =
    cesoth87 * pdicesoth*.01

[054] CESOTH87 (ST, Blk 2) Consumption Expenditures, Other Services

log(cesoth87/np) =
    0.32603 * log(ttrend)
  + 0.1830 * from0 to3 degree1 far log(jcs)
  + 0.8488 * from0 to7 degree1 far log(ydpxmed87/np)
  − 0.3147 * from0 to3 degree1 far log(pdicesoth/pdices)
  − 3.94974

[055] CESTAR (ID, Blk 3) Consumption Expenditures, Transportation Services, Auto Repair

cestar =
    cestar87 * pdicestar*.01

[056] CESTAR87 (ST, Blk 2) Consumption Expenditures, Transportation Services, Auto Repair

```
log(cestar87/kucarnew) =
      0.0047 * ttrend
    + 0.93332 * log(ydpperm87/np)
    + 1.54719 * log((ydpxmed87/ydpperm87)/np)
    + 0.1198 * from0 to3 degree1 far
        log(jcs)
    - 1.5482 * from0 to3 degree1 far
        log(pdicestar/pdice)
    + 4.19056
```

[057] CESTRN (ID, Blk 2) Consumption Expenditures, Transportation Services, Total

```
cestrn =
    (cestar87 * pdicestar+cestrnxar87 * pdicestrnxar)/100
```

[058] CESTRN87 (ID, Blk 2) Consumption Expenditures, Transportation Services, Total

```
cestrn87 =
    cestar87 + cestrnxar87
```

[059] CESTRNXAR (ID, Blk 3) Consumption Expenditures, Transportation Services, Other

```
cestrnxar =
    cestrnxar87 * pdicestrnxar*.01
```

[060] CESTRNXAR87 (ST, Blk 2) Consumption Expenditures, Transportation Services, Other

```
log(cestrnxar87/np) =
      0.6723 * log(ydpperm87/np)
    + 0.0703 * from0 to3 degree1 far
        log(jcs)
    - 0.3898 * from0 to3 degree1 far
        log(pdicestrnxar/pdice)
    - 3.62746
```

1.2. *Fixed investment and changes in inventory*

1.2.1. *Nonresidential fixed investment*

Nonresidential investment is determined based on the neo-classical formulation as outlined by Hall and Jorgenson, and others. Output variable (usually GNP), user cost of capital, defined on the basis of Dale Jorgenson's work (see Chapters II and IV), and corporate cash flow, which reflects the cost of financing investment projects.

[061] IFX (ID, Blk 3) Fixed Investment, Total

ifx =
    ip + ir

[062] IFX87 (ID, Blk 3) Fixed Investment, Total

ifx87 =
    ipe87 + ips87 + ir87

[063] IGD (ID, Blk 3) Gross Private Domestic Investment

igd =
    ifx + ii

[064] IGD87 (ID, Blk 3) Gross Private Domestic Investment

igd87 =
    ifx87 + ii87

[065] IP (ID, Blk 2) Fixed Investment, Nonres, Total

ip =
    ipe + ips

[066] IP87 (ID, Blk 2) Fixed Investment, Nonres, Total

ip87 =
    ipe87 + ips87

[067] IPE (ID, Blk 2) Fixed Investment, Nonres, Prod Dur Equip, Total

ipe =
    (ipeinf87 * pdiipeinf + ipetrn87 * pdiipetrn +
    ipeoas87 * pdiipeoas + ipeind87 * pdiipeind)/100

[068] IPE87 (ID, Blk 2) Fixed Investment, Nonres, Prod Dur Equip, Total

ipe87 =
    ipeinf87 + ipeind87 + ipetrn87 + ipeoas87

[069] IPEIND (ID, Blk 2) Fixed Investment, Nonres, Prod Dur Equip, Industrial

ipeind =
    ipeind87 * pdiipeind*.01

[070] IPEIND87 (ST, Blk 2) Fixed Investment, Nonres, Prod Dur Equip, Industrial

log(ipeind87) =
    + 0.7119 * from0 to5 degree2 near far
        log(gdp87)
    − 0.2332 * from0 to5 degree1 far
        log(uckeind/pdignp)
    −1.9849

[071] IPEINF (ID, Blk 3) Fixed Investment, Nonres, Prod Dur Equip, Info. Processing

ipeinf =
    ipeinf87 * pdiipeinf*.01

[072] IPEINF87 (ST, Blk 2) Fixed Investment, Nonres, Prod Dur Equip, Info. Processing

log(ipeinf87) =
    1.6606 * log(ttrend)
    + 1.2125 * from0 to5 degree2 near far
        log(gdp87)
    + 0.8477 * from0 to7 degree1 far
        log(kpopt87/gdp87)
    − 13.8863

[073] IPEOAS (ID, Blk 2) Fixed Investment, Nonres, Prod Dur Equip, Other

ipeoas =
    ipeoas87 * pdiipeoas*.01

[074] IPEOAS87 (ST, Blk 2) Fixed Investment, Nonres, Prod Dur Equip, Other

log(ipeoas87) =
    + 1.0157 * from0 to5 degree2 near far
        log(gdp87)
    − 0.4300 * from0 to5 degree1 far
        log(uckeoas/pdignp)
    − 4.9458

[075] IPETRN (ID, Blk 3) Fixed Investment, Nonres, Prod Dur Equip, Motor Vehicles and Parts

ipetrn =
    ipetrn87 * pdiipetrn*.01

[076] IPETRN87 (ST, Blk 2) Fixed Investment, Nonres, Prod Dur Equip, Motor Vehicles and Parts

log(ipetrn87) =
    + 1.0450 * from0 to5 degree2 near far
        log(gdp87)
    − 0.6804 * from0 to5 degree1 far
        log(ucketrn/pdignp)
    − 5.1527

[077] IPS (ID, Blk 2) Fixed Investment, Nonres, Structures, Total

ips =
    (ipsbldg87 * pdiipsbldg + ipsmap87 * pdiipsmap +
    ipsutl87 * pdiipsutl + ipsoaf87 * pdiipsoaf)/100

[078] IPS87 (ID, Blk 2) Fixed Investment, Nonres, Structures, Total

ips87 =
    ipsbldg87 + ipsmap87 + ipsutl87 + ipsoaf87

[079] IPSBLDG (ID, Blk 3) Fixed Investment, Nonres, Structures, Buildings

ipsbldg =
    ipscom + ipsind + ipsbldgoth

[080] IPSBLDG87 (ID, Blk 2) Fixed Investment, Nonres, Structures, Buildings

ipsbldg87 =
    ipscom87 + ipsind87 + ipsbldgoth87

[081] IPSBLDGOTH (ID, Blk 2) Fixed Investment, Nonres, Structures, Other Buildings

ipsbldgoth =
    ipsbldgoth87 * pdiipsbldgoth*.01

[082] IPSBLDGOTH87 (ST, Blk 2) Fixed Investment, Nonres, Structures, Other Buildings

log(ipsbldgoth87) =
    + 1.4926 * from0 to5 degree2 near far
        log(gdp87/kpsnetbldgoth87.1)
    + 0.8390* from0 to19 degree2 near far
        log(kpopt87/gdp87)
    + 0.2241

[083] IPSCOM (ID, Blk 2) Fixed Investment, Nonres, Structures, Commercial

ipscom =
    ipscom87 * pdiipsiac*.01

[084] IPSCOM87 (ST, Blk 2) Fixed Investment, Nonres, Structures, Commercial

log(ipscom87) =
    + 0.7911* from0 to3 degree2 near far
        log(gdp87)
    + 2.0017* from0 to19 degree2 near far
        log(kpopt87/gdp87)
    – 2.5473

[085] IPSIND (ID, Blk 2) Fixed Investment, Nonres, Structures, Industrial

ipsind =
 ipsind87 * pdiipsiac*.01

[086] IPSIND87 (ST, Blk 2) Fixed Investment, Nonres, Structures, Industrial

log(ipsind87) =
 + 1.2943 * from0 to5 degree2 near far
  log(gdp87/kpsnetind87.1)
 + 0.9183 * from0 to19 degree2 near far
  log(kpopt87/gdp87)
 + 0.5695 * from0 to3 degree1 far
  log(cashflow/pdiipsiac)
 − 0.5299

[087] IPSMAP (ID, Blk 3) Fixed Investment, Nonres, Structures, Min Expl, Shafts, Wells

ipsmap =
 ipsmap87 * pdiipsmap*.01

[088] IPSMAP87 (ST, Blk 2) Fixed Investment, Nonres, Structures, Min Expl, Shafts, Wells

log(ipsmap87) =
 − 0.0033 * step(86,4) * ttrend
 + 0.6923 * from0 to5 degree1 far
  log(puvoilrac/pdiipsmap)
 + 4.2149

[089] IPSOAF (ID, Blk 3) Fixed Investment, Nonres, Structures, Other

ipsoaf =
 ipsoaf87 * pdiipsoaf*.01

[090] IPSOAF87 (ST, Blk 2) Fixed Investment, Nonres, Structures, Other

log(ipsoaf87) =
    0.4286 * step(82,1)
  + 1.0438* from0 to11 degree2 near far
      log(gdp87)
  – 7.3542

[091] IPSUTL (ID, Blk 3) Fixed Investment, Nonres, Structures, Utilities

ipsutl =
  ipsutl87 * pdiipsutl*.01

[092] IPSUTL87 (ST, Blk 2) Fixed Investment, Nonres, Structures, Utilities

log(ipsutl87) =
  + 0.9382 * from0 to19 degree2 near far
      log(kpopt87/kpsnetutl87.1)
  + 1.4314

1.2.2. *User cost of capital*

[093] UCK (ID, Blk 2) User Cost of Capital, CES Equation

uck =
pdiip * ((.34 * ratrrips + .66 * ratrripe) + .2-.01 * pchya(pdignp)) * (1−(.05 * itcsind + .14 * itcscom + .01 * itcsoaf + .06 * itcsbldgoth +.05 * itcsutl + .15 * itcetrn + .22 * itceinf + .15 * itceoas +.15 * itceind)-rmcpt * (((.34 * dmps + .66 * dmpe)/((.34 * ratrrips +.66 * ratrripe) * (.05 * tlsind + .14 * tlscom + .01 * tlsoaf + .06 * tlsbldgoth + .05 * tlsutl + .02 * tlsmap + .15 * tletrn + .22 * tleinf + .15 * tleoas + .15 * tleind) + (.34 * dmps + .66 * dmpe))) * (1−exp(−((.34 * ratrrips + .66 * ratrripe) * (.05 * tlsind + .14 * tlscom + .01 * tlsoaf + .06 * tlsbldgoth + .05 * tlsutl +.02 * tlsmap + .15 * tletrn + .22 * tleinf + .15 * tleoas + .15 * tleind) * (((.34 * dmps + .66 * dmpe)−1)/(.34 * dmps + .66 * dmpe)) + (.34 * dmps + .66 * dmpe)−1))) + ((.34 * dmps + .66 * dmpe)/((.34 * ratrrips + .66 * ratrripe) * (.05 * tlsind + .14 * tlscom + .01 * tlsoaf

+ .06 * tlsbldgoth + .05 * tlsutl + .02 * tlsmap + .15 * tletrn + .22 * tleinf + .15 * tleoas + .15 * tleind))) * (exp(−((.34 * ratrrips + .66 * ratrripe) * (.05 * tlsind + .14 * tlscom + .01 * tlsoaf + .06 * tlsbldgoth + .05 * tlsutl + .02 * tlsmap + .15 * tletrn + .22 * tleinf + .15 * tleoas + .15 * tleind) * (((.34 * dmps + .66 * dmpe)−1)/(.34 * dmps + .66 * dmpe)) + (.34 * dmps + .66 * dmpe)−1))− exp(−((.34 * ratrrips + .66 * ratrripe) * (.05 * tlsind + .14 * tlscom + .01 * tlsoaf + .06 * tlsbldgoth + .05 * tlsutl + .02 * tlsmap + .15 * tletrn + .22 * tleinf + .15 * tleoas + .15 * tleind) + (.34 * dmps + .66 * dmpe)−1)))))/(1−rmcpt)

[094] UCKEIND (ID, Blk 2) User Cost of Capital, Nonres, Prod Dur Equip, Industrial Equipment

uckeind =

pdiipeind * (ratrripe + .1263-.01 * rpdignphat) * (1−itceind− rmcpt * ((dmpe/(ratrripe * tleind + dmpe)) * (1−exp(−(ratrripe * tleind * ((dmpe−1)/dmpe) + dmpe−1))) + (dmpe/(ratrripe * tleind)) * (exp(−(ratrripe * tleind * ((dmpe−1)/dmpe) + dmpe-1))−exp(−(ratrripe * tleind + dmpe−1)))))/(1−rmcpt)

[095] UCKEINF (ID, Blk 3) User Cost of Capital, Nonres, Prod Dur Equip, Info Processing

uckeinf =

pdiipeinf * (ratrripe + .1263-.01 * rpdignphat) * (1−itceinf−rmcpt * ((dmpe/(ratrripe * tleinf + dmpe)) * (1−exp(−(ratrripe * tleinf * ((dmpe−1)/dmpe) + dmpe−1))) + (dmpe/(ratrripe * tleinf)) * (exp(−(ratrripe * tleinf * ((dmpe−1)/dmpe) + dmpe−1))−exp(−(ratrripe * tleinf + dmpe−1)))))/(1−rmcpt)

[096] UCKEOAS (ID, Blk 2) User Cost of Capital, Nonres, Prod Dur Equip, Other

uckeoas =

pdiipeoas * (ratrripe + .1263-.01 * rpdignphat) * (1−itceoas−rmcpt * ((dmpe/(ratrripe * tleoas + dmpe)) * (1−exp(−(ratrripe * tleoas * ((dmpe−1)/dmpe) + dmpe−1))) + (dmpe/(ratrripe * tleoas)) * (exp(−(ratrripe * tleoas * ((dmpe−1)/dmpe) + dmpe−1)) − exp(−(ratrripe * tleoas + dmpe−1)))))/(1−rmcpt)

[097] UCKETRN (ID, Blk 2) User Cost of Capital, Nonres, Prod Dur Equip, Transportation

ucketrn =
pdiipetrn * (ratrripe + .2830-.01 * rpdignphat) * (1−itcetrn−rmcpt * ((dmpe/(ratrripe * tletrn + dmpe)) * (1−exp(−(ratrripe * tletrn * ((dmpe−1)/dmpe) + dmpe−1))) + (dmpe/(ratrripe * tletrn)) * (exp(−(ratrripe * tletrn * ((dmpe−1)/dmpe) + dmpe−1))− exp(−(ratrripe * tletrn + dmpe−1)))))/(1−rmcpt)

[098] UCKIRSGE2 (ID, Blk 3) User Cost of Capital, Residential, New Hous, Multi-Unit Str

uckirsge2 =
pdiirstom * ratrrirs * (1−((txpf + txpn)/yptax) * ((dmps/(ratrrirs * (tlsind + tlscom) + dmps)) * (1−exp(−(ratrrirs * (tlsind + tlscom) * ((dmps−1)/dmps) + dmps−1))) + (dmps/(ratrrirs * (tlsind + tlscom))) * (exp(−(ratrrirs * (tlsind + tlscom) * ((dmps−1)/dmps) + dmps−1))−exp(−(ratrrirs * (tlsind + tlscom) + dmps−1)))))/(1−((txpf + txpn)/yptax))

[099] UCKIRSONE (ID, Blk 3) User Cost of Capital, Residential, New Hous, Single Unit Str

uckirsone =
pdiirsone * ratrrirs

[100] UCKSBLDGOTH (ID, Blk 3) User Cost of Capital, Nonres, Structures, Buildings, Other

ucksbldgoth =
pdiipsbldgoth * (ratrrips + .0264-.01 * rpdignphat) * (1−itcsbldgoth−rmcpt * ((dmps/(ratrrips * tlsbldgoth + dmps)) * (1−exp(−(ratrrips * tlsbldgoth * ((dmps−1)/dmps) + dmps−1))) + (dmps/(ratrrips * tlsbldgoth)) * (exp(−(ratrrips * tlsbldgoth * ((dmps−1)/dmps) + dmps−1))−exp(−(ratrrips * tlsbldgoth + dmps−1)))))/(1−rmcpt)

[101] UCKSCOM (ID, Blk 3) User Cost of Capital, Nonres Structures, Commercial

uckscom =
pdiipsiac * (ratrrips + .0264-.01 * rpdignphat) * (1−itcscom − rmcpt * ((dmps/ (ratrrips * tlscom + dmps)) * (1−exp(−(ratrrips * tlscom * ((dmps−1)/dmps) + dmps−1))) + (dmps/(ratrrips * tlsind)) * (exp(−(ratrrips * tlsind * ((dmps−1)/dmps) + dmps−1))−exp(−(ratrrips * tlsind + dmps−1)))))/(1−rmcpt)

[102] UCKSIND (ID, Blk 3) User Cost of Capital, Nonres Structures, Industrial

ucksind =
pdiipsiac * (ratrrips + .0264-.01 * rpdignphat) * (1−itcsind−rmcpt * ((dmps/(ratrrips * tlsind + dmps)) * (1−exp(−(ratrrips * tlsind * ((dmps−1)/dmps) + dmps−1))) +(dmps/(ratrrips * tlsind)) * (exp(−(ratrrips * tlsind * ((dmps−1)/dmps) + dmps−1))− exp(−(ratrrips * tlsind + dmps−1)))))/(1−rmcpt)

[103] UCKSMAP (ID, Blk 3) User Cost of Capital, Nonres Structures, Mining Expl, Shafts, Wells

ucksmap =
pdiipsmap * (ratrrips + .0663-.01 * rpdignphat) * (1−itcsmap− rmcpt * ((dmps/(ratrrips * tlsmap + dmps)) * (1−exp(−(ratrrips * tlsmap * ((dmps−1)/dmps) + dmps−1))) + (dmps/(ratrrips * tlsmap)) * (exp(−(ratrrips * tlsmap * ((dmps−1)/dmps) + dmps−1))−exp(−(ratrrips * tlsmap + dmps−1)))))/(1−rmcpt)

[104] UCKSOAF (ID, Blk 3) User Cost of Capital, Nonres, Structures, Other

ucksoaf =
pdiipsoaf * (ratrrips + .0360-.01 * rpdignphat) * (1−itcsoaf−rmcpt * ((dmps/(ratrrips * tlsoaf + dmps)) * (1−exp(−(ratrrips * tlsoaf * ((dmps−1)/dmps) + dmps−1))) + (dmps/(ratrrips * tlsoaf)) * (exp(−(ratrrips * tlsoaf * ((dmps−1)/dmps) + dmps−1))− exp(−(ratrrips * tlsoaf + dmps−1)))))/(1−rmcpt)

[105] UCKSUTL (ID, Blk 3) User Cost of Capital, Nonres, Structures, Utilities

ucksutl =
pdiipsutl * (ratrrips + .0360-.01 * rpdignphat) * (1−itcsutl−rmcpt * ((dmps/(ratrrips * tlsutl + dmps)) * (1−exp(−(ratrrips * tlsutl * ((dmps−1)/dmps) + dmps−1))) + (dmps/(ratrrips * tlsutl)) * (exp(−(ratrrips * tlsutl * ((dmps−1)/dmps) + dmps−1))− exp(−(ratrrips * tlsutl + dmps−1))))))/(1−rmcpt)

1.2.3. *Capital stock (nonresidential)*

[106] KPENET87 (ID, Blk 2) Net Capital Stock, Nonres, Prod Dur Equip, Total

kpenet87 =
kpenetinf87 + kpenetind87 + kpenettrn87 + kpenetoas87

[107] KPENETIND87 (ID, Blk 2) Net Capital Stock, Nonres, Prod Dur Equip, Industrial

kpenetind87 =
kpenetind87.1 * (1−((1+rdepeind87)**.25-1))+ipeind87/4

[108] KPENETINF87 (ID, Blk 2) Net Capital Stock, Nonres, Prod Dur Equip, Information Processing

kpenetinf87 =
kpenetinf87.1 * (1−((1+rdepeinf87)**.25-1))+ipeinf87/4

[109] KPENETOAS87 (ID, Blk 2) Net Capital Stock, Nonres, Prod Dur Equip, Other

kpenetoas87 =
kpenetoas87.1 * (1−((1+rdepeoas87)**.25-1))+ipeoas87/4

[110] KPENETTRN87 (ID, Blk 2) Net Capital Stock, Nonres, Prod Dur Equip, Transportation

kpenettrn87 =
kpenettrn87.1 * (1−((1+rdepetrn87)**.25-1))+ipetrn87/4

[111] KPNET87 (ID, Blk 2) Net Capital Stock, Nonres, Total

kpnet87 =
kpenet87 + kpsnet87

[112] KPNETCON87 (ID, Blk 2) Net Capital Stock, Nonres, Construction

kpnetcon87 =
kpnetcon87.1
+ 0.0143 * diff(kpenetinf87)
+ 0.1170 * diff(kpenettrn87)
+ 0.0954 * diff((kpenetoas87+kpenetind87))
+ 0.0387 * diff(kpsnetcom87)

[113] KPNETMFG87 (ID, Blk 2) Net Capital Stock, Nonres, Manufacturing

kpnetmfg87 =
kpnetmfg87.1
+ 0.3210 * diff(kpenetinf87)
+ 0.1943 * diff(kpenettrn87)
+ 0.2696 * diff((kpenetoas87+kpenetind87))
+ 0.8745 * diff(kpsnetind87) 0.1479 diff(kpsnetcom87)
+ 0.0011* diff(kpsnetbldgoth87+kpsnetutl87+kpsnetoaf87)

[114] KPNETMIN87 (ID, Blk 2) Net Capital Stock, Nonres, Mining

kpnetmin87 =
kpnetmin87.1
+ 0.0083 * diff(kpenetinf87)
+ 0.0183 * diff(kpenettrn87)
+ 0.0442 * diff((kpenetoas87+kpenetind87))
+ 0.1223* diff(kpsnetind87+kpsnetmap87)

[115] KPNETOTH87 (ID, Blk 2) Net Capital Stock, Nonres, Other

kpnetoth87 =
kpnetoth87.1
+ 0.4077 * diff(kpenetinf87)
+ 0.1497 * diff(kpenettrn87)
+ 0.1679 * diff((kpenetoas87+kpenetind87))

+ 0.0016 * diff(kpsnetind87)
+ 0.3913 * diff(kpsnetcom87)
+ 0.1867 * diff(kpsnetbldgoth87+kpsnetutl87+kpsnetoaf87)

[116] KPNETTPU87 (ID, Blk 2) Net Capital Stock, Nonres, Transportation & Utilities

kpnettpu87 =
kpnettpu87.1
+ 0.0675 * diff(kpenetinf87)
+ 0.1697 * diff(kpenettrn87)
+ 0.2538 * diff((kpenetoas87+kpenetind87))
+ 0.0278 * diff(kpsnetcom87)
+ 0.6240 * diff(kpsnetbldgoth87+kpsnetutl87+kpsnetoaf87)

[117] KPNETWRT87 (ID, Blk 2) Net Capital Stock, Nonres, Wholesale & Retail Trade

kpnetwrt87 =
kpnetwrt87.1
+ 0.1813 * diff(kpenetinf87)
+ 0.3510 * diff(kpenettrn87)
+ 0.1692 * diff((kpenetoas87+kpenetind87))
+ 0.0016 * diff(kpsnetind87)
+ 0.3944 * diff(kpsnetcom87)
+ 0.1882 * diff(kpsnetbldgoth87+kpsnetutl87+kpsnetoaf87))

[118] KPOPT87 (ST, Blk 2) Net Capital Stock, Nonres, Optimal

log(kpopt87) =
1.1565 * log(gdp87 * (.13058 * *(.64673)) *
((((((.13058 **(.64673)) * (uck**(1−(.64673)))+
(.61726**(.64673)) * (jqwrhnfm**(1−(.64673)))) **
(1/(1−(.64673))))/((1.0045)**((ttrend−158.5)/4)))/
uck) **(.64673)) * ((.99841) * *((ttrend−158.5)/4)))
− 0.6234

[119] KPSNET87 (ID, Blk 2) Net Capital Stock, Nonres, Structures, Total

kpsnet87 =
kpsnetbldg87 + kpsnetmap87 + kpsnetutl87 + kpsnetoaf87

[120] KPSNETBLDG87 (ID, Blk 2) Net Capital Stock, Nonres, Buildings

kpsnetbldg87 =
kpsnetind87 + kpsnetcom87 + kpsnetbldgoth87

[121] KPSNETBLDGOTH87 (ID, Blk 2) Net Capital Stock, Nonres, Other Building

kpsnetbldgoth87 =
kpsnetbldgoth87.1 * (1−((1+rdepsbldgoth87)**.25-1))+ ipsbldgoth87/4

[122] KPSNETCOM87 (ID, Blk 2) Net Capital Stock, Nonres, Structures, Commercial

kpsnetcom87 =
kpsnetcom87.1 * (1−((1+rdepscom87)**.25-1))+ipscom87/4

[123] KPSNETIND87 (ID, Blk 2) Net Capital Stock, Nonres, Structures, Industrial

kpsnetind87 =
kpsnetind87.1 * (1−((1+rdepsind87)**.25-1))+ipsind87/4

[124] KPSNETMAP87 (ID, Blk 2) Net Capital Stock, Nonres, Mining Expl, Shafts & Wells

kpsnetmap87 =
kpsnetmap87.1 * (1−((1+rdepsmap87)**.25-1))+ipsmap87/4

[125] KPSNETOAF87 (ID, Blk 2) Net Capital Stock, Nonres, Structures, Other

kpsnetoaf87 =
kpsnetoaf87.1 * (1−((1+rdepsoaf87)**.25-1))+ipsoaf87/4

[126] KPSNETUTL87 (ID, Blk 2) Net Capital Stock, Nonres, Utilities

```
kpsnetutl87 =
    kpsnetutl87.1 * (1−((1+rdepsutl87)**.25-1))+ipsutl87/4
```

1.2.4. *Residential investment*

[127] IR (ID, Blk 2) Fixed Investment, Residential, Total

```
ir =
    (irsone87 * pdiirsone+irstom87 * pdiirstom+iroth87 * pdiiroth)/100
```

[128] IR87 (ID, Blk 2) Fixed Investment, Residential, Total

```
ir87 =
    irsone87 + irstom87 + iroth87
```

[129] IROTH (ID, Blk 2) Fixed Investment, Residential, Other

```
iroth =
    iroth87 * pdiiroth*.01
```

[130] IROTH87 (ST, Blk 2) Fixed Investment, Residential, Other

```
log((iroth87−2.09451 * puvholdmed_u/puvholdmed_sf/pdice−4.37290 *
uhesld−2.15708 * spike(86,4)+1.17616)/nhhdcsu) =
        0.6945 * log(ydp87/nhhdcsu)
      + 0.6168 * log(puvholdmed_u/puvholdmed_sf/pdice)
      − 0.0155 * rprime-rpdicehat
      − 0.1345 * spike(73,2)
      − 0.1235 * spike(73,3)
      − 0.1923 * spike(74,4)
      − 0.1384 * spike(76,3)
      − 0.1262 * spike(82,3)
      + 0.2387
```

[131] IRSONE (ID, Blk 3) Fixed Investment, Residential, New Housing, Single Unit Structures

```
irsone =
    irsone87 * pdiirsone*.01
```

[132] IRSONE87 (ST, Blk 2) Fixed Investment, Residential, New Housing, Single Unit Structures

```
log(irsone87) =
      1.1393 * log(ydpperm87/nhhdcsu)
    - 0.1126 * spike(80,2)
    + 1.1393 * log(ydpperm87/nhhdcsu)
    + 0.3012 * log(uhsone)
    + 0.4862 * log(uhsone)[-1]
    + 0.1712 * log(uhsone)[-2]
    + 0.0827* log(uhsone)[-3]
    + 0.4979
```

[133] IRSTOM (ID, Blk 3) Fixed Investment, Residential, New Housing, Multi-Unit Structures

```
irstom =
    irstom87 * pdiirstom*.01
```

[134] IRSTOM87 (ST, Blk 2) Fixed Investment, Residential, New Housing, Multi-Unit Structures

```
log(irstom87) =
      0.0153 * log(ydpperm87/nhhdcsu)
    + 0.2003 * (1-step(75,1)) * log(uhsge2)
    + 0.2038 * (1-step(75,1)) * log(uhsge2)[-1]
    + 0.2615 * (1-step(75,1)) * log(uhsge2)[-2]
    + 0.2333 * (1-step(75,1)) * log(uhsge2)[-3]
    + 0.0587 * (1-step(75,1)) * log(uhsge2)[-4]
    + 1.0010 * from0 to4 degree2 far
          step(75,1) * log(uhsge2)
    + 3.8580
```

[135] KRNET87 (ID, Blk 2) Net Capital Stock, Residential, Total

```
krnet87 =
    0.9946 * krnet87.1 + ((irstom87+irsone87)/4) + 0.6610 *
          (iroth87/4)
```

[136] UHC (ID, Blk 3) Housing Units Completed, Total

uhc =
    uhcone + uhcge2

[137] UHCGE2 (ST, Blk 3) Housing Units Completed, Multi-Unit

uhcge2 =
    + 0.9646* from0 to9 degree2 far
        uhsge2

[138] UHCONE (ST, Blk 3) Housing Units Completed, Single Unit

uhcone =
    + 0.9779 * from0 to6 degree2 far
        uhsone

[139] UHESLD (ST, Blk 2) Homes Sold, Existing Single Unit

log(uhesld/nhhld) =
    0.08353 * dcredit
    + 2.92595 * log((nhhld2534+nhhld3544)/nhhld)
    + 0.80385 * movavg(4,log(1+pchya(puvholdmed_u)/rmorefw))
    + 0.2651 * log(jcs)
    + 2.17012 * log(ydpperm87/np)
    + 1.67958 * log((ydp87/ydpperm87)/np)
    + 4.7724 * from0 to2 degree1 far
        dlog(eme)
    −1.2165

[140] UHS (ID, Blk 2) Housing Starts, Total

uhs =
    uhsone + uhsge2

[141] UHSGE2 (ST, Blk 2) Housing Starts, Multi-Unit

log(uhsge2) =
    0.3791 * log(max(0,ratrrirs.2 * 100-rprime.2)+1)
    − 0.4266 * log(tlsoaf.2)
    − 0.8645 * log(vrfr*nhhld)
    + 5.4773

[142] UHSONE (ST, Blk 2) Housing Starts, Single Unit

```
log(uhsone/nhhld) =
      0.57463 * log(ratrrirs)
    + 0.99086 * log(uhesld/nhhld)
    + 0.02709 * dcredit
    - 0.60418 * log(rmorefw/100 * puvhnewmed_u/(ydp/nhhld))
    - 2.79605 * log(krnet87.1/nhhld.1)
    + 0.40836 * log(jcs)
    + 8.03633
```

1.2.5. *Changes in inventory*

[143] II (ID, Blk 2) Change in Business Inventories, Total

```
ii =
    iifrm + iinfm
```

[144] II87 (ID, Blk 2) Change in Business Inventories, Total

```
ii87 =
    iifrm87 + iinfm87
```

[145] IICAR87 (ST, Blk 2) Change in Business Inventories, Automotive

```
iicar87/4 =
      0.8575 * (ukcardom*puvcar87-ukcardom[-1]*puvcar87[-1])
    + 0.1185
```

[146] IIFRM (ID, Blk 1) Change in Business Inventories, Farm

```
iifrm =
    iifrmaccc + gpfnnonccc
```

[147] IIFRM87 (ID, Blk 1) Change in Business Inventories, Farm

```
iifrm87 =
    iifrmaccc87 + gpfnnonccc87
```

[148] IIFRMACCC (ST, Blk 1) Change in Business Inventories, Farm Plus CCC Purchases

```
iifrmaccc =
      1.3038 * iifrmaccc87 * ((ppifrm[-1]+ppifrm)/2/100)
    + 0.0422
```

[149] IIMFG (ST, Blk 2) Change in Business Inventories, Manufacturing

```
iimfg =
      0.9867 * iimfg87 * (pdikimfg+pdikimfg[-1])/2 * .01
    + 0.0751
```

[150] IIMFG87 (ID, Blk 2) Change in Business Inventories, Manufacturing

```
iimfg87 =
    4 * (kimfg87-kimfg87.1)
```

[151] IINFM (ID, Blk 2) Change in Business Inventories, Nonfarm

```
iinfm =
    iimfg + iinfmxmfg
```

[152] IINFM87 (ID, Blk 2) Change in Business Inventories, Nonfarm

```
iinfm87 =
    iimfg87 + iicar87 + iinfmoth87
```

[153] IINFMOTH87 (ID, Blk 2) Change in Business Inventories, Nonfarm, Nonmanufacturing, Other

```
iinfmoth87 =
    4 * (kinfmoth87-kinfmoth87.1)
```

[154] IINFMXMFG (ST, Blk 2) Change in Business Inventories, Nonfarm, Nonmanufacturing

```
iinfmxmfg =
      0.9728 * iinfmxmfg87 * (pdikinfmxmfg+
         pdikinfmxmfg[-1])/2 * .01
    - 0.1717
```

[155] IINEFMXMFG87 (ID, Blk 2) Change in Business Inventories, Nonfarm, Nonmanufacturing

```
iinfmxmfg87 =
    iinfm87−iinfg87
```

1.2.6. *Inventory stock*

Stock of inventories and nonfarm spending on services are divided into seven categories: *three* household operations; *two* transportation services; a medical care; and other services.

[156] KIMFG87 (ST, Blk 2) Stock of Inventories, Manufacturing

```
log(kimfg87) =
    + 0.6981 * from0 to8 degree2 near far
          log(xiomfg87)
    + 0.2855
```

[157] KINFM (ST, Blk 2) Stock of Inventories, Nonfarm

```
kinfm =
       1.0527 * kimfg87 * (pdikimfg+pdikimfg.1)/2 * .01
    + 0.9660 * ((kinfm87.1−kimfg87.1)+iinfmxmfg87/4) *
          (pdikinfmxmfg+pdikinfmxmfg.1)/2 * .01
```

[158] KINFM87 (ID, Blk 2) Stock of Inventories, Nonfarm

```
kinfm87 =
    kimfg87 + kinfmoth87 + (kinfm87.1−kimfg87.1−
    kinfmoth87.1+iicar87/4)
```

[159] KINFMOTH87 (ST, Blk 2) Stock of Inventories, Other, Nonfarm

```
log(kinfmoth87) =
    + 1.0718 * from0 to8 degree2 near far
          log(gdp87)
    −2.8696
```

1.3. *Government expenditure*

[160] GP (ID, Blk 3) Govt Purchases, Total

```
gp =
    gpf + gpn
```

[161] GP87 (ID, Blk 3) Govt Purchases, Total

gp87 =
gpf87 + gpn87

[162] GPF (ID, Blk 2) Govt Purchases, Federal, Total

gpf =
gpfd + gpfn

[163] GPF87 (ID, Blk 2) Govt Purchases, Federal, Total

gpf87 =
gpfd87 + gpfn87

[164] GPFD (ID, Blk 2) Govt Purchases, Federal, Defense, Total

gpfd =
gpfdxpay + gpfdpay

[165] GPFD87 (ID, Blk 2) Govt Purchases, Federal, Defense, Total

gpfd87 =
gpfdpay87 + gpfdxpay87

[166] GPFDPAY (ID, Blk 2) Govt Purchases, Federal, Defense, Comp of Employees, Total

gpfdpay =
gpfdpaymil + gpfdpayciv

[167] GPFDPAY87 (ID, Blk 2) Govt Purchases, Federal, Defense, Comp of Employees, Total

gpfdpay87 =
gpfdpaymil87 + gpfdpayciv87

[168] GPFDPAYCIV (ID, Blk 2) Govt Purchases, Federal, Defense, Comp of Employees, Civilian

gpfdpayciv =
(wrgpfdpayciv*40 * 52) * (emegfd/1000)

[169] GPFDPAYCIV87 (ID, Blk 2) Govt Purchases, Federal, Defense, Comp of Employees, Civilian

gpfdpayciv87 =
 100 * (gpfdpayciv/pdigpfdpayciv)

[170] GPFDPAYMIL (ID, Blk 2) Govt Purchases, Federal, Defense, Comp of Employees, Military

gpfdpaymil =
 (wrgpfdpaymil*40 * 52) * (emgfdmil/1000)

[171] GPFDPAYMIL87 (ID, Blk 2) Govt Purchases, Federal, Defense, Comp of Employees, Military

gpfdpaymil87 =
 100 * (gpfdpaymil/pdigpfdpaymil)

[172] GPFDXPAY (ID, Blk 2) Govt Purchases, Federal, Defense, Noncompensation

gpfdxpay =
 (1−dumgef) * (gpfdxpay87exo*pdigpfdxpay/100) +
 dumgef*gpfdxpayexo

[173] GPFDXPAY87 (ID, Blk 2) Govt Purchases, Federal, Defense, Noncompensation

gpfdxpay87 =
 ((1−dumgef) * gpfdxpay87exo) +
 (dumgef*(gpfdxpayexo/pdigpfdxpay) * 100)

[174] GPFN (ID, Blk 2) Govt Purchases, Federal, Nondefense, Total

gpfn =
 gpfnpay + gpfnxpay

[175] GPFN87 (ID, Blk 2) Govt Purchases, Federal, Nondefense, Total

gpfn87 =
 gpfnpay87 + gpfnxpay87

[176] GPFNNONCCC (ST, Blk 1) Govt Purchases, Federal, Nondefense, CCC Payments

gpfnnonccc =
1.3069 * gpfnnonccc87 * ((ppifrm[−1]+ppifrm)/2/100)
− 0.2286

[177] GPFNOTH (ID, Blk 2) Govt Purchases, Federal, Nondefense, Noncompensation, Other

gpfnoth =
((1−dumgef) * (gpfnoth87exo*pdigpfnoth/100)) +
(dumgef*gpfnothexo)

[178] GPFNOTH87 (ID, Blk 2) Govt Purchases, Federal, Nondefense, Noncompensation, Other

gpfnoth87 =
((1−dumgef) * gpfnoth87exo) + (dumgef *(gpfnothexo/pdigpfnoth) *
100)

[179] GPFNPAY (ID, Blk 2) Govt Purchases, Federal, Nondefense, Comp of Employees

gpfnpay =
(wrgpfnpay*40 * 52) * (emegfn/1000)

[180] GPFNPAY87 (ID, Blk 2) Govt Purchases, Federal, Nondefense, Comp of Employees

gpfnpay87 =
100 * (gpfnpay/pdigpfnpay)

[181] GPFNXCCC (ID, Blk 3) Govt Purchases, Federal, Nondefense, Less CCC Payments

gpfnxccc =
gpfnpay + gpfnoth

[182] GPFNXCCC87 (ID, Blk 3) Govt Purchases, Federal, Nondefense, Less CCC Payments

gpfnxccc87 =
gpfnpay87 + gpfnoth87

[183] GPFNXPAY (ID, Blk 2) Govt Purchases, Federal, Nondefense, Noncompensation

gpfnxpay =
gpfnnonccc + gpfnoth

[184] GPFNXPAY87 (ID, Blk 2) Govt Purchases, Federal, Nondefense, Noncompensation

gpfnxpay87 =
gpfnnonccc87 + gpfnoth87

[185] GPFPAY (ID, Blk 2) Govt Purchases, Federal, Compensation of Employees

gpfpay =
gpfdpay + gpfnpay

[186] GPFPAY87 (ID, Blk 2) Govt Purchases, Federal, Compensation of Employees

gpfpay87 =
gpfdpay87 + gpfnpay87

[187] GPN (ID, Blk 2) Govt Purchases, State & Local, Total

gpn =
gpnpay + gpnxpay

[188] GPN87 (ID, Blk 2) Govt Purchases, State & Local, Total

gpn87 =
gpnpay87 + gpnxpay87

[189] GPNPAY (ID, Blk 2) Govt Purchases, State & Local, Comp of Employees

```
gpnpay =
    (wrgpnpay*40 * 52) * (emegn/1000)
```

[190] GPNPAY87 (ID, Blk 2) Govt Purchases, State & Local, Comp of Employees

```
gpnpay87 =
    100 * (gpnpay/pdigpnpay)
```

[191] GPNXPAY (ID, Blk 2) Govt Purchases, State & Local, Noncompensation

```
gpnxpay =
    .01 * pdigpnxpay*gpnxpay87
```

[192] GPPAY (ID, Blk 3) Govt Purchases, Total, Compensation of Employees

```
gppay =
    gpfpay + gpnpay
```

[193] GPPAY87 (ID, Blk 3) Govt Purchases, Total, Compensation of Employees

```
gppay87 =
    gpfpay87 + gpnpay87
```

1.4. *International exports and imports*

1.4.1. *Exports*

[194] EX (ID, Blk 2) Exports, Total

```
ex =
    exmer + exser
```

[195] EX87 (ID, Blk 2) Exports, Total

```
ex87 =
    exmer87 + exser87
```

[196] EXCAPOTH (ID, Blk 3) Exports, Merchandise, Other Capital Goods

excapoth =
    excapoth87 * pdiexcapoth/100

[197] EXCAPOTH87 (ST, Blk 2) Exports, Merchandise, Other Capital Goods

log(excapoth87) =
    + 1.2695 * from0 to4 degree1 none
        log(gdp15w87)
    − 1.2053 * from0 to9 degree2 far
        log(pdiexcapoth*rexmor15/ppirow15)
    + 4.05768

[198] EXCAR87 (ST, Blk 2) Exports, Merchandise, Autos

log(excar87) =
    + 2.3556 * from0 to4 degree1 far
        log(gdp15w87)
    − 0.6945 * from0 to4 degree1 far
        log(puvcardom87 * pdice*rexmor15/ppirow15)
    − 3.98

[199] EXCOMPEQU (ID, Blk 3) Exports, Merchandise, Computers, Peripherals, and Parts

excompequ =
    excompequ87 * pdiexcompequ/100

[200] EXCOMPEQU87 (ST, Blk 2) Exports, Merchandise, Computers, Peripherals, and Parts

log(excompequ87 * pdiexcompequ*.01) =
    1.88263 * log(ppirow15 * gdp15w87)
    − 0.3024 * from0 to6 degree2 near far
        log(rexmor15)
    − 13.2641

[201] EXCONXMVP (ID, Blk 3) Exports, Merchandise, Consumer Goods Except MVP

```
exconxmvp =
    exconxmvp87 * pdiexconxmvp*.01
```

[202] EXCONXMVP87 (ST, Blk 2) Exports, Merchandise, Consumer Goods Except MVP

```
log(exconxmvp87) =
      0.18995 * spike(74,1)+spike(74,2)
    - 0.17363 * spike(75,2)
    + 0.2963 * spike(80,1)
    + 1.6423 * from0 to3 degree1 far
        log(gdp15w87)
    - 2.0462 * from0 to12 degree2 far
        log(pdiexconxmvp*rexmor15/ppirow15)
    + 4.84421
```

[203] EXFFB (ID, Blk 3) Exports, Merchandise, Foods, Feeds, & Beverages

```
exffb =
    exffb87 * pdiexffb*.01
```

[204] EXFFB87 (ST, Blk 2) Exports, Merchandise, Foods, Feeds, & Beverages

```
log(exffb87) =
      0.69138 * log(exgrain)
    + 0.22993 * spike(78,2)
    - 0.21314 * spike(74,1)+spike(74,2)+spike(74,3)+spike(74,4)
    - 0.19668 * spike(85,2)+spike(85,3)
    - 0.25844 * spike(75,2)
    - 0.3708 * from0 to12 degree2 near far
        log(pdiexffb*rexmor15/ppirow15)
    + 2.2454
```

[205] EXISM (ID, Blk 3) Exports, Merchandise, Industrial Supplies & Materials

exism =
    exism87 * pdiexism*.01

[206] EXISM87 (ST, Blk 2) Exports, Merchandise, Industrial Supplies & Materials

log(exism87) =
    − 0.1463 * spike(77,4)+spike(78,1)
    + 0.14713 * spike(79,4)+spike(80,1)+spike(80,2)+spike(80,3)
    + 1.1214 * from0 to4 degree2 near far
        log(gdp15w87)
    −0.3911 * from0 to8 degree2 near far
        log(pdiexism*rexmor15/ppirow15)
    + 0.92957

[207] EXMER (ID, Blk 2) Exports, Merchandise, Total

exmer =
    (exffb87 * pdiexffb + exism87 * pdiexism +
    excapoth87 * pdiexcapoth + excompequ87 * pdiexcompequ +
    exmvp87 * pdiexmvp + exconxmvp87 * pdiexconxmvp +
    exoth87 * pdiexoth)/100

[208] EXMER87 (ID, Blk 2) Exports, Merchandise, Total

exmer87 =
    exffb87 + exism87 + excapoth87 + excompequ87 + exmvp87 +
    exconxmvp87 + exoth87

[209] EXMVP (ID, Blk 3) Exports, Merchandise, Motor Vehicles & Parts

exmvp =
    exmvp87 * pdiexmvp*.01

[210] EXMVP87 (ST, Blk 2) Exports, Merchandise, Motor Vehicles & Parts

```
log(exmvp87−excar87) =
    − 0.27572 * spike(82,4)+spike(83,1)
    + 0.6262 * from0 to2 degree1 far
        log(gdp15w87)
    − 0.6352 * from0 to5 degree2 near far
        log(pdiexmvp*rexmor15/ppirow15)
    + 3.00545
```

[211] EXOTH (ID, Blk 3) Exports, Merchandise, Other

```
exoth =
    exoth87 * pdiexoth*.01
```

[212] EXOTH87 (ST, Blk 2) Exports, Merchandise, Other

```
log(exoth87) =
      0.35095 * log(exffb87+exism87+excapoth87+excompequ87+
        exconxmvp87+exmvp87−excar87)
    − 0.47381 * (1−step(82,4))
    − 0.1071 * (1−step(89,1))
    + 1.19672
```

[213] EXRFI (ST, Blk 2) Exports, Services, Factor Income

```
exrfi/(gdp15w87 * ppirow15) =
      0.8253 * exrfi/(gdp15w87 * ppirow15)[−1]
    + 0.0001 * rlibor3m
    + 0.0000 * rexmor15
    − 0.0010 * spike(75,1)
    + 0.0019
```

[214] EXRFI87 (ID, Blk 2) Exports, Services, Factor Income

```
exrfi87 =
    exrfi/pdiexrfi*100
```

[215] EXSER (ID, Blk 2) Exports, Services, Total

```
exser =
    exser87 * pdiexser*.01
```

[216] EXSER87 (ST, Blk 2) Exports, Services, Total

```
log(exser87) =
    − 0.10038 * spike(79,4)
    − 0.06251 * (1−step(86,1))
    + 1.7961 * from0 to4 degree1 far
        log(gdp15w87)
    − 0.2583 * from0 to9 degree2 near far
        log(pdiexser*rexmor15/ppirow15)
    − 2.42119
```

1.4.2. *Imports*

[217] IM (ID, Blk 2) Imports, Total

```
im =
    immer + imser
```

[218] IM87 (ID, Blk 2) Imports, Total

```
im87 =
    immer87 + imser87
```

[219] IMCAPOTH (ID, Blk 3) Imports, Merchandise, Capital Goods, Other

```
imcapoth =
    imcapoth87 * pdiimcapoth/100
```

[220] IMCAPOTH87 (ST, Blk 2) Imports, Merchandise, Other Capital Goods

```
log(imcapoth87) =
    + 1.8047 * from0 to3 degree1 far
        log(ipeoas87+ipeind87)
    − 1.8416 * from0 to11 degree2 near far
        log(pdiimcapoth/((ipeoas+ipeind)/(ipeoas87+ipeind87)))
    + 3.6831
```

[221] IMCAR87 (ST, Blk 2) Imports, Merchandise, Autos

```
log(imcar87) =
    − 0.8562 * log(pdiimmvp/pdicedmvp)
    − 0.2082 * spike(82,4)
    − 0.2182 * spike(77,2)
    + 1.0080 * log(puvcarimp87 * uscarimp)
    − 0.2287
```

[222] IMCOMPEQU (ID, Blk 3) Imports, Merchandise, Computers, Peripherals and Parts

```
imcompequ =
    imcompequ87 * pdiimcompequ/100
```

[223] IMCOMPEQU87 (ST, Blk 2) Imports, Merchandise, Computers, Peripherals and Parts

```
log(imcompequ87/ipeinf87)+
.15 * (pdiimcompequ/pdiipeinf)+
.2 * (pdiimcompequ.1/pdiipeinf.1)+
.3 * (pdiimcompequ.2/pdiipeinf.2)+
.2 * (pdiimcompequ.1/pdiipeinf.1)+
.15 * (pdiimcompequ.2/pdiipeinf.2) =
        1.0029 * log(ttrend)
    − 6.0367
```

[224] IMCONXMVP (ID, Blk 3) Imports, Merchandise, Consumer Goods

```
imconxmvp =
    imconxmvp87 * pdiimconxmvp*.01
```

[225] IMCONXMVP87 (ST, Blk 2) Imports, Merchandise, Consumer Goods

```
log(imconxmvp87/np) =
        0.0050 * ((1−step(88,1)) * ttrend+step(88,1) * 160−108)
    + 1.8062 * from0 to2 degree2 far
            log((ced87−cedmvp87+cencas87+cenoth87)/np)
```

```
    - 1.4836 * from0 to8 degree2 far
          log(pdiimconxmvp/((ced-cedmvp+cencas+cenoth /
          (ced87-cedmvp87+cencas87+cenoth87)))
    + 3.7946
```

[226] IMFFB (ID, Blk 3) Imports, Merchandise, Foods, Feeds, & Beverages

```
imffb =
    imffb87 * pdiimffb*.01
```

[227] IMFFB87 (ST, Blk 2) Imports, Merchandise, Foods, Feeds, & Beverages

```
log(imffb87/np) =
        1.04048 * log(cenfab87/np)
    + 0.5608 * log(cenfab87/np)[-1]
    - 0.09184 * log(runc)
    - 0.0843 * spike(88,4)+spike(89,1)
    - 0.19819 * spike(75,1)+spike(75,2)
    - 0.14326 * spike(82,1)
    + 0.11042 * spike(74,1)
    - 0.4110 * from0 to2 degree2 far
          log(pdiimffb/pdicenfab)
    - 3.3021
```

[228] IMISMXOIL (ID, Blk 3) Imports, Merchandise, Indust Supplies & Materials, Excl Petroleum

```
imismxoil =
    imismxoil87 * pdiimismxoil*.01
```

[229] IMISMXOIL87 (ST, Blk 2) Imports, Merchandise, Indust Supplies & Materials, Excl Petroleum

```
log((imismxoil87)/np) =
    - 0.1527 * spike(75,2)+spike(75,3)
    - 0.1181 * spike(80,3)
    + 1.1001  * from0 to3 degree1 far
          log((xiomfg87)/np)
```

− 0.7551 * from0 to4 degree2 far
log(pdiimismxoil/(.0784 * ppicap+.02504 * ppirap+.0164 * ppilwp+.08464 * ppippa+.10062 * ppimmp))
− 3.2531

[230] IMMER (ID, Blk 2) Imports, Merchandise, Total

immer =
(imoil87 * pdiimoil+imffb87 * pdiimffb+imismxoil87 * pdiimismxoil+imcompequ87 * pdiimcompequ+imcapoth87 * pdiimcapoth+immvp87 * pdiimmvp+imconxmvp87 * pdiimconxmvp+imoth87 * pdiimoth)/100

[231] IMMER87 (ID, Blk 2) Imports, Merchandise, Total

immer87 =
imoil87 + imffb87 + imismxoil87 + imcapoth87
+ imcompequ87+ immvp87 + imconxmvp87 + imoth87

[232] IMMVP (ID, Blk 3) Imports, Merchandise, Motor Vehicles & Parts

immvp =
immvp87 * pdiimmvp*.01

[233] IMMVP87 (ST, Blk 2) Imports, Merchandise, Motor Vehicles & Parts

log((immvp87−imcar87)/np) =
+ 1.3465 * from0 to2 degree1 far
log((cedmvp87−cedmnc87)/np)
− 0.6449

[234] IMOIL (ID, Blk 3) Imports, Merchandise, Petroleum & Products

imoil =
imoil87 * pdiimoil*.01

[235] IMOIL87 (ST, Blk 2) Imports, Merchandise, Petroleum & Products

log(imoil87) =
0.9784 * log(qebloil−qebloildom)
− 0.0542 * dqtr1
− 0.0360 * dqtr2
+ 0.0159 * dqtr3
+ 0.0840* spike(77,1)
− 0.0805 * spike(89,1)
+ 1.9357

[236] IMOTH (ID, Blk 3) Imports, Merchandise, Other

imoth =
imoth87 * pdiimoth*.01

[237] IMOTH87 (ST, Blk 2) Imports, Merchandise, Other

log(imoth87/np) =
0.9847 *
log((imffb87+imcapoth87+imcompequ87+imismxoil87 + immvp87+imconxmvp87)/np)
− 0.2732 * spike(76,4)
− 0.2732 * spike(80,2)
− 0.4536 * 1−step(80,1)
− 2.7009

[238] IMPFI (ST, Blk 2) Imports, Services, Factor Income

(impfi−exrfi) =
− 0.0033 * movavg(2,rcp3m) * knetexcab
− 25.4928

[239] IMPFI87 (ID, Blk 2) Imports, Services, Factor Income

impfi87 =
impfi/pdiimpfi*100

[240] IMSER (ID, Blk 2) Imports, Services, Total

imser =
imser87 * pdiimser*.01

[241] IMSER87 (ST, Blk 2) Imports, Services, Total

```
log(imser87/np) =
      0.0349 * spike(87,2)+spike(87,3)
    + 0.0574 * spike(87,4)+spike(88,1)
    + 1.7929 * from0 to3 degree2 far
         log(ydp87/np)
    – 0.8345 * from0 to6 degree2 far
         log(pdiimser/pdices)
    – 5.6809
```

[242] IMXOIL (ID, Blk 2) Imports, Merchandise, Nonpetroleum Products

```
imxoil =
    immer–imoil87 * pdiimoil/100
```

[243] IMXOIL87 (ID, Blk 2) Imports, Merchandise, Nonpetroleum Products

```
imxoil87 =
    immer87– imoil87
```

1.4.3. *Net exports (international)*

[244] NETEX (ID, Blk 2) Net Exports, Goods & Services, NIPA Basis

```
netex =
    ex–im
```

[245] NETEX87 (ID, Blk 3) Net Exports, Goods & Services, NIPA Basis

```
netex87 =
    ex87 – im87
```

[246] NETEXCAB (ID, Blk 2) Net Exports, Current Account Balance

```
netexcab =
    inf + netcadif
```

[247] NETEXMER (ID, Blk 3) Net Exports, Merchandise, NIPA Basis

```
netexmer =
    exmer - immer
```

[248] NETEXMER87 (ID, Blk 3) Net Exports, Merchandise, NIPA Basis

```
netexmer87 =
    exmer87 - immer87
```

1.5. *GDP, GNP and potential capacity*

[249] GDP (ID, Blk 2) Gross Domestic Product

```
gdp =
    ce + ipe + ips + ir + ii + gpf + gpn + ex - im
```

[250] GDP87 (ID, Blk 2) Gross Domestic Product

```
gdp87 =
    ce87 + ipe87 + ips87 + ir87 + ii87 + gpf87 + gpn87 + ex87 - im87
```

[251] GDPPOT87 (ID, Blk 2) Potential Gross Domestic Product

```
gdppot87 =
    18.25 * (.13058 * ((kpnet87+kgnet87) * *(-.54623))+.61726 *
    (((1-runcn/100.) * nlfc) * *(-.54623))) * *(1/(-.54623)) *
    (1+(rtechchg/100)) * *((ttrend-158.5)/4)
```

[252] RKUMFGFRB (ST, Blk 2) Capacity Utilization Rate, Manufacturing

```
rkumfgfrb =
    - 9.7219 * from0 to9 degree2 near far
          log(1.1 * (gdppot87)-gdp87)
    + 144.3920
```

[253] GDPXNETEX (ID, Blk 3) Gross Domestic Purchases

```
gdpxnetex =
    gdp - netex
```

[254] GDPXNETEX87 (ID, Blk 3) Gross Domestic Purchases

gdpxnetex87 =
    gdp87 − netex87

[255] GNP (ID, Blk 2) Gross National Product

gnp =
    gdp − impfi + exrfi

[256] GNP87 (ID, Blk 2) Gross National Product

gnp87 =
    gdp87 − impfi87 + exrfi87

[257] SFXNETEX (ID, Blk 3) Final Sales to Domestic Purchasers

sfxnetex =
    gnp − netex − ii

[258] SFXNETEX87 (ID, Blk 3) Final Sales to Domestic Purchasers

sfxnetex87 =
    gnp87 − netex87 − ii87

[259] SVPER (ID, Blk 2) Personal Saving

svper =
    ydp − ce − yipper − trfp

[260] NNP (ID, Blk 2) Net National Product

nnp =
    gnp − cfx

[261] NNP87 (ID, Blk 2) Net National Product

nnp87 =
    gnp87 − cfx87

2. Income Determination

All the details from the main National Income and Product Account tables are available, including profits, total wages and salaries, proprietors' income, rental income, interest income, personal and disposable personal income, etc.

2.1. *Personal income*

[262] YDP (ID, Blk 2) Disposable Personal Income

ydp =
 yp − txp

[263] YDP87 (ID, Blk 2) Disposable Personal Income

ydp87 =
 ydp/(.01 * pdice)

[264] YDPPERM87 (ID, Blk 2) Disposable Personal Income, Smoothed

ydpperm87 =
 0.1500 * ydp87 + 0.1400 * ydp87.1 + 0.1300 * ydp87.2 + 0.1200 * ydp87.3 + 0.1050 * ydp87.4 + 0.0850 * ydp87.5 + 0.0700 * ydp87.6 + 0.0600 * ydp87.7 + 0.0500 * ydp87.8 + 0.0400 * ydp87.9 + 0.0300 * ydp87.10 + 0.0200 * ydp87.11

[265] YDVN (ID, Blk 2) Profits after Tax, Dividends

ydvn =
 ydvper + ydvrgn

[266] YDVPER (ST, Blk 2) Personal Dividend Income

dlog(ydvper+ydvrgn) =
 0.6918 * dlog(ydvper+ydvrgn)[−1]
 + 0.0162 * dlog(za.1)
 + 0.0163 * log(za.1)
 − 0.0180 * log(ydvper.1+ydvrgn.1)
 + 0.0058

[267] YIN (ID, Blk 2) Net Interest

```
yin =
    yirper - yipper - yingf - yingn
```

[268] YINGF (ST, Blk 2) Net Interest Paid, Federal Govt

```
log(yingf/kdebtgfnet.1) =
    - 0.1691 * (1-step(86,1))
    + 0.1553 * from0 to5 degree2 near far
          log(rtbill3m)
    + 0.7521 * from0 to2 degree1 far
          log(rtbond30y)
    - 4.4928
```

[269] YINGN (ST, Blk 2) Net Interest PAID, State & Local Govt

```
yingn =
    - 1.1488 * movavg(4,kasstgnnet_u) * .01 *
          (movavg(4,rtbill3m)+movavg(4,rtbond30y))/2
    - 4.3829
```

[270] YIPPER (ST, Blk 2) Interest Paid by Consumers to Business

```
log(yipper/lconi) =
    + 0.2832 * from0 to8 degree2 near far
          log(rtbill3m)
    - 2.4078
```

[271] YIRPER (ST, Blk 2) Personal Interest Income

```
log(yirper/(lconi+lcbcai+netgef+netgen)) =
      0.1609 * spike(83,3)+spike(83,4)
    - 0.1832 * (1-step(84,1))
    + 0.7264 * from0 to8 degree2 near far
          log(rtbond30y)
    - 2.2079
```

[272] YN (ID, Blk 2) National Income

```
yn =
    nnp - txi - trpb - trfb - gnpsdx + gsls
```

[273] YOL (ST, Blk 2) Other Labor Income

log(yol/wd)−log(jqwrhnfm/jecwap) =
 + 1.2043 * from0 to3 degree1 far
 log((za+cfxcor+adjcor)/wd)
 − 0.8480

[274] YOTH (ST, Blk 2) Other Income

log(yoth) =
 + 1.1436 * from0 to8 degree2 near far
 log(cen+iroth+cesmed+cesoth+svper+za)
 − 1.9896

[275] YP (ID, Blk 2) Personal Income

yp =
 wd + yol + ypr + yf + yr + yirper + ydvper + trp − txsp

[276] YPR (ID, Blk 2) Proprietors Income with IVA & CCADJ, Nonfarm

ypr =
 yoth − yirper − ydvper

[277] YPTAX (ID, Blk 2) Taxable Personal Income

yptax =
 yp − trp + txsp

[278] YR (ST, Blk 2) Rental Income of Persons with CCADJ

diff(yr/np) =
 0.0031 * movavg(4,diff(puvoilrac))
 + 0.3776 * diff((ceshou−cfxnon)/np)
 − 0.0078

2.2. *Wage actuals*

[279] WB (ID, Blk 3) Compensation of Employees

wb =
 wd + ws

[280] WD (ST, Blk 2) Wage & Salary Disbursements, Total

```
log(wd−wdgov) =
      1.0239 * log(jecwap*(ememfg*hrwpmfg+emecon*hrwpcon+
         ememin*hrwpmin+emewrt*hrwpwrt+emetpu*hrwptpu+
         emefir*hrwpfir+emeser*hrwpser))
   − 5.3285
```

[281] WDCPIOTH (ST, Blk 3) Wage & Salary Disbursements, Other Commodity Industries (Excluding Mfg)

```
dlog(wdcpioth) =
      0.5224 * dlog(emecon*hrwpcon*wrhpcon)
   + 0.1972 * dlog(ememin*hrwpmin*wrhpmin)
```

[282] WDGOV (ST, Blk 2) Wage & Salary Disbursements, Govt. & Govt. Industries

```
log(wdgov) =
      0.9514 * log(gpfpay+gpnpay)
   + 0.1702
```

[283] WDMFG (ST, Blk 3) Wage & Salary Disbursements, Manufacturing

```
dlog(wdmfg) =
      0.8571 * dlog(ememfg*hrwpmfg*wrhpmfg)
```

[284] WDPSP (ST, Blk 3) Wage & Salary Disbursements, Private Service Producing

```
log(wdpsp) =
      0.9862 * log(wdpsp)[−1]
   + 0.0120 * log((emewrt*hrwpwrt*wrhpwrt)+(emetpu*hrwptpu*
         wrhptpu)+(emefir*hrwpfir*wrhpfir)+(emeser*hrwpser*
         wrhpser))
```

[285] WD_DIFF (ID, Blk 3) Wage & Salary Disbursements, Total, Difference Calculation, Internal

```
wd_diff =
   wd − wdgov − wd_sum
```

[286] WD_SUM (ST, Blk 3) Wage & Salary Disbursements, Total, Bottom Up Calculation, Internal

```
wd_sum =
      1.1275 * wdcpioth.1 * exp(.6052529 *
         dlog(emecon*hrwpcon*wrhpcon)+
         .1968838 * dlog(ememin*hrwpmin*wrhpmin))
    + 0.9709  * wdmfg.1 * exp(.8542760 * dlog(ememfg*hrwpmfg*
         wrhpmfg))
    + 0.9975 * wdpsp.1 * exp(.3038242 *
         dlog(emewrt*hrwpwrt*wrhpwrt)+
         .1260621 * dlog(emetpu*hrwptpu*wrhptpu)+
         .2696483 * dlog(emefir*hrwpfir*wrhpfir)+
         .3405092 * dlog(emeser*hrwpser*wrhpser))
```

[287] WALD (ID, Blk 1) Wage Accruals Less Disbursements, Total

```
wald =
    waldgf + waldgn + waldpri
```

2.3. *Corporate profit*

[288] Z (ID, Blk 2) Corporate Profits with IVA & CCADJ

```
z =
    yn − wd − txse − yol − ypr − yf − yr − yin − wald
```

[289] ZA (ID, Blk 2) Profits after Tax

```
za =
    zb − txcf − txcn
```

[290] ZB (ID, Blk 2) Profits before Tax

```
zb =
    z − (adjcor+ivacor)
```

[291] ZROW (ST, Blk 2) Corporate Profits with IVA, Rest of the World

```
diff(zrow/gnp) =
      0.7925 * diff((exrfi−impfi)/gnp)
    + 0.0001
```

[292] ZXADJ (ID, Blk 3) Corporate Profits with IVA, Total

```
zxadj =
    z − adjcor
```

[293] ZXADJ6011 (ST, Blk 2) Corporate Profits with IVA, Federal Reserve Banks

```
log(zxadj6011) =
       0.9051 * log(movavg(4,rtnote5y))
    + 0.2560 * log(pdigdpnfm)
    − 5.4386
```

[294] ZXADJDOM (ID, Blk 3) Corporate Profits with IVA, Domestic Industries

```
zxadjdom =
    zxadj − zrow
```

2.4. *Capital consumption allowance*

[295] CFX (ID, Blk 2) Capital Consumption Allowance with CCADJ

```
cfx =
    cfxcor + cfxnon
```

[296] CFX87 (ST, Blk 2) Capital Consumption Allowance with CCADJ

```
log(cfx87) =
       0.6604 * log(cfxcor/pdiip)
    + 0.3193 * log(cfxnon/pdiir)
    + 5.2647
```

[297] CFXCOR (ST, Blk 2) Capital Consumption Allowance with CCADJ, Corporate

```
log(cfxcor) =
       0.8894 * log(pdiipeinf*rdepeinf87 * kpenetinf87+
          pdiipetrn*rdepetrn87 * kpenettrn87+
          pdiipeind*rdepeind87 * kpenetind87+
          pdiipeoas*rdepeoas87 * kpenetoas87+
```

pdiipsiac*rdepsind87 * kpsnetind87+
pdiipsutl*rdepsutl87 * kpsnetutl87+
pdiipsbldgoth*rdepsbldgoth87 * kpsnetbldgoth87+
pdiipsi)
−3.8373

[298] CFXNON (ST, Blk 2) Capital Consumption Allowance with CCADJ, Noncorporate

log(cfxnon) =
1.0416 * log(pdiir*krnet87)
+ 0.0604 * dumagnes
− 8.0986

[299] ADJCOR (ST, Blk 2) Capital Consumption Adjustment, Corporate Business

diff(adjcor) =
0.0128 * ttrend
+ 0.1661 * from0 to3 degree2 near far
diff(dpve*ipe87)
+ 0.3528 * from0 to 11 degree2 near far
diff(dpvs*ips87)
− 1.6021

[300] CASHFLOW (ID, Blk 2) Corporate Cash Flow

cashflow =
z − zrow − zxadj6011 − ivacor + cfxcor − adjcor − txcf − txcn − ydvn

[301] CCACOR (ID, Blk 3) Capital Consumption Allowance, Corporate

ccacor =
cfxcor + adjcor

2.5. *Inventory valuation*

[302] IVACOR (ST, Blk 2) Inventory Valuation Adjustment, Corporate

ivacor =
− 0.0100 * (pdikimfg-pdikimfg.2) * kimfg87
− 0.0068 * (pdikimfg-pdikimfg.3) * kimfg87

```
    – 0.0061 * diff(pdikinfmxmfg) * (kinfm87–kimfg87)
    – 3.2489
```

3. Labor Market

3.1. *Employment*

[303] EME (ID, Blk 2) Employment, Establishment, Total

```
eme =
    emepri + emegge
```

[304] EMECON (ST, Blk 2) Employment, Construction

```
dlog(emecon*hrwpcon) =
      0.6015 * log(xiocon87)
    – 0.3292 * log(emecon.1 * hrwpcon.1)+.315 * log(kpnetcon87)
    – 0.0120 * log(ttrend)
    + 0.0537 * spike(78,2)
    – 1.2959
```

[305] EMEFIR (ST, Blk 2) Employment, Finance, Insurance, & Real Estate

```
dlog(emefir*hrwpfir) =
      0.1744 * log(xiofsr87)
    –0.1080 * log(emefir.1 * hrwpfir.1)+.315 * log(kpnetoth87)
    –0.0163 * step(87,3)
    –0.5260
```

[306] EMEGF (ID, Blk 1) Employment, Federal Govt, Total

```
emegf =
    emegfd + emegfn
```

[307] EMEGGE (ID, Blk 1) Employment, Govt & Govt Enterprises

```
emegge =
    emegf + emegn
```

[308] EMEMFG (ST, Blk 2) Employment, MFG, Total

dlog(ememfg*hrwpmfg) =
 0.6336 * log(xiomfg87)
 − 0.6888 * log(ememfg.1 * hrwpmfg.1)
 + 0.315 * log(kpnetmfg87)
 + 0.0046 * spike(81,4)
 −0.3110 * log(ttrend)
 + 2.5941

[309] EMEMIN (ST, Blk 2) Employment, Mining

dlog(ememin*hrwpmin) =
 0.3988 * log(xiomin87)
 − 0.1015 * log(ememin.1 * hrwpmin.1)
 + 0.315 * log(kpnetmin87)
 − 0.5829 * log(ttrend)
 + 1.1396

[310] EMEPRI (ID, Blk 2) Employment, Total Private

emepri =
 ememfg + emecon + ememin + emetpu + emewrt + emefir + emeser

[311] EMESER (ST, Blk 2) Employment, Services, Total

dlog(emeser*hrwpser) =
 0.3425 * log(xiofsr87)
 − 0.1921 * log(emeser.1 * hrwpser.1)
 + 0.315 * log(kpnetoth87)
 − 0.9626

[312] EMETPU (ST, Blk 2) Employment, Trans & Pub Util, Total

dlog(emetpu*hrwptpu) =
 0.4861 * log(xiotpu87)
 − 0.6307 * log(emetpu.1 * hrwptpu.1)
 + 0.315 * log(kpnettpu87)
 − 0.0002 * ttrend
 − 0.0510 * spike(83,3)
 + 1.4980

[313] EMEWRT (ST, Blk 2) Employment, Wholesale & Retail Trade

dlog(emewrt*hrwpwrt) =
  0.3619 * log(xiowrt87)
  − 0.5448 * log(emewrt.1 * hrwpwrt.1)
  + 0.315 * log(kpnetwrt87)
  + 0.0020 * ttrend
  + 1.9697

[314] EMHC (ID, Blk 2) Employment, Household Basis, Civilian

emhc =
  eme + emhcxe

3.2. *Average weekly hours*

[315] HRWPCON (ST, Blk 2) Average Weekly Hours, Construction

log(hrwpcon) =
  0.0694 * log(xiocon87)
  + 0.0003 * ttrend
  + 3.1691

[316] HRWPFIR (ST, Blk 2) Average Weekly Hours, Finance, Insurance, & Real Estate

log(hrwpfir) =
  0.0461 * log(xiofsr87)
  − 0.0005 * ttrend
  − 0.0072 * step(87,3)
  + 3.3039

[317] HRWPMFG (ST, Blk 2) Average Weekly Hours, Manufacturing

hrwpmfg =
  0.0529 * xiomfg87/ememfg
  + 0.0862 * rkumfgfrb
  − 0.0292 * ttrend
  + 30.1312

[318] HRWPMIN (ST, Blk 2) Average Weekly Hours, Mining

```
log(hrwpmin) =
        0.1536 * log(xiomin87/kpnetmin87)
    + 0.0010 * rkumfgfrb
    + 0.0694 * movavg(2,log(pdicenene/pdice))
    − 0.0657 * spike(74,4)
    + 3.6445
```

[319] HRWPNFMPRI (ST, Blk 3) Average Weekly Hours, Nonfarm Private

```
hrwpnfmpri =
        1.0531 * (hrwpmfg*ememfg+hrwpcon*emecon+
            hrwpmin*ememin+hrwpwrt*emewrt+hrwptpu*emetpu+
            hrwpfir*emefir+hrwpser*emeser)/(emepri)
    − 2.2048
```

[320] HRWPSER (ST, Blk 2) Average Weekly Hours, Services

```
hrwpser =
        0.0013 * xiofsr87
    + 689.6550 *1/ttrend
    + 24.7992
```

[321] HRWPTPU (ST, Blk 2) Average Weekly Hours, Transportation & Public Utilities

```
hrwptpu =
        379.0540 * 1/ttrend
    + 0.0358  * movavg(2,rkumfgfrb)
    + 33.7437
```

[322] HRWPWRT (ST, Blk 2) Average Weekly Hours, Wholesale & Retail Trade

```
hrwpwrt =
        0.0023 * xiowrt87
    + 2.0859 * xiowrt87/xiowrt87.2
    + 1147.1600 *  1/ttrend
    + 20.0084
```

3.3. *Unemployment*

[323] NUN (ID, Blk 2) Number of Unemployed

nun =
nlfc − emhc

[324] RUNC (ID, Blk 2) Unemployment Rate, Civilian

runc =
100 * (1−emhc/nlfc)

3.4. *Labor force*

[325] NLFC (ID, Blk 1) Labor Force, Civilian, Total

nlfc =
nlfcm1619 + nlfcf1619 + nlfcm20a + nlfcf20a

[326] NLFCF (ID, Blk 1) Labor Force, Civilian, Femails, Total

nlfcf =
nlfcf1619 + nlfcf2024 + nlfcf2534 + nlfcf3544 +
nlfcf4554 + nlfcf5564 + nlfcf65a

[327] NLFCF1619 (ID, Blk 1) Labor Force, Civilian, Femails, 16–19

nlfcf1619 =
rplcf1619 * npf1619

[328] NLFCF2024 (ID, Blk 1) Labor Force, Civilian, Femails, 20–24

nlfcf2024 =
rplcf2024 * npf2024

[329] NLFCF20A (ID, Blk 1) Labor Force, Civilian, Femails, 20 & Over

nlfcf20a =
rplcf20a*npf20a

[330] NLFCF2534 (ID, Blk 1) Labor Force, Civilian, Femails, 25–34

nlfcf2534 =
    rplcf2534 * npf2534

[331] NLFCF3544 (ID, Blk 1) Labor Force, Civilian, Femails, 35–44

nlfcf3544 =
    rplcf3544 * npf3544

[332] NLFCF4554 (ID, Blk 1) Labor Force, Civilian, Femails, 45–54

nlfcf4554 =
    rplcf4554 * npf4554

[333] NLFCF5564 (ID, Blk 1) Labor Force, Civilian, Femails, 55–64

nlfcf5564 =
    rplcf5564 * npf5564

[334] NLFCF65A (ID, Blk 1) Labor Force, Civilian, Femails, 65 & Over

nlfcf65a =
    rplcf65a * npf65a

[335] NLFCM (ID, Blk 1) Labor Force, Civilian, Males, Total

nlfcm =
    nlfcm1619 + nlfcm2024 + nlfcm2534 + nlfcm3544 +
    nlfcm4554 + nlfcm5564 + nlfcm65a

[336] NLFCM1619 (ID, Blk 1) Labor Force, Civilian, Males, 16–19

nlfcm1619 =
    rplcm1619 * npm1619

[337] NLFCM2024 (ID, Blk 1) Labor Force, Civilian, Males, 20–24

nlfcm2024 =
    rplcm2024 * npm2024

[338] NLFCM20A (ID, Blk 1) Labor Force, Civilian, Males, 20 & Over

nlfcm20a =
rplcm20a * npm20a

[339] NLFCM2534 (ID, Blk 1) Labor Force, Civilian, Males, 25–34

nlfcm2534 =
rplcm2534 * npm2534

[340] NLFCM3544 (ID, Blk 1) Labor Force, Civilian, Males, 35–44

nlfcm3544 =
rplcm3544 * npm3544

[341] NLFCM4554 (ID, Blk 1) Labor Force, Civilian, Males, 45–54

nlfcm4554 =
rplcm4554 * npm4554

[342] NLFCM5564 (ID, Blk 1) Labor Force, Civilian, Males, 55–64

nlfcm5564 =
rplcm5564 * npm5564

[343] NLFCM65A (ID, Blk 1) Labor Force, Civilian, Males, 65 & Over

nlfcm65a =
rplcm65a * npm65a

3.5. *Labor force participation rate*

[344] RPLC (ID, Blk 1) Labor Force Participation Rate, Total

rplc =
nlfc/np16a

[345] RPLCF (ID, Blk 1) Labor Force Participation Rate, Femails, Total

rplcf =
nlfcf/npf16a

[346] RPLCF1619 (ID, Blk 1) Labor Force Participation Rate, Femails, 16–19

rplcf1619 =
rplcf1619exo*(nlfpcnt/100)

[347] RPLCF2024 (ID, Blk 1) Labor Force Participation Rate, Femails, 20–24

rplcf2024 =
rplcf2024exo*(nlfpcnt/100)

[348] RPLCF20A (ID, Blk 1) Labor Force Participation Rate, Femails, 20 & Over

rplcf20a =
(nlfcf2024+nlfcf2534+nlfcf3544+nlfcf4554 +nlfcf5564+nlfcf65a)/
(npf16a−npf1619)

[349] RPLCF2534 (ID, Blk 1) Labor Force Participation Rate, Femails, 25–34

rplcf2534 =
rplcf2534exo*(nlfpcnt/100)

[350] RPLCF3544 (ID, Blk 1) Labor Force Participation Rate, Femails, 35–44

rplcf3544 =
rplcf3544exo*(nlfpcnt/100)

[351] RPLCF4554 (ID, Blk 1) Labor Force Participation Rate, Femails, 45–54

rplcf4554 =
rplcf4554exo*(nlfpcnt/100)

[352] RPLCF5564 (ID, Blk 1) Labor Force Participation Rate, Femails, 55–64

rplcf5564 =
rplcf5564exo*(nlfpcnt/100)

[353] RPLCF65A (ID, Blk 1) Labor Force Participation Rate, Femails, 65 & Over

rplcf65a =
rplcf65aexo*(nlfpcnt/100)

[354] RPLCM (ID, Blk 1) Labor Force Participation Rate, Males, Total

rplcm =
nlfcm/npm16a

[355] RPLCM1619 (ID, Blk 1) Labor Force Participation Rate, Males, 16–19

rplcm1619 =
rplcm1619exo*(nlfpcnt/100)

[356] RPLCM2024 (ID, Blk 1) Labor Force Participation Rate, Males, 20–24

rplcm2024 =
rplcm2024exo*(nlfpcnt/100)

[357] RPLCM20A (ID, Blk 1) Labor Force Participation Rate, Males, 20 & Over

rplcm20a =
(nlfcm2024+nlfcm2534+nlfcm3544+nlfcm4554+nlfcm5564+
nlfcm65a)/(npm16a−npm1619)

[358] RPLCM2534 (ID, Blk 1) Labor Force Participation Rate, Males, 25–34

rplcm2534 =
rplcm2534exo*(nlfpcnt/100)

[359] RPLCM3544 (ID, Blk 1) Labor Force Participation Rate, Males, 35-44

rplcm3544 =
rplcm3544exo*(nlfpcnt/100)

[360] RPLCM4554 (ID, Blk 1) Labor Force Participation Rate, Males, 45–54

rplcm4554 =
  rplcm4554exo*(nlfpcnt/100)

[361] RPLCM5564 (ID, Blk 1) Labor Force Participation Rate, Males, 55–64

rplcm5564 =
  rplcm5564exo*(nlfpcnt/100)

[362] RPLCM65A (ID, Blk 1) Labor Force Participation Rate, Males, 65 & Over

rplcm65a =
  rplcm65aexo*(nlfpcnt/100)

4. Price and Costs

4.1. *Prices*

4.1.1. *PPI (Producer price index)*

[363] PPI (ST, Blk 2) PPI, All Commodities

ppi =
  0.9976 * 1.0 * ((5.098 * ppifrm/95.0+12.033 * ppipff/106.5+4.641 * ppitpa/103.3+0.518 * ppihsl/114.0+ 13.005 * ppifap/63.3+7.284 * ppicap/102.2+2.504 * ppirap/101.3+1.640 * ppilwp/108.0+8.464 * ppippa/117.9+ 10.062 * ppimmp/103.4+15.385 * ppimae/109.4+2.603 * ppifhe/108.7+2.232 * ppinmp/109.7+9.684*ppiteq/113.0+ 4.845*ppimis/ 112.4)/100*99.8)

[364] PPICAP (ST, Blk 2) PPI, Chemicals

log(ppicap) =
  0.2182 * log(pdigdpnfm)
  + 0.7992 * from0 to1 degree1 far
  log(picap)

[365] PPICAP_U (ID, Blk 3) PPI, Chemicals

ppicap_u =
ppicap*ppicap_sf/100

[366] PPICEQ (ST, Blk 3) PPI, Finished Goods, Capital Equipment

log(ppiceq) =
1.0267 * log(piceq)
− 0.1172

[367] PPICEQ_U (ID, Blk 3) PPI, Finished Goods, Capital Equipment

ppiceq_u =
ppiceq*ppiceq_sf/100

[368] PPICMP (ST, Blk 2) PPI, Crude Materials

log(ppicmp) =
0.9518 * (0.414 * log(ppifrm)+0.204 * log(ppifap)+0.382 * log(ppimmp))
+ 0.2113

[369] PPICMP_U (ID, Blk 3) PPI, Crude Materials

ppicmp_u =
ppicmp*ppicmp_sf/100

[370] PPICOL_U (ST, Blk 2) PPI, Fuels & Related Products, Coal

log(ppicol_u) =
0.2584 * log(pdigdpnfm)
+ 0.1683 * from1 to4 degree2 near far log(ppirpp_u)
+ 2.6716

[371] PPIELP_U (ST, Blk 1) PPI, Fuels & Related Products, Electric Power

log(ppielp_u) =
0.0195 * dqtr2
+ 0.0411 * dqtr3

+ 0.0111 * dqtr4
+ 0.7105 * from0 to3 degree1 far
log(ppirpp_u)
+1.5159

[372] PPIFAP (ST, Blk 2) PPI, Fuels & Related Products, Total

log(ppifap*ppifap_sf) =
1.0384 * log(pifap_u)
+ 4.3788

[373] PPIFAP_U (ID, Blk 3) PPI, Fuels & Related Products, Total

ppifap_u =
ppifap*ppifap_sf/100

[374] PPIFCG (ST, Blk 2) PPI, Finished Goods, Consumer Goods

log(ppifcg) =
1.0170 * log(pifcg)
− 0.0902

[375] PPIFCG_U (ID, Blk 3) PPI, Finished Goods, Consumer Goods

ppifcg_u =
ppifcg*ppifcg_sf/100

[376] PPIFHE (ST, Blk 2) PPI, Furniture & Household Equipment

log(ppifhe) =
0.5427 * log(pifhe)
+ 0.2279 * log(pdigdpnfm)
+ 1.0944

[377] PPIFHE_U (ID, Blk 3) PPI, Furniture & Household Equipment

ppifhe_u =
ppifhe*ppifhe_sf/100

[378] PPIFIN (ID, Blk 3) PPI, Finished Goods, Total

ppifin =
ppifin_u/ppifin_sf*100

[379] PPIFIN_U (ID, Blk 3) PPI, Finished Goods, Total

```
ppifin_u =
   ((75.583 * ppifcg_u/101.5+24.417 * ppiceq_u/111.1)/100 * 103.6)
```

[380] PPIFPF (ID, Blk 2) PPI, Farm Products & Processed Foods & Feeds, Total

```
ppifpf =
   ppifpf_u/ppifpf_sf*100
```

[381] PPIFPF_U (ST, Blk 2) PPI, Farm Products & Processed Foods & Feeds, Total

```
ppifpf_u =
   1.0014 * (5.098 * ppifrm_u/95.0+12.033 * ppipff_u/106.5)/
     17.131 * 102.7
```

[382] PPIFRM_U (ID, Blk 1) PPI, Farm Products

```
ppifrm_u =
   ppifrm*ppifrm_sf/100
```

[383] PPIGas_U (ST, Blk 1) PPI, Fuels & Related Products, Gas Fuels

```
log(ppigas_u) =
     0.2650 * step(85,1)
   + 1.1758 * from0 to3 degree2 near far
       log(ppirpp_u)
   - 0.7925
```

[384] PPIHSL_U (ID, Blk 3) PPI, Hides, Skins, & Leather

```
ppihsl_u =
   ppihsl*ppihsl_sf/100
```

[385] PPIIND (ST, Blk 2) PPI, Industrial Commodities, Total

```
ppiind =
   1.0*((100*ppi/99.8-5.098*ppifrm/95.0-12.033*ppipff/106.5)/
       82.869*99.2)
   + 0.9987
```

[386] PPIIND_U (ST, Blk 3) PPI, Industrial Commodities, Total

ppiind_u =
    1.0017 * ((100 * ppi_u/99.8−5.098 * ppifrm_u/95.0−
        12.033 * ppipff_u/106.5)/82.869 * 99.2)
    − 0.2417

[387] PPIINT (ST, Blk 3) PPI, Intermediate Materials

log(ppiint) =
    0.9911 * log(piint)
    + 0.0288

[388] PPIINT_U (ID, Blk 3) PPI, Intermediate Materials

ppiint_u =
    ppiint*ppiint_sf/100

[389] PPILWP (ST, Blk 2) PPI, Lumber & Wood Products

log(ppilwp) =
    0.7141 * log(rkumfgfrb)
    + 0.8872 * log(pdiimxoil)
    + 0.1103 * log(uhs)
    − 2.4974

[390] PPILWP_U (ID, Blk 3) PPI, Lumber & Wood Products

ppilwp_u =
    ppilwp*ppilwp_sf/100

[391] PPIMAE (ST, Blk 2) PPI, Machinery & Equipment

log(ppimae) =
    0.4404 * log(pimae)
    + 0.1504 * log(pdigdpnfm)
    + 0.4089 * log(julcnfmpriavg)

[392] PPIMAE_U (ID, Blk 3) PPI, Machinery & Equipment

ppimae_u =
    ppimae*ppimae_sf/100

[393] PPIMIS (ST, Blk 2) PPI, Miscellaneous Commodities

log(ppimis) =
    1.2486 * log(ppiind)
  – 1.0647

[394] PPIMIS_U (ID, Blk 3) PPI, Miscellaneous Commodities

ppimis_u =
  ppimis*ppimis_sf/100

[395] PPIMMP (ST, Blk 2) PPI, Metals & Metal Products

log(ppimmp) =
    0.4836 * log(pimmp.1)
  + 0.1157 * log(rkumfgfrb)
  + 0.4729 * log(pdiimismxoil)
  + 0.1085 * log(ipe87/gnp87)

[396] PPIMMP_U (ID, Blk 3) PPI, Metals & Metal Products

ppimmp_u =
  ppimmp*ppimmp_sf/100

[397] PPINMP (ST, Blk 2) PPI, Nonmetallic Mineral Products

log(ppinmp) =
  + 1.0125 * from0 to2 degree1 far
      log(pinmp)
  – 0.0787

[398] PPINMP_U (ID, Blk 3) PPI, Nonmetallic Mineral Products

ppinmp_u =
  ppinmp*ppinmp_sf/100

[399] PPIPFF (ST, Blk 2) PPI, Processed Foods & Feeds

log(ppipff) =
    0.4007 * log(ppifrm)
  + 0.4191 * log(pdigdpnfm)
  + 0.1329 * log(pdiimffb.1)
  + 0.3041

[400] PPIPFF_U (ID, Blk 2) PPI, Processed Foods & Feeds

```
ppipff_u =
    ppipff*ppipff_sf/100
```

[401] PPIPPA (ST, Blk 2) PPI, Pulp, Paper, & Allied Products

```
log(ppippa) =
      0.9579 * log(pippa)
    + 0.0472 * log(pdiimismxoil.1)
```

[402] PPIPPA_U (ID, Blk 3) PPI, Pulp, Paper, & Allied Products

```
ppippa_u =
    ppippa*ppippa_sf/100
```

[403] PPIRAP (ST, Blk 2) PPI, Rubber & Plastics

```
log(ppirap) =
    + 0.8272 * from0 to1 degree1 far
          log(pirap)
    + 0.7656
```

[404] PPIRAP_U (ID, Blk 3) PPI, Rubber & Plastics

```
ppirap_u =
    ppirap*ppirap_sf/100
```

[405] PPIRPP (ID, Blk 1) PPI, Fuels & Related Products, Refined Petroleum Prod

```
ppirpp =
    ppirpp_u/ppirpp_sf*100
```

[406] PPIRPP_U (ST, Blk 1) PPI, Fuels & Related Products, Refined Petroleum Prod

```
log(ppirpp_u) =
      0.0016 * ttrend
    + 0.6771 * log(puvoilrac)
    + 0.1945 * log(puvoilrac)[-1]
    + 1.3403
```

[407] PPITEQ (ST, Blk 2) PPI, Transportation Equipment

log(ppiteq) =
0.5868 * log(pdigdpnfm)
+ 0.4285 * log(piteq)

[408] PPITEQ_U (ID, Blk 3) PPI, Transportation Equipment

ppiteq_u =
ppiteq*ppiteq_sf/100

[409] PPITPA (ST, Blk 2) PPI, Textiles & Apparel

log(ppitpa) =
0.6669 * log(pitpa)
+ 0.1030 * log(rkumfgfrb)
+ 1.0683

[410] PPITPA_U (ID, Blk 3) PPI, Textiles & Apparel

ppitpa_u =
ppitpa*ppitpa_sf/100

[411] PPIXFAE (ST, Blk 2) PPI, All Items less Food & Energy

log(ppixfae) =
1.0023 * log((100 * ppi/99.8−5.098 * ppifrm/95−12.033 * ppipff/106.5−13.005 * ppifap/63.3)/69.864 * 108)

[412] PPIXFAE_U (ID, Blk 3) PPI, All Items less Food & Energy

ppixfae_u =
ppixfae*ppixfae_sf/100

[413] PPI_U (ST, Blk 3) PPI, All Commodities
ppi_u =
0.9976 * 1.0*((5.098*ppifrm_u/95.0+12.033*ppipff_u/106.5 +
4.641*ppitpa_u/103.3+0.518*ppihsl_u/114.0+
13.005*ppifap_u/63.3+7.284*ppicap_u/10+2.2
2.504*ppirap_u/101.3+1.640*ppilwp_u/108.0+
8.464*ppippa_u/117.9+10.062*ppimmp_u/103.4+
15.385*ppimae_u/109.4+2.603*ppifhe_u/108.7+

2.232*ppinmp_u/109.7+9.684*ppiteq_u/113.0+
4.845*ppimis_u/112.4)/100*99.8)

4.1.2. *CPI (Consumer price index)*

[414] PCIU (ST, Blk 3) CPI, All Urban Consumers, All Items

```
pciu =
      1.0004 * 1.0 * ((17.396 * pciufab/139.9+41.404 *
         pciuhou/138.9+6.005 * pciuapp/131.9+17.012 *
         pciutrn/128.5+6.931 * pciumed/195.5+4.350 *
         pciuent/143.8+6.902 * pciuogs/189.4)/100 * 142.2)
    −10461.7
```

[415] PCIUAPP (ST, Blk 3) CPI, All Urban Consumers, Apparel & Upkeep

```
log(pciuapp) =
      1.1156 * (0.908 * log(pdicencas)+0.092 * log(pdicesoth))
    − 0.4317
```

[416] PCIUCOM (ST, Blk 3) CPI, All Urban Consumers, Commodities

```
pciucom =
      1.0405 * (100 * pciu/142.2−55.905 * pciuser/154.7)/
        44.095 * 130.2
    − 5.0338
```

[417] PCIUENE (ST, Blk 3) CPI, All Urban Consumers, Energy

```
log(pciuene) =
      0.5185 * log(pdicengas)
    + 0.1097 * log(pdicenfoc)
    + 0.1903 * log(pdiceshhogas)
    + 0.1815 * log(pdiceshhoele)
    − 0.1265
```

[418] PCIUENT (ST, Blk 3) CPI, All Urban Consumers, Entertainment

```
log(pciuent) =
      0.8757 * (0.467 * log(pdicesoth)+0.533 *
         log((pdicenoth+pdicedoth)/2))
    + 0.7252
```

[419] PCIUFAB (ST, Blk 3) CPI, All Urban Consumers, Food & Beverages

log(pciufab) =
    1.0006 * log(pdicenfab)
  + 0.1257

[420] PCIUFOO (ST, Blk 3) CPI, All Urban Consumers, Food

log(pciufoo) =
    1.0085 * log(pciufab)
  − 0.0391

[421] PCIUHOU (ST, Blk 3) CPI, All Urban Consumers, Housing

log(pciuhou) =
    0.9127 * (.669 * log(pdiceshou)+.013 * log(pdicenfoc)+
    .090 * log(pdicedfhe)+.028 * log(pdicenoth)+
    .112 * log(pdiceshhooth)+.088 * log((ceshhoele+
    ceshhogas) * 100/(ceshhoele87+ceshhogas87)))
  + 0.5440

[422] PCIUMED (ST, Blk 3) CPI, All Urban Consumers, Medical Care

log(pciumed) =
    1.0930 * (0.812 * log(pdicesmed)+0.188 * log(pdicenoth))
  − 0.1729

[423] PCIUOGS (ST, Blk 3) CPI, All Urban Consumers, Other Goods & Services

log(pciuogs) =
    1.2710 * (0.342 * log(pdicenoth)+0.621 * log(pdicesoth)+
    0.037 * log(pdicedoth))
  − 0.9803

[424] PCIUREN (ST, Blk 3) CPI, All Urban Consumers, Housing, Rent, Residential

log(pciuren) =
    0.9141 * log(pdiceshou)
  + 0.5959

[425] PCIUSER (ST, Blk 3) CPI, All Urban Consumers, Services

log(pciuser) =
1.0382 * (.494 * log(pdiceshou)+.160 * log(pdiceshho)+
.126 * log(pdicestrn)+.095 * log(pdicesmed)+
.125 * log(pdicesoth))
+ 0.0131

[426] PCIUTRN (ST, Blk 3) CPI, All Urban Consumers, Transportation

log(pciutrn) =
1.0735 * (.227 * log(pdicedmnc)+.055 * log(pdicedmtr)+
.064 * log(pdicedmuc)+.228 * log(pdicengas)+
.303 * log(pdicestrnxar)+.039 * log(pdicedmtp)+
.084 * log(pdicestar))
− 0.2814

[427] PCIUXENE (ST, Blk 3) CPI, All Urban Consumers, All Items less Energy

pciuxene =
0.9977 * (100 * pciu/142.2−7.294 * pciuene/103.9)/
92.706 * 147.5

[428] PCIUXFAE (ST, Blk 3) CPI, All Urban Consumers, All Items less Food & Energy

pciuxfae =
0.9967 * (100 * pciu/142.2−7.294 * pciuene/103.9−
15.777 * pciufoo/139.2)/76.929 * 149.6

[429] PCIUXFOO (ID, Blk 3) CPI, All Urban Consumers, All Items less Food

pciuxfoo =
(100 * pciu/115.3−16.055 * pciufoo/114.8)/83.945 * 115.4

[430] PCIUXMED (ST, Blk 3) CPI, All Urban Consumers, All Items less Medical Care

pciuxmed =
1.0006 * (100 * pciu/142.2−6.931 * pciumed/195.5)/
93.069 * 139.0

[431] PCIW (ST, Blk 3) CPI, Urban Wage Eaners, All Items

log(pciw) =
0.9646 * log((19.310 * pciufab/139.9+38.948 * pciuhou/138.9+
6.015 * pciuapp/131.9+18.947 * pciutrn/128.5+
5.888 * pciumed/195.5+4.022 * pciuent/143.8
+6.871 * pciuogs/189.4)/100 * 142.2)
+ 0.1582

4.1.3. *PDG (Implicit price deflator)*

[432] PDFGDP (ST, Blk 3) Fixed Weight Price Index, Gross Domestic Product

log(pdfgdp) =
0.9907 * log((94.3*pdicedmnc+pdicedmuc*26.8+
pdicedmtr*48.0+pdicedmtp*14.4+pdicedfhe*144.0+
pdicedoth*76.2+pdicencas*174.5+pdicenfah*341.6+
pdicenfmb*159.2+pdicengas*84.7+pdicenfoc*12.0+
pdicenoth*239.1+pdiceshou*452.5+pdiceshhoele*63.0+
pdiceshhogas*25.5+pdiceshhooth*99.2+pdicestar*65.5+
pdicestrnxar*51.1+pdicesmed*384.8+pdicesoth*495.7+
pdiipsiac* 93.3+pdiipsmap*13.1+pdiipsoaf*7.4+
pdiipsutl*26.5+ pdiipsbldgoth*31.1+pdiipeinf*109.4+
pdiipetrn*73.6+pdiipeoas*68.8+pdiipeind*74.8+
pdiirsone*113.8+pdiirstom*25.5+pdiiroth*86.0+
pdiexffb*25.2+pdiexism*67.4+pdiexmvp*27.6+
pdiexcapoth*73.9+pdiexcompequ*18.8+pdiexconxmvp*20.3+
pdiexoth*24.5+pdiexser*106.2+pdiexrfi*105.1−
pdiimoil*43.0−pdiimffb*24.8−pdiimismxoil*66.1−
pdiimmvp*85.2−pdiimcapoth*70.3−pdiimcompequ*14.9−
pdiimconxmvp*88.8−pdiimoth*21.8−pdiimser*92.2+
pdigpfd*292.0+pdigpfn*92.9+pdigpn*496.6)/4513.6)
+ 0.0215

[433] PDFGNP (ST, Blk 3) Fixed Weight Price Index, Gross National Product

log(pdfgnp) =
0.9915 * log((94.3*pdicedmnc+pdicedmuc*26.8+
pdicedmtr*48.0+pdicedmtp*14.4+pdicedfhe*144.0+
pdicedoth*76.2+pdicencas*174.5+pdicenfah*341.6+
pdicenfmb*159.2+pdicengas*84.7+pdicenfoc*12.0+

pdicenoth*239.1+pdiceshou*452.5+pdiceshhoele*63.0+
pdiceshhogas*25.5+pdiceshhooth*99.2+pdicestar*65.5+
pdicestrnxar*51.1+pdicesmed*384.8+pdicesoth*495.7+
pdiipsiac*93.3+pdiipsmap*13.1+pdiipsoaf*7.4+
pdiipsutl*26.5+pdiipsbldgoth*31.1+pdiipeinf*109.4+
pdiipetrn*73.6+pdiipeoas*68.8+pdiipeind*74.8+
pdiirsone*113.8+pdiirstom*25.5+pdiiroth*86.0+
pdiexffb*25.2+pdiexism*67.4+pdiexmvp*27.6+
pdiexcapoth*73.9+pdiexcompequ*18.8+pdiexconxmvp*20.3+
pdiexoth*24.5+pdiexser*106.2+pdiexrfi*105.1−
pdiimoil*43.0−pdiimffb*24.8−pdiimismxoil*66.1−
pdiimmvp*85.2−pdiimcapoth*70.3−pdiimcompequ*14.9−
pdiimconxmvp*88.8−pdiimoth*21.8−pdiimser*92.2−
pdiimpfi*100.5+pdigpfd*292.0+pdigpfn*92.9
+pdigpn*496.6)/4518.2)
\+ 0.0403

[434] PDICE (ID, Blk 2) Impl Price Deflator, Cons Expend, Total

pdice =
ce/ce87 * 100

[435] PDICED (ID, Blk 3) Impl Price Deflator, Cons Expend, Durable Goods

pdiced =
ced/ced87 * 100

[436] PDICEDFHE (ST, Blk 2) Impl Price Deflator, Cons Expend, Furniture & Household Equipment

log(pdicedfhe) =
\+ 0.7521 * from0 to2 degree1 far
log(ppifhe)
\+ 1.0739

[437] PDICEDMNC (ST, Blk 2) Impl Price Deflator, Cons Expend, New Cars

log(pdicedmnc)-.43 * log(pdigdpnfm) =
0.2961 * ((1−rimpcar) * log(ppiteq))+(rimpcar*log(pdiimmvp.1))

```
        + 0.1290 * log(ttrend)
        + 0.5645
```

[438] PDICEDMTP (ST, Blk 2) Impl Price Deflator, Cons Expend, Tires, Tubes, Accessories & Parts

```
  log(pdicedmtp) =
        − 0.0138 * spike(84,1)
        + 0.5714 * from0 to6 degree2 near far
              log(.5 * ppiteq+.5 * ppirap)
        + 1.9677
```

[439] PDICEDMTR (ST, Blk 2) Impl Price Deflator, Cons Expend, New & Used Trucks, Rec. Vehicles

```
  log(pdicedmtr)−.3 * log(pdigdpnfm) =
          0.4784 * log(ppiteq)
        + 0.0544 * log(ppimmp.1)
        + 0.6987
```

[440] PDICEDMUC (ST, Blk 2) Impl Price Deflator, Cons Expend, Net Purchases of Used Cars

```
  log(pdicedmuc) =
        + 0.9870 * from0 to2 degree1 far
              log(ppiteq)
        − 0.1162
```

[441] PDICEDMVP (ID, Blk 2) Impl Price Deflator, Cons Expend, Motor Vehicles & Parts

```
  pdicedmvp =
        cedmvp/cedmvp87 * 100
```

[442] PDICEDOTH (ST, Blk 2) Impl Price Deflator, Cons Expend, Other Dur Goods

```
  log(pdicedoth) =
          0.8444 * log(pdigdpnfm)
        + 0.7346
```

[443] PDICEN (ID, Blk 3) Impl Price Deflator, Cons Expend, Nondurable Goods

```
pdicen =
    cen/cen87 * 100
```

[444] PDICENCAS (ST, Blk 2) Impl Price Deflator, Cons Expend, Clothing & Shoes

```
log(pdicencas) =
       0.0526 * log(pdiimconxmvp)
    + 0.0057 * spike(87,2)−spike(87,3)
    − 0.0067 * spike(84,1)+spike(84,2)+spike(86,1)+spike(86,2)
    + 0.5127 * log(pdigdpnfm)
    + 0.0840 * from0 to3 degree2 near far
           log(ppitpa)
```

[445] PDICENENE (ID, Blk 2) Impl Price Deflator, Cons Expend, Energy

```
pdicenene =
    cenene/cenene87 * 100
```

[446] PDICENFAB (ID, Blk 2) Impl Price Deflator, Cons Expend, Food & Beverages

```
pdicenfab =
    cenfab/cenfab87 * 100
```

[447] PDICENFAH (ST, Blk 2) Impl Price Deflator, Cons Expend, Food & Beverages at Home

```
log(pdicenfah) =
       0.6396 * log(pdigdpnfm)
    + 0.4106 * from0 to3 degree2 near far
           log(.29 * ppifrm+.66 * ppipff+.05 * pdiimffb)
    − 0.2463
```

[448] PDICENFMB (ST, Blk 2) Impl Price Deflator, Cons Expend, Purchased Meals & Beverages

log(pdicenfmb) =
    1.0358 * log(pdigdpnfm)
  + 0.0405 * from0 to4 degree1 far
      log(.29 * ppifrm+.66 * ppipff+.05 * pdiimffb)
  − 0.3614

[449] PDICENFOC (ST, Blk 1) Impl Price Deflator, Cons Expend, Fuel Oil & Coal

log(pdicenfoc) =
    0.9185 * log(ppirpp)
  + 0.7512

[450] PDICENGAS (ST, Blk 1) Impl Price Deflator, Cons Expend, Gasoline & Oil

log(pdicengas) =
    0.0052 * ttrend
  + 0.5557 * log(ppirpp)
  + 1.5569

[451] PDICENOTH (ST, Blk 2) Impl Price Deflator, Cons Expend, Other Nondurable Goods

log(pdicenoth)-.3 * log(pdigdpnfm) =
    1.2093 * log(ttrend)
  + 0.2580 * from0 to3 degree2 near far
      log(.5 * ppiind+.5 * ppippa)
  − 4.1280

[452] PDICES (ID, Blk 2) Impl Price Deflator, Cons Expend, Services

pdices =
  ces/ces87 * 100

[453] PDICESHHO (ID, Blk 2) Impl Price Deflator, Cons Expend, Household Operation, Total

pdiceshho =
  ceshho/ceshho87 * 100

[454] PDICESHHOELE (ST, Blk 1) Impl Price Deflator, Cons Expend, Household Operation, Electricity

log(pdiceshhoele) =
    0.9552 * log(ppielp_u)
  − 0.0386 * dqtr3
  − 0.0036 * dqtr4
  − 0.0157 * dqtr2
  + 0.1101

[455] PDICESHHOGAS (ST, Blk 1) Impl Price Deflator, Cons Expend, Household Operation, Gas

log(pdiceshhogas) =
    0.7884 * log(ppigas_u)
  + 0.0121 * dqtr1
  + 0.0189 * dqtr2
  + 0.0130 * dqtr3
  + 1.0583

[456] PDICESHHOOTH (ST, Blk 2) Impl Price Deflator, Cons Expend, Household Operation, Other

log(pdiceshhooth) =
    0.9999 * log(pdigdpnfm)
  − 0.0996 * spike(80,2)
  − 0.0091 * spike(84,1)

[457] PDICESHOU (ST, Blk 2) Impl Price Deflator, Cons Expend, Housing Services

log(pdiceshou) =
    0.7718 * log(pdigdpnfm)
  + 0.2176 * log((pdiirsone+pdiirsone.1+pdiirsone.2+pdiirsone.3+
      pdiirsone.4+pdiirsone.5+pdiirsone.6)/7)

[458] PDICESMAO (ID, Blk 2) Impl Price Deflator, Cons Expend, Medical & Other Services

pdicesmao =
  cesmao/cesmao87 * 100

[459] PDICESMED (ST, Blk 2) Impl Price Deflator, Cons Expend, Medical Care

log(pdicesmed) =
0.6453 * log(pdigdpnfm)
+ 0.0104 * ttrend
− 0.0014 * spike(77,2)

[460] PDICESOTH (ST, Blk 2) Impl Price Deflator, Cons Expend, Other Services

log(pdicesoth) =
1.1099 * log(pdigdpnfm)
− 0.5386

[461] PDICESTAR (ST, Blk 2) Impl Price Deflator, Cons Expend, Transportation Services, Auto Repair

log(pdicestar) =
1.0964 * log(pdigdpnfm)
− 0.4502

[462] PDICESTRN (ID, Blk 2) Impl Price Deflator, Cons Expend, Transportation Services, Total

pdicestrn =
cestrn/cestrn87 * 100

[463] PDICESTRNXAR (ST, Blk 2) Impl Price Deflator, Cons Expend, Transportation Services, Other

log(pdicestrnxar) =
0.0702 * log(ppirpp)
+ 1.9210 * log(ttrend)
+ 0.1557 * log(pdigdpnfm)
− 6.1165

[464] PDIEX (ID, Blk 3) Impl Price Deflator, Exports, Total

pdiex =
ex/ex87 * 100

[465] PDIEXCAPOTH (ST, Blk 2) Impl Price Deflator, Exports, Merch, Other Capital Goods

log(pdiexcapoth) =
    0.5702 * log(ppimae)
  + 0.4532 * log(ppiteq)
  − 0.2119

[466] PDIEXCOMPEQU (ST, Blk 2) Impl Price Deflator, Exports, Merch, Computers

log(pdiexcompequ/ppimae) =
    874.1610 * 1/ttrend
  − 5.5913

[467] PDIEXCONXMVP (ST, Blk 2) Impl Price Deflator, Exports, Merch, Consumer Goods

log(pdiexconxmvp) =
    0.8374 * movavg(2,log(ppifcg))
  − 0.1653 * log(rexmor15r)
  + 0.0179 * 1/(1−rkumfgfrb*.01)
  − 0.0710 * spike(77,4)
  + 1.3658

[468] PDIEXFFB (ST, Blk 2) Impl Price Deflator, Exports, Merch, Foods, Feeds, & Beverages

log(pdiexffb) =
  + 0.5027 * from0 to3 degree2 near far
      log(ppifrm)
  + 2.4353

[469] PDIEXISM (ST, Blk 2) Impl Price Deflator, Exports, Merch, Indust. Supplies & Materials

log(pdiexism) =
    0.4693 * movavg(2,log(ppixfae))
  + 0.2515 * movavg(2,log(ppifap))
  − 0.4524 * movavg(2,log(rexmor15r))
  + 0.0104 * movavg(2,1/(1−rkumfgfrb*.01))
  + 3.3386

[470] PDIEXMER (ID, Blk 3) Impl Price Deflator, Exports Merch, Total

```
pdiexmer =
    exmer/exmer87 * 100
```

[471] PDIEXMVP (ST, Blk 2) Impl Price Deflator, Exports, Merch, Motor Vehicles & Parts

```
log(pdiexmvp) =
      1.1809 * movavg(2,log(ppiteq))
    - 0.9658
```

[472] PDIEXOTH (ST, Blk 2) Impl Price Deflator, Exports, Merch, Other

```
log(pdiexoth) =
    - 0.0689 * log(rexmor15r)
    + 0.0714 * movavg(2,log(ppifap))
    + 0.5479 * movavg(2,log(ppixfae))
    + 0.1962 * movavg(2,log(ppifpf))
    + 1.1332
```

[473] PDIEXRFI (ST, Blk 2) Impl Price Deflator, Exports, Services, Factor Income

```
log(pdiexrfi) =
      1.0000 * log(pdinnp)
    - 0.0002
```

[474] PDIEXSER (ST, Blk 2) Impl Price Deflator, Exports, Services, Total

```
log(pdiexser) =
      0.9893 * movavg(2,log(pdigdpnfm))
    + 0.0528
```

[475] PDIGDP (ID, Blk 2) Impl Price Deflator, Gross Domestic Product

```
pdigdp =
    gdp/gdp87 * 100
```

[476] PDIGDPNFM (ST, Blk 2) Impl Price Deflator, Gross Domestic Product, Nonfarm Business

```
log(pdigdpnfm) =
    + 0.2816 * from0 to6 degree1 far
          log(rkumfgfrb)
    + 1.0245 * from0 to3 degree1 far
          log(.05 * ppirpp_u+.12 * pdiimxoil+.83 * julcnfmpriavg)
    - 1.4502
```

[477] PDIGNP (ID, Blk 2) Impl Price Deflator, Gross National Product

```
pdignp =
    gnp/gnp87 * 100
```

[478] PDIGP (ID, Blk 3) Impl Price Deflator, Govt Purchases, Total

```
pdigp =
    100 * (gp/gp87)
```

[479] PDIGPF (ID, Blk 3) Impl Price Deflator, Govt Purchases, Federal

```
pdigpf =
    100 * gpf/gpf87
```

[480] PDIGPFD (ID, Blk 3) Impl Price Deflator, Govt Purchases, Federal, Defense, Total

```
pdigpfd =
    100 * gpfd/gpfd87
```

[481] PDIGPFDPAY (ID, Blk 3) Impl Price Deflator, Govt Purchases, Federal, Defense, Comp, Total

```
pdigpfdpay =
    100 * (gpfdpay/gpfdpay87)
```

[482] PDIGPFDPAYCIV (ST, Blk 2) Impl Price Deflator, Govt Purchases, Federal, Defense, Comp, Civilian

```
log(pdigpfdpayciv) =
      0.8343 * log(wrgpfdpayciv)
    + 0.3515 * log(emegfd)
    + 2.2233
```

[483] PDIGPFDPAYMIL (ST, Blk 2) Impl Price Deflator, Govt Purchases, Federal, Defense, Comp, Military

log(pdigpfdpaymil) =
 0.9403 * log(wrgpfdpaymil)
 − 0.0725 * log(emgfdmil)
 + 2.0819

[484] PDIGPFDXPAY (ST, Blk 2) Impl Price Deflator, Govt Purchases, Federal, Defense, Noncomp

log(pdigpfdxpay) =
 1.0151 * movavg(4,log(ppiind))
 − 0.1150

[485] PDIGPFN (ID, Blk 3) Impl Price Deflator, Govt Purchases, Federal, Nondefense, Total

pdigpfn =
 100 * gpfn/gpfn87

[486] PDIGPFNOTH (ST, Blk 2) Impl Price Deflator, Govt Purchases, Federal, Nondefense, Noncomp, Other

log(pdigpfnoth) =
 1.0625 * movavg(4,log(ppiind))
 − 0.3473

[487] PDIGPFNPAY (ST, Blk 2) Impl Price Deflator, Govt Purchases, Federal, Nondefense, Compensation

log(pdigpfnpay) =
 0.9165 * log(wrgpfnpay)
 + 0.2677 * log(emegfn)
 + 2.2467

[488] PDIGPFNXPAY (ID, Blk 3) Impl Price Deflator, Govt Purchases, Federal, Nondefense, Noncomp

pdigpfnxpay =
 100 * (gpfnxpay/gpfnxpay87)

[489] PDIGPN (ID, Blk 2) Impl Price Deflator, Govt Purchases, State & Local, Total

pdigpn =
100 * gpn/gpn87

[490] PDIGPNPAY (ST, Blk 2) Impl Price Deflator, Govt Purchases, State & Local, Compensation

log(pdigpnpay) =
0.9730 * log(wrgpnpay)
+ 2.2623

[491] PDIGPNXPAY (ST, Blk 2) Impl Price Deflator, Govt Purchases, State & Local, Noncompensation

log(pdigpnxpay) =
0.8998 * movavg(4,log(ppi))
+ 0.4290

[492] PDIIFX (ID, Blk 3) Impl Price Deflator, Fixed Investment, Total

pdiifx =
ifx/ifx87 * 100

[493] PDIIGD (ID, Blk 3) Impl Price Deflator, Gross Private Domestic Investment

pdiigd =
igd/igd87 * 100

[494] PDIIM (ID, Blk 2) Impl Price Deflator, Imports, Total

pdiim =
100 * (im/im87)

[495] PDIIMCAPOTH (ST, Blk 2) Impl Price Deflator, Imports, Merch, Other Capital Goods

log(pdiimcapoth) =
0.6956 * log(ppirow15/rexmor15)
+ 4.4777

[496] PDIIMCOMPEQU (ST, Blk 2) Impl Price Deflator, Imports, Merch, Computers

log(pdiimcompequ) =
0.9756 * log(pdiexcompequ)
+ 0.1439

[497] PDIIMCONXMVP (ST, Blk 2) Impl Price Deflator, Imports, Merch, Consumer Goods

log(pdiimconxmvp) =
0.7335 * log(ppirow15/rexmor15)
+ 4.4748

[498] PDIIMFFB (ST, Blk 2) Impl Price Deflator, Imports, Merch, Foods, Feeds, & Beverages

log(pdiimffb) =
0.4841 * log(ppirow15/rexmor15)
− 0.2511 * spike(75,3)+spike(75,4)
+ 4.5418

[499] PDIIMISMXOIL (ST, Blk 2) Impl Price Deflator, Imports, Merch, Indust Suppl & Matls less Petrol

log(pdiimismxoil) =
0.6923 * log(ppicmp)
+ 0.3267 * from0 to 4 degree2 far
log(ppirow15/rexmor15)
+ 1.4607

[500] PDIIMMER (ID, Blk 3) Impl Price Deflator, Imports, Merch, Total

pdiimmer =
immer/immer87 * 100

[501] PDIIMMVP (ST, Blk 2) Impl Price Deflator, Imports, Merch, Motor Vehicles & Parts

log(pdiimmvp) =
1.1579 * log(ppirow15/rexmor15)
+ 4.3648

[502] PDIIMOIL (ST, Blk 1) Impl Price Deflator, Imports, Merch, Petroleum & Products

log(pdiimoil) =
    1.0063 * log(puvoilrac)
  + 0.0133 * dqtr1
  + 0.0187 * dqtr2
  − 0.0151 * dqtr3
  + 1.7092

[503] PDIIMOTH (ST, Blk 2) Impl Price Deflator, Imports, Merch, Other

log(pdiimoth) =
    0.6018 * log(ppirow15/rexmor15)
  + 4.5097

[504] PDIIMPFI (ST, Blk 2) Impl Price Deflator, Imports, Services, Factor Income

log(pdiimpfi) =
    log(pdinnp)
  − 0.0128 * (1−step(85,1))
  − 0.0009

[505] PDIIMSER (ST, Blk 2) Impl Price Deflator, Imports, Services, Total

log(pdiimser) =
    0.1339 * log(puvoilrac)
  + 0.9100 * log(ppirow15/rexmor15)
  + 4.0541

[506] PDIIMXOIL (ID, Blk 2) Impl Price Deflator, Imports, Merch, Nonpetroleum Products

pdiimxoil =
  imxoil/imxoil87 * 100

[507] PDIIP (ID, Blk 2) Impl Price Deflator, Fixed Invest, Nonres, Total

pdiip =
  ip/ip87 * 100

[508] PDIIPE (ID, Blk 2) Impl Price Deflator, Fixed Invest, Nonres, Prod Dur Eq, Total

pdiipe =
  ipe/ipe87 * 100

[509] PDIIPEIND (ST, Blk 2) Impl Price Deflator, Fixed Invest, Nonres, Prod Dur Eq, Industrial

log(pdiipeind) =
  + 1.0554 * from0 to4 degree1 far
    log(.571 * ppimae+.143 * ppifhe+.286 * ppiteq)
  − 0.3468

[510] PDIIPEINF (ST, Blk 2) Impl Price Deflator, Fixed Invest, Nonres, Prod Dur Eq, Info. Processing

log(pdiipeinf) =
  0.2921 * log(pdigdpnfm/julcnfmpriavg)
  + 0.3784 * log(julcnfmpriavg)
  − 0.0111 * ttrend
  + 4.6234

[511] PDIIPEOAS (ST, Blk 2) Impl Price Deflator, Fixed Invest, Nonres, Prod Dur Eq, Other

log(pdiipeoas) =
  0.1621 * log(pdigdpnfm/(.571 * ppimae+.143 * ppifhe+.286 * ppiteq))
  + 1.0016 * from0 to1 degree1 far
    log(.571 * ppimae+.143 * ppifhe+.286 * ppiteq)
  − 0.0860

[512] PDIIPETRN (ST, Blk 2) Impl Price Deflator, Fixed Invest, Nonres, Prod Dur Eq, Transportation

log(pdiipetrn) =
  1.1104 * log(pdicedmnc)
  + 0.3410 * log(pdigdpnfm/pdicedmnc)
  − 0.5009

[513] PDIIPS (ID, Blk 2) Impl Price Deflator, Fixed Invest, Nonres, Str, Total

pdiips =
ips/ips87 * 100

[514] PDIIPSBLDG (ID, Blk 2) Impl Price Deflator, Fixed Invest, Nonres, Str, Buildings

pdiipsbldg =
100 *
(ipsind+ipscom+ipsbldgoth)/(ipsind87+ipscom87+ipsbldgoth87)

[515] PDIIPSBLDGOTH (ST, Blk 2) Impl Price Deflator, Fixed Invest, Nonres, Str, Other Bldgs

log(pdiipsbldgoth) =
0.1253 * log(.013 * ppitpa+.074 * ppifap+.037 * ppicap+
.022 * ppirap+.188 * ppilwp+.008 * ppippa+
.341 * ppimmp+.110 * ppimae+.018 * ppifhe+
.190 * ppinmp)
+ 0.8687 * log(pdigdpnfm)

[516] PDIIPSIAC (ST, Blk 2) Impl Price Deflator, Fixed Invest, Nonres, Str, Commercial & Industrial

log(pdiipsiac) =
0.8688 * log(pdigdpnfm)
+ 0.1747 * from0 to3 degree1 far
log(.325 * ppilwp+.325 * ppinmp+.1 * ppicap+.25 * ppimmp)
− 0.2328

[517] PDIIPSMAP (ST, Blk 2) Impl Price Deflator, Fixed Invest, Nonres, Str, Min Expl, Shfts, Wells

log(pdiipsmap) =
0.4578 * log(.013 * ppitpa+.074 * ppifap+.037 * ppicap+
.022 * ppirap+.188 * ppilwp+.008 * ppippa+
.341 * ppimmp+.110 * ppimae+.018 * ppifhe+
.190 * ppinmp)

+ 0.3128 * log(ipsmap87.1+ipsmap87.2+ipsmap87.3)
+ 1.6023 * log(pdigdpnfm)
− 6.2416

[518] PDIIPSOAF (ST, Blk 2) Impl Price Deflator, Fixed Invest, Nonres, Str, Other

log(pdiipsoaf) =
0.7253 * log(.013 * ppitpa+.074 * ppifap+.037 * ppicap+
.022 * ppirap+.188 * ppilwp+.008 * ppippa+
.341 * ppimmp+.110 * ppimae+.018 * ppifhe+
.190 * ppinmp)
+ 0.3114 * log(pdigdpnfm)
− 0.2260

[519] PDIIPSUTL (ST, Blk 2) Impl Price Deflator, Fixed Invest, Nonres, Str, Utilities

log(pdiipsutl) =
0.3195 * log(.013 * ppitpa+.074 * ppifap+.037 * ppicap+
.022 * ppirap+.188 * ppilwp+.008 * ppippa+
.341 * ppimmp+.110 * ppimae+.018 * ppifhe+
.190 * ppinmp)
+ 0.5229 * log(pdigdpnfm)
+ 0.7420

[520] PDIIR (ID, Blk 2) Impl Price Deflator, Fixed Invest, Res, Total

pdiir =
ir/ir87 * 100

[521] PDIIROTH (ST, Blk 2) Impl Price Deflator, Fixed Invest, Res, Other

log(pdiiroth) =
0.2542 * log(jecwap)
+ 0.5430 * log(pdigdpnfm)
+ 0.1984 * from0 to3 degree1 far
log(.325 * ppilwp+.325 * ppinmp+.100 * ppicap+.250 * ppimmp)

[522] PDIIRSONE (ST, Blk 2) Impl Price Deflator, Fixed Invest, Res, New Hous, Single Unit Str

```
log(pdiirsone) =
      0.2876 * log(pdigdpnfm)
    + 0.8675 * from0 to3 degree1 far
         log(.325 * ppilwp+.325 * ppinmp+.100 * ppicap+
         .250 * ppimmp)
    - 0.8180
```

[523] PDIIRSTOM (ST, Blk 2) Impl Price Deflator, Fixed Invest, Res, Two or More Unit Structures

```
pdiirstom =
      1.0227 * pdiirsone
    - 2.7229
```

[524] PDIKIMFG (ST, Blk 2) Impl Price Deflator, Inventories, Mfg

```
log(pdikimfg) =
      0.6281 * log(ppiind)
    + 1.7252
```

[525] PDIKINFMXMFG (ST, Blk 2) Impl Price Deflator, Inventories, Nonfarm less Manufacturing

```
log(pdikinfmxmfg) =
    + 0.8688 * from0 to3 degree1 far
         log(.5 * ppiteq+.5 * ppifcg)
    + 0.5791
```

[526] PDINNP (ID, Blk 2) Impl Price Deflator, Net National Product

```
pdinnp =
    100 * nnp/nnp87
```

4.2. *Wage and average compensation*

The key equation to determine the rate of wages (the employment cost index for private nonfarm wages and salaries) is a Phillips curve specification. See Chapter 2, Section 4.2.

4.2.1. *Average compensation per manhour (public)*

[527] WRGPFDPAYCIV (ST, Blk 2) Average Compensation per Manhour, Federal Govt, Defense, Civilian

```
log(wrgpfdpayciv) =
      0.0641 * (1−step(81,4))
    + 1.0867 * log(wrgpfpay)
    − 0.0040 * runc.1−runcn.1
    + 0.0001
```

[528] WRGPFDPAYMIL (ST, Blk 2) Average Compensation per Manhour, Federal Govt, Defense, Military

```
dlog(wrgpfdpaymil) =
      1.0590 * dlog(wrgpfpay)
```

[529] WRGPFNPAY (ST, Blk 2) Average Compensation per Manhour, Federal Govt, Nondefense

```
dlog(wrgpfnpay) =
      1.0282 * dlog(wrgpfpay)
```

[530] WRGPFPAY (ST, Blk 2) Average Compensation per Manhour, Federal Govt

```
log(wrgpfpay) =
      1.0132 * log(movavg(4,jqwrhnfm))
    − 2.1930
```

[531] WRGPNPAY (ST, Blk 2) Average Compensation per Manhour, State & Local Govt

```
log(wrgpnpay) =
      1.0303 * log(movavg(4,jqwrhnfm))
    − 0.0128 * runc–runcn[−1]
    − 2.5261
```

4.2.2. *Average hourly earnings*

[532] WRHPCON (ST, Blk 3) Average Hourly Earnings, Construction

dlog(wrhpcon) =
1.0770 * dlog(jecwap)
− 0.0015 * runc−runcn
− 0.0023

[533] WRHPFIR (ST, Blk 3) Average Hourly Earnings, Finance, Insurance & Real Estate

dlog(wrhpfir) =
0.6634 * dlog(jecwap)
+ 0.0044

[534] WRHPMFG (ST, Blk 3) Average Hourly Earnings, Manufacturing

dlog(wrhpmfg) =
1.2093 * dlog(jecwap)
+ 0.0010 * log((xiomfg87.1/(ememfg.1 * hrwpmfg.1)+
xiomfg87.2/(ememfg.2 * hrwpmfg.2)+
xiomfg87.3/(ememfg.3 * hrwpmfg.3)+
xiomfg87.4/(ememfg.4 * hrwpmfg.4))/
(jomhnfm.1+jomhnfm.2+jomhnfm.3+jomhnfm.4))

[535] WRHPMIN (ST, Blk 3) Average Hourly Earnings, Mining

dlog(wrhpmin) =
1.0853 * dlog(jecwap)
− 0.0239 * diff(spike(81,2))

[536] WRHPSER (ST, Blk 3) Average Hourly Earnings, Services

dlog(wrhpser) =
0.7787 * dlog(jecwap)
+ 0.0041

[537] WRHPTPU (ST, Blk 3) Average Hourly Earnings, Transportation & Public Utilities

dlog(wrhptpu) =
0.9966 * dlog(jecwap)

[538] WRHPWRT (ST, Blk 3) Average Hourly Earnings, Wholesale & Retail Trade

```
dlog(wrhpwrt) =
      0.9029 * dlog(jecwap)
    + 0.0345 * dlog(wrhmnm)
    + 0.0033 * diff(spike(78,4))
    − 0.0006 * runc−runcn
```

[539] WS (ID, Blk 3) Supplements to Wages & Salaries

```
ws =
    txse + yol
```

4.2.3. *Input cost term*

[540] PICAP (ID, Blk 2) Input Cost Term Used in PPICAP

```
picap =
      (.5 * julcnfmpriavg+.3 * ppifap+.1 * ppirap+.1 * ppimmp) *
      ppipcnt/100
```

[541] PICEQ (ID, Blk 3) Input Cost Term Used in PPICEQ

```
piceq =
          0.0010 * ppirap
    +     0.0250 * ppimmp
    +     0.5540 * ppimae
    +     0.0710 * ppifhe
    +     0.3370 * ppiteq
    +     0.0120 * ppimis
```

[542] PIFAP_U (ID, Blk 2) Input Cost Term Used in PPIFAP_U

```
pifap_u =
    (.095 * ppicol_u+.221 * ppigas_u+.262 * ppielp_u+.422 *
    ppirpp_u) * (ppipcnt/100)
```

[543] PIFCG (ID, Blk 2) Input Cost Term Used in PPIFCG

pifcg =
    0.0210 * ppifrm
+ 0.3140 * ppipff
+ 0.0890 * ppitpa
+ 0.1450 * ppifap
+ 0.0500 * ppicap
+ 0.0180 * ppirap
+ 0.0120 * ppilwp
+ 0.0460 * ppippa
+ 0.0080 * ppimmp
+ 0.0160 * ppimae
+ 0.0650 * ppifhe
+ 0.0020 * ppinmp
+ 0.2140 * ppimis

[544] PIFHE (ID, Blk 2) Input Cost Term Used in PPIFHE

pifhe =
(.001 * ppipff+.038 * ppitpa+.006 * ppifap+.028 * ppicap+.075 * ppirap+.060 * ppilwp+.025 * ppippa+.186 * ppimmp+.228 * ppimae+.010 * ppinmp+.001 * ppiteq+.006 * ppimis+.328 * julcnfmpriavg+.008 * txi/2.58825) * (ppipcnt/100)

[545] PIINT (ID, Blk 3) Input Cost Term Used in PPIINT

piint =
    0.0500 * ppipff
+ 0.0480 * ppitpa
+ 0.1410 * ppifap
+ 0.1000 * ppicap
+ 0.0370 * ppirap
+ 0.0370 * ppilwp
+ 0.1000 * ppippa
+ 0.2410 * ppimmp
+ 0.1180 * ppimae
+ 0.0140 * ppifhe
+ 0.0530 * ppinmp
+ 0.0430 * ppiteq
+ 0.0180 * ppimis

[546] PIMAE (ID, Blk 2) Input Cost Term Used in PPIMAE

pimae =
(.002 * ppipff+.010 * ppitpa+.022 * ppifap+.042 * ppicap+.086 * ppirap+.007 * ppilwp+.034 * ppippa+.702 * ppimmp+.027 * ppinmp+.022 * ppiteq+.007 * ppimis+.039 * txi/2.58825) * (ppipcnt/100)

[547] PIMMP (ID, Blk 2) Input Cost Term Used in PPIMMP

pimmp =
(.006 * ppitpa+.065 * ppifap+.052 * ppicap+.018 * ppirap+.007* ppilwp+.013 * ppippa+.078 * ppimae+.005 * ppifhe+.019 * ppinmp+.004 * ppiteq+.002 * ppimis+.695 * julcnfmpriavg+.036 * txi/2.58825) * (ppipcnt/100)

[548] PINMP (ID, Blk 2) Input Cost Term Used in PPINMP

pinmp =
(.001 * ppipff+.007 * ppitpa+.057 * ppifap+.072 * ppicap+.013 * ppirap+.014 * ppilwp+.061 * ppippa+.047 * ppimmp+.048 * ppimae+.006 * ppiteq+.012 * ppimis+.620 * julcnfmpriavg+.042 * txi/2.58825) * (ppipcnt/100)

[549] PIPPA (ID, Blk 2) Input Cost Term Used in PPIPPA

pippa =
(.001 * ppifrm+.006 * ppipff+.020 * ppitpa+.044 * ppifap+.010 * ppicap+.032 * ppirap+.069 * ppilwp+.012 * ppimmp+.016 * ppimae+.005 * ppinmp+.017 * ppimis+.733 * julcnfmpriavg+.035 * txi/2.58825) * (ppipcnt/100)

[550] PIRAP (ID, Blk 2) Input Cost Term Used in PPIRAP

pirap =
(.059 * ppitpa+.022 * ppifap+.361 * ppicap+.004 * ppilwp+.036 * ppippa+.033 * ppimmp+.015 * ppimae+.014 * ppinmp+.001 * ppiteq+.001 * ppimis+.407 * julcnfmpriavg+.047 * txi/2.58825) * (ppipcnt/100)

[551] PITEQ (ID, Blk 2) Input Cost Term Used in PPITEQ

piteq =
(.033 * ppitpa+.007 * ppifap+.014 * ppicap+.067 * ppirap+.012 * ppilwp+.007 * ppippa+.349 * ppimmp+.161 * ppimae+.048 * ppifhe+.014 * ppinmp+.003 * ppimis+.280 * julcnfmpriavg+.005 * txi/2.58825) * (ppipcnt/100)

[552] PITPA (ID, Blk 2) Input Cost Term Used in PPITPA

pitpa =
(.062 * ppifrm+.013 * ppifap+.229 * ppicap+.024 * ppirap+.022 * ppilwp+.021 * ppippa+.001 * ppimmp+.013 * ppimae+.001 * ppifhe+.003 * ppinmp+.023 * ppimis+.574 * julcnfmpriavg+.014 * txi/2.58825) * (ppipcnt/100)

4.2.4. *Unit labor cost*

[553] JOMHNFM (ST, Blk 2) Output per Hour, Private Business Sector

log(jomhnfm) =
0.9740 * log((gdp87−iifrmaccc87−gpfpay87−gpnpay87−ceshou87−gnpsdx87)/(ememfg*hrwpmfg+emecon*hrwpcon+ememin*hrwpmin+emewrt*hrwpwrt+emetpu*hrwptpu+emefir*hrwpfir+emeser*hrwpser))
+ 4.4927

[554] JQWRHNFM (ST, Blk 2) Compensation per Hour, Nonfarm Business Sector

log(jqwrhnfm/jecwap) =
0.1166 * log(rtxssp)
+ 0.0149 * log(za.1/yn.1+za.2/yn.2+za.3/yn.3+za.4/yn.4)
+ 0.1289 * log(pdicesmed/jecwap)
+ 0.0448 * step(74,1)
+ 0.5482

[555] JULCNFMPRI (ID, Blk 3) Unit Labor Costs, Nonfarm Business Sector

julcnfmpri =
jqwrhnfm/jomhnfm*100

[556] JULCNFMPRIAVG (ID, Blk 2) Unit Labor Costs, Nonfarm Business Sector, Smoothed

```
julcnfmpriavg =
    100 * jqwrhnfm/(.125 * (jomhnfm+jomhnfm.1+jomhnfm.2+
    jomhnfm.3+jomhnfm.4+jomhnfm.5+jomhnfm.6+jomhnfm.7))*
    1.00412
```

4.2.5. *Employment cost index*

[557] JECWAP (ST, Blk 2) Employment Cost Index, Wages & Salary, Private Nonfarm

```
log(jecwap) =
      0.00637 * dlog(wrhmnm)
    – 0.0009 * from0 to7 degree2 near far
        runc-runcn
    + 0.4985 * from0 to 11 degree2 near far
        dlog(movavg(4,jomhnfm))
    + 0.0021 * from0 to3 degree1 none
        rpdicehat
    + 0.00177
```

4.3. *Anticipated inflation*

[558] RPDICEHAT (ID, Blk 2) Anticipated Inflation Rate, Impl Price Deflator, Consumption Expend

```
rpdicehat =
    40 * (((pdice/pdice.1)**4)–1)+30 * (((pdice.1/pdice.2)**4)–1)+
    20 * (((pdice.2/pdice.3)**4)–1)+10 * (((pdice.3/pdice.4)**4)–1)
```

[559] RPDIGNPHAT (ID, Blk 2) Anticipated Inflation Rate, Impl Price Deflator, GNP

```
rpdignphat =
    10*(((pdignp/pdignp.1)**4)–1)+10 *(((pdignp.1/pdignp.2)**4)–1)+
    10*(((pdignp.2/pdignp.3)**4)–1)+10 *(((pdignp.3/pdignp.4)**4)–
    1)+10 * (((pdignp.4/pdignp.5)**4)–1)+10*(((pdignp.5/
    pdignp.6) **4)–1)+10*(((pdignp.6/pdignp.7)**4)–1)+
    10*(((pdignp.7/pdignp.8)**4)–1)+10*(((pdignp.8/pdignp.9) **4)–
    1)+10*(((pdignp.9/pdignp.10)**4)–1)
```

4.4. *Unit value*

[560] PUVCAR (ST, Blk 3) Unit Value, Average Price, New Cars, Retail, Domestics & Imports

log(puvcar) =
    0.8470 * log(puvcar87 * pdice)
  − 3.5398

[561] PUVCAR87 (ST, Blk 2) Unit Value, Average Price, New Cars, Retail, Domestics & Imports

puvcar87 =
    0.9127 * (.5 * (rimpcar*puvcarimp87+(1-rimpcar) *
      puvcardom87)+.3 * (rimpcar.1 * puvcarimp87.1+
      (1−rimpcar.1) * puvcardom87.1)+.2 * (rimpcar.2 *
      puvcarimp87.2+(1−rimpcar.2) * puvcardom87.2))
  + 0.76894

[562] PUVCARDOM87 (ST, Blk 2) Unit Value, Average Price, New Cars, Wholesale, Domestics

log(puvcardom87) =
    0.7104 * log(ydpperm87/np16a)+log(ttrend)
  − 3.1045

[563] PUVCARIMP87 (ST, Blk 2) Unit Value, Average Price, New Cars, Retail, Imports

log(puvcarimp87) =
    1.0671 * log(ydpperm87/np16a)+log(ttrend)
  − 5.5488

[564] PUVHNewMED_U (ST, Blk 2) Unit Value, Median Price, New Single Unit Homes Sold

log(puvhnewmed_u/puvhnewmed_sf) =
    1.0334 * log(puvholdmed_u/puvholdmed_sf)
  + 0.1529

[565] PUVHOLDMED_U (ST, Blk 2) Unit Value, Median Price, Existing Single Unit Homes Sold

```
log(puvholdmed_u/puvholdmed_sf) =
    0.9349 * log(pdiirsone)
  + 0.2560 * log(pdigdpnfm)
  – 0.0906 * from0 to8 degree2 near far
      log(rmorefw)
  – 5.4386
```

5. Government Revenues and Expenditures

Mark 10 has a great amount of government policy detail. See some expositions in Chapter 2, Section 3.

5.1. *Government receipt*

[566] TXC (ID, Blk 3) Govt Receipts, Profits Tax Accruals, Total

```
txc =
  txcf + txcn
```

[567] TXCF (ST, Blk 2) Govt Receipts, Profits Tax Accruals, Federal

```
txcf =
  0.01 * rtxcf_eff*(zb–zrow–zxadj6011)+zxadj6011
```

[568] TXCN (ST, Blk 2) Govt Receipts, Profits Tax Accruals, State & Local

```
txcn =
  (rtxcn_eff/100) * (zb–zrow–zxadj6011)
```

[569] TXF (ID, Blk 2) Govt Receipts, Federal, NIPA Basis

```
txf =
  txpf + txcf + txif + txsf
```

[570] TXFUBB (ID, Blk 2) Govt Receipts, Federal, Unified Budget Basis

```
txfubb =
  txf + txfadj
```

[571] TXI (ID, Blk 2) Govt Receipts, Ind Bus Tax & Nontax Accruals, Total

txi =
 txif + txin

[572] TXIF (ST, Blk 2) Govt Receipts, Ind Bus Tax & Nontax Accruals, Federal

log(txif-txifoil) =
 0.6383 * log(ce)
 − 1.1658

[573] TXIN (ST, Blk 2) Govt Receipts, Ind Bus Tax & Nontax Accruals, State & Local

log(txin−txinpty) =
 1.0837 * log(ce)
 − 3.4466

[574] TXINPTY (ST, Blk 2) Govt Receipts, Ind Bus Tax & Nontax Accruals, Prop Tax, State & Local

txinpty =
 + 3.3264 * from0 to11 degree2 near far
 .0001 * puvholdmed_u*(krnet87)
 + 20.0271

[575] TXIXOIL (ID, Blk 3) Govt Receipts, Ind Bus Tax & Nontax Accruals, Xcl Wndfall Prof, Total

txixoil =
 txi − txifoil

[576] TXN (ID, Blk 2) Govt Receipts, State & Local

txn =
 txpn + txcn + txin + txsn + gia

[577] TXP (ID, Blk 2) Govt Receipts, Personal Tax & Nontax Receipts, Total

txp =
 txpf + txpn

[578] TXPAV (ID, Blk 3) Govt Receipts, Personal Tax & Nontax Receipts, Total, 4 Qtr Mov Avg

txpav =
    0.2500 * (txp+txp.1+txp.2+txp.3)

[579] TXPF (ST, Blk 2) Govt Receipts, Personal Tax & Nontax Receipts, Federal

txpf =
    .01 * rtxpf_eff*yptax

[580] TXPN (ST, Blk 2) Govt Receipts, Personal Tax & Nontax Receipts, State & Local

txpn =
    (rtxpn_eff/100) * yptax

[581] TXS (ID, Blk 2) Govt Receipts, Contributions for Social Insurance, Total

txs =
    txsf + txsn

[582] TXSE (ID, Blk 2) Govt Receipts, Contributions for Social Insurance, Employer

txse =
    .01 * rtxse*(txsf+txsn)

[583] TXSF (ST, Blk 2) Govt Receipts, Contributions for Social Insurance, Federal

dlog(txsf) =
    0.6737 * dlog(.01 * txosecovr*(200 * rtxssp) * (wd+txse+yol−(gpfdpay+gpfnpay)))
    + 0.2667 * dlog(ybasssp*(eme-emegf-emgfdmil)/(wd+txse+yol−(gpfdpay+gpfnpay)))
    + 0.0085

[584] TXSN (ST, Blk 2) Govt Receipts, Contributions for Social Insurance, State & Local

log(txsn) =
    0.9737 * log(txsn)[−1]
  + 0.0207 * log(txsf)

[585] TXSP (ID, Blk 2) Govt Receipts, Contributions for Social Insurance, Persons

txsp =
  txs − txse

5.2. *Government expenditure*

[586] GEF (ID, Blk 2) Govt Expenditures, Federal, Total, NIPA Basis

gef =
  gpf + trgf + gia + yingf + gslsf − waldgf

[587] GEFUBB (ID, Blk 2) Govt Expenditures, Federal, Total, Unified Budget Basis

gefubb =
  gef + gefadj

[588] GEN (ID, Blk 2) Govt Expenditures, State & Local, Total

gen =
  gpn + trpgn + yingn + gslsn − waldgn − ydvrgn

[589] GIA (ID, Blk 2) Federal Grants in Aid to State & Local Govts

gia =
  dumgef*(giaothexo+giamedcai)+(1.0−dumgef) * (.01 * pdigpn*giaoth87exo+giamedcai)

[590] GIA87 (ID, Blk 3) Federal Grants in Aid to State & Local Govts

gia87 =
  dumgef*100 * gia/pdigpn+(1.0−dumgef) * (giaoth87exo+100 * giamedcai/pdigpn)

[591] GIAMEDCAI (ST, Blk 2) Federal Grants-in-Aid to State and Local Govts, MEDICAID

log(giamedcai/(.01 * pdicesmed*np)) =
    0.20783 * step(91,1)
  + 0.42979 * log(nun)
  + 1.9497 * from0 to6 degree2 near far
      log(ydp87/np)
  – 8.00254

[592] GPDUR87 (ID, Blk 2) Govt Purchases, Durable Equipment, Total

gpdur87 =
  (gpnxpay87 * rgpndur) + (gpfdxpay87 * rgpfddur) + (gpfnoth87 * rgpfndur)

[593] GPSTR87 (ID, Blk 2) Govt Purchases, Structures, Total

gpstr87 =
  (gpnxpay87 * rgpnstr) + (gpfdxpay87 * rgpfdstr) + (gpfnoth87 * rgpfnstr)

5.3. *Government surplus*

[594] NETGEF (ID, Blk 2) Govt Surplus or Deficit, Federal, NIPA Basis

netgef =
  txf – gef

[595] NETGEFUBB (ID, Blk 2) Govt Surplus or Deficit, Federal, Unified Budget Basis

netgefubb =
  txfubb – gefubb

[596] NETGEN (ID, Blk 2) Govt Surplus or Deficit, State & Local, Total

netgen =
  txn – gen

[597] NETGENOTH (ID, Blk 3) Govt Surplus or Deficit, State & Local, Other

netgenoth =
    netgen − netgensif

[598] NETGENSIF (ST, Blk 3) Govt Surplus or Deficit, State & Local, Social Insurance Fund

log(netgensif/(.01 * pdice)) =
    + 0.2692 * from0 to2 degree1 far
        log(emegn)
    + 0.2414 * from0 to15 degree2 near far
        log(rmunibb20)
    + 2.8445

[599] KGNET87 (ID, Blk 2) Net Capital Stock, Public, Structures

kgnet87 =
    kgsnet87 + kgenet87

[600] KGENET87 (ID, Blk 2) Net Capital Stock, Public, Equipment

kgenet87 =
    kgenet87.1 * (1−((1+rdepge87) * *.25-1))+gpdur87/4

[601] KGSNET87 (ID, Blk 2) Net Capital Stock, Public, Total

kgsnet87 =
    kgsnet87.1 * (1−((1+rdepgs87) * *.25-1))+gpstr87/4

[602] KASSTGNNET_U (ST, Blk 2) State and Local Net Financial Assets,

(kasstgnnet_u-kasstgnnet_u.4) =
    1.1381 * movavg(4,netgen)
    − 1.8008

[603] KDEBTGFNET (ST, Blk 2) Net Federal Debt, Net of Agency Holdings

(kdebtgfnet-kdebtgfnet.4) =
    − 1.0155 * movavg(4,netgefubb)
    + 8.2679

5.4. *Subsidies*

[604] GSLS (ID, Blk 1) Subsidies less Curr Surplus of Govt Enterprises, Total

```
gsls =
    gslsf + gslsn
```

5.5. *Tax rate*

[605] RTXCF_ADJ (ST, Blk 2) Tax Rate, Corporate Profits Tax, Federal, Rate Adjustment

```
rtxcf_adj*z =
        121.9410 * (itcetrn*ipetrn87 * pdiipetrn/100+
         itceind*ipeind87 * pdiipeind/100+itceinf*ipeinf87 *
         pdiipeinf/100+itceoas*ipeoas87 * pdiipeoas/100)
    - 602.9720 * step(87,1)
    + 678.9710
```

[606] RTXCF_EFF (ID, Blk 2) Tax Rate, Corporate Profits Tax, Federal, Effective Rate

```
rtxcf_eff =
    rtxcf_stat - rtxcf_adj
```

5.6. *Transfer payment*

[607] TRF (ID, Blk 3) Transfer Payments, To Foreigners (Net), Total

```
trf =
    trfp + trfg + trfb
```

[608] TRGF (ID, Blk 2) Transfer Payments, Total, From Govt. Federal

```
trgf =
    trpgf + trfg
```

[609] TRP (ID, Blk 2) Transfer Payments, To Persons, Total

```
trp =
    trpgf + trpgn + trpb
```

[610] TRP87 (ID, Blk 3) Transfer Payments, To Persons, Total

```
trp87 =
    trp/(.01 * pdice)
```

[611] TRPB (ST, Blk 2) Transfer Payments, To Persons, From Business

```
trpb/(.01 * pdignp*np) =
       0.0006 * ttrend
    + 0.0009 * from0 to2 degree2 far
          rprime−rpdignphat
    − 0.0087
```

[612] TRPG (ID, Blk 3) Transfer Payments, To Persons, From Govt, Total

```
trpg =
    trpgf + trpgn
```

[613] TRPGF (ID, Blk 2) Transfer Payments, To Persons, From Govt, Federal, Total

```
trpgf =
    trpgfoasdi + trpgfhi + trpgfuib + trpgfret + trpgfvet + trpgfoth
```

[614] TRPGFHI (ST, Blk 2) Transfer Payments, To Persons, From Govt, Federal, Health Insurance

```
log((trpgfhi/np65a)/(pdicesmed*.01)) =
       0.1230 * (1−step(87,1))
    + 5.6988 * log((nptf7579+nptf8084+nptf85a+nptm7579+
          nptm8084+nptm85a)/np65a)
    + 5.7832
```

[615] TRPGFOASDI (ST, Blk 2) Transfer Payments, To Persons, From Govt, Federal, OASDI

```
log(trpgfoasdi/(np65a*pdice*.01)) =
       0.0989 * (step(74,1)−step(83,1)) * dqtr3
    − 0.1208 * step(84,1)
    + 0.0410 * dqtr1 * step(84,1)
```

+ 0.0280 * dqtr2 * step(84,1)
+ 0.0165 * dqtr3 * step(84,1)
+ 1.1725 * from0 to3 degree2 near far
log(pdicesmed/pdice)
+ 2.0559

[616] TRPGFOTH (ST, Blk 2) Transfer Payments, To Persons, From Govt, Federal, Other

log((trpgfoth/np)/(pdice*.01)) =
2.1212 * log(ttrend)
+ 0.1867 * spike(75,2)-spike(75,3)
− 0.5790 * step(81,1)
+ 0.5702 * from0 to3 degree2 near far
log(nun)
− 12.9811

[617] TRPGFRET (ST, Blk 2) Transfer Payments, To Persons, From Govt, Federal, Fed Empl Retirement

log(trpgfret/(np65a*.01 * pdice)) =
1.4181 * log(ttrend)
− 0.3302 * step(88,1)
+ 0.0610 * dqtr1 * step(88,1)
+ 0.0342 * dqtr2 * step(88,1)
+ 0.0105 * dqtr3 * step(88,1)
− 6.5005

[618] TRPGFSSP (ID, Blk 3) Transfer Payments, To Persons, From Govt, Federal, OASDHI

trpgfssp =
trpgfoasdi + trpgfhi

[619] TRPGFUIB (ST, Blk 2) Transfer Payments, To Persons, From Govt, Federal, Unempl Insurance

log(trpgfuib/(pdice*.01)) =
+ 1.0846 * from0 to3 degree1 far
log(nun)
+ 0.8191

[620] TRPGFVET (ID, Blk 2) Transfer Payments, To Persons, From Govt, Federal, Veterans Benefits

trpgfvet =
    trpgfvetoth + trpgfvetmed

[621] TRPGFVETMED (ST, Blk 2) Transfer Payments, To Persons, From Govt, Federal, Veterans Benefits, Medical

log(trpgfvetmed/(np*.01 * pdicesmed)) =
    0.80902 * log(ttrend)
    + 0.16576 * step(88,1)
    + 0.00317 * dqtr1 * step(88,1)
    + 0.0055 * dqtr2 * step(88,1)
    + 0.00452 * dqtr3 * step(88,1)
    − 8.97673

[622] TRGFVETOTH (ST, Blk 2) Transfer Payments, To Persons, From Govt, Federal, Veterans Benefits, Other

log(trpgfvetoth/(np*.01 * pdice)) =
    − 0.61616 * log(ttrend)
    − 0.34301 * step(88,1)
    + 0.04902 * dqtr1 * step(88,1)
    + 0.03556 * dqtr2 * step(88,1)
    + 0.01476 * dqtr3 * step(88,1)
    + 0.54048

[623] TRPGN (ID, Blk 2) Transfer Payments, To Persons, From Govt, State & Local

trpgn =
    trpgnoth + trpgnmedcai

[624] TRPGNMEDCAI (ST, Blk 2) Transfer Payments, To Persons, From Govt, State and Local, MEDICAID

log(trpgnmedcai) =
    0.96622 * log(giamedcai)
    + 0.66288

[625] TRPGNOTH (ST, Blk 2) Transfer Payments, To Persons, From Govt, State and Local, Other

```
log(trpgnoth/(np*pdice*.01)) =
      2.91717 * log(np65a/np)
    + 0.0045 * from0 to3 degree2 near far
        log(nun)
    + 5.11177
```

5.7. *Profit tax rate*

[626] RMCPT (ID, Blk 2) Marginal Corporate Profits Tax Rate

```
rmcpt =
    .01 * (rtxcf_stat(1-.01 * rtxcf_stat) * 100 *
          txcn/(zb-zrow-zxadj6011))
```

6. Production and Sectoral Demand

6.1. *IP (Industrial production index)*

[627] JIP (ST, Blk 3) IP Index, Industrial Production, Total

```
log(jip) =
        0.8844 * .845 * log(xiomfg87)+.079 * log(xiomin87)+
         .076 * log(xiotpu87)
    - 0.4049 * log(ttrend)
```

6.2. *Total demand*

[628] XIOCON187 (ID, Blk 2) Final Demand, Construction, Part One

```
xiocon187 =
    0.0236 * cedmnc87 + 0.0083 * cedmuc87 + 0.0228 * cedmtr87 +
    0.0229 * cedmtp87 + 0.0212 * cedfhe87 + 0.0214 * cedoth87 +
    0.0225 * cenfah87 + 0.0263 * cenfmb87 + 0.0210 * cencas87 +
    0.0228 * cenene87 + 0.0214 * cenoth87 + 0.0263 * ceshou87 +
    0.0542 * ceshho87 + 0.0358 * cestrn87 + 0.0265 * cesmao87
```

[629] XIOCON287 (ID, Blk 2) Final Demand, Construction, Part Two

xiocon287 =
0.0234 * ipeinf87 + 0.0300 * ipetrn87 + 0.0265 * (ipeind87 + ipeoas87) + 0.4840 * ipsmap87 + 0.4185 * ipscom87 + 0.4559 * ipsind87 + 0.4563 * (ipsbldgoth87 + ipsutl87 + ipsoaf87) + 0.3879 * irsone87 + 0.3872 * irstom87 + 0.2929 * iroth87 + 0.0240 * iifrmaccc87 + 0.0242 * iinfm87 + 0.1288 * (gpfdpayciv87 + gpfdpaymil87) + 0.0405 * gpfdxpay87 + 0.1288 * gpfnpay87 + 0.2668 * gpfnoth87 + 0.1288 * gpnpay87 + 0.3684 * gpnxpay87

[630] XIOCON387 (ID, Blk 2) Final Demand, Construction, Part Three

xiocon387 =
0.0250 * exffb87 + 0.0272 * exism87 + 0.0251 * (excapoth87 + excompequ87) + 0.0251 * exmvp87 + 0.0251 * exconxmvp87 + 0.0276 * exoth87 + 0.0139 * exser87 − 0.0387 * imoil87 − 0.0245 * imffb87 −0.0270 * imismxoil87 − 0.0245 * (imcapoth87 + imcompequ87) − 0.0245 * immvp87 − 0.0245 * imconxmvp87 − 0.0253 * imoth87 − 0.0067 * imser87

[631] XIOCON87 (ID, Blk 2) Final Demand, Construction, Total

xiocon87 =
xiocon187 + xiocon287 + xiocon387

[632] XIOFSR187 (ID, Blk 2) Final Demand, Fin, Insur, Real Estate, & Other Services, Part One

xiofsr187 =
0.1946 * cedmnc87 + 0.1286 * cedmuc87 + 0.1960 * cedmtr87 + 0.2248 * cedmtp87 + 0.2172 * cedfhe87 + 0.2252 * cedoth87 + 0.2081 * cenfah87 + 1.2111 * cenfmb87 + 0.2226 * cencas87 + 0.2057 * cenene87 + 0.2129 * cenoth87 + 1.2126 * ceshou87 + 0.2253 * ceshho87 + 0.8655 * cestrn87 + 1.1439 * cesmao87

[633] XIOFSR287 (ID, Blk 2) Final Demand, Fin, Insur, Real Estate, & Other Services, Part Two

xiofsr287 =
0.1938 * ipeinf87 + 0.2375 * ipetrn87 + 0.2105 * (ipeind87 + ipeoas87) + 0.3347 * ipsmap87 + 0.3026 * ipscom87 + 0.2959 *

ipsind87 + 0.3324 * (ipsbldgoth87 + ipsutl87 + ipsoaf87) + 0.2686 * irsone87 + 0.2681 * irstom87 + 0.2619 * iroth87 + 0.2047 * iifrmaccc87 + 0.1809 * iinfm87 + 0.1478 * (gpfdpayciv87 + gpfdpaymil87) + 0.2272 * gpfdxpay87 + 0.1478 * gpfnpay87 + 0.7327 * gpfnoth87 + 0.1478 * gpnpay87 0.4302 * gpnxpay87

[634] XIOFSR387 (ID, Blk 2) Final Demand, Fin, Insur, Real Estate, & Other Services, Part Three

xiofsr387 =

0.2115 * exffb87 + 0.1929 + xism87 + 0.1976 * (excapoth87 + excompequ87) + 0.1976 * exmvp87 + 0.1976 * exconxmvp87 + 0.3951 * exoth87 + 0.2084 * exser87 − 0.1423 * imoil87 − 0.1849 * imffb87 − 0.1745 * imismxoil87 − 0.1812 * (imcapoth87 + imcompequ87) − 0.1812 * immvp87 − 0.1812 * imconxmvp87 − 0.5787 * imoth87 − 0.0773 * imser87

[635] XIOFSR87 (ID, Blk 2) Final Demand, Fin, Insur, Real Estate, & Other Services, Total

xiofsr87 =

xiofsr187 + xiofsr287 + xiofsr387

[636] XIOMFG187 (ID, Blk 2) Final Demand, Manufacturing, Part One

xiomfg187 =

1.3832 * cedmnc87 + 0.0729 * cedmuc87 + 1.2981 * cedmtr87 + 1.0133 * cedmtp87 + 0.9740 * cedfhe87 + 1.0050 * cedoth87 + 1.0923 * cenfah87 + 0.2349 * cenfmb87 + 0.9373 * cencas87 + 1.1670 * cenene87 + 0.9988 * cenoth87 + 0.2348 * ceshou87 + 0.2807 * ceshho87 + 0.2502 * cestrn87 + 0.2317 * cesmao87

[637] XIOMFG287 (ID, Blk 2) Final Demand, Manufacturing, Part Two

xiomfg287 =

1.4462 * ipeinf87 + 1.8266 * ipetrn87 + 1.5466 * (ipeind87 + ipeoas87)+ 0.8771 * ipsmap87 + 0.9822 * ipscom87 + 0.9714 * ipsind87 + 0.9208 * (ipsbldgoth87 + ipsutl87 + ipsoaf87) + 0.9764 * irsone87 + 0.9816 * irstom87 + 1.1039 * iroth87 +

0.4877 * iifrmaccc87 + 1.6733 * iinfm87+ 0.3216 * (gpfdpayciv87 + gpfdpaymil87) + 1.3265 * gpfdxpay87 + 0.3216 * gpfnpay87 + 0.4703 * gpfnoth87 + 0.3216 * gpnpay87 + 0.8269 * gpnxpay87

[638] XIOMFG387 (ID, Blk 2) Final Demand, Manufacturing, Part Three

xiomfg387 =
0.8068 * exffb87 + 1.3371 * exism87 + 1.4962 * (excapoth87 + excompequ87) + 1.4962 * exmvp87 + 1.4962 * exconxmvp87 + 1.0780 * exoth87 + 0.1262 * exser87 − 0.6176 * imoil87 − 1.5211 * imffb87 − 1.5141 * imismxoil87 − 1.7014 * (imcapoth87 + imcompequ87) − 1.7014 * immvp87 − 1.7014 * imconxmvp87 − 1.1479 * imoth87 − 0.0521 * imser87

[639] XIOMFG87 (ID, Blk 2) Final Demand, Manufacturing, Total

xiomfg87 =
xiomfg187 + xiomfg287 + xiomfg387

[640] XIOMIN187 (ID, Blk 2) Final Demand, Mining, Part One

xiomin187 =
0.1449 * cedmnc87 * 0.0125 + cedmuc87 + 0.1361 * cedmtr87 + 0.1113 * cedmtp87 + 0.1047 * cedfhe87 + 0.1072 * cedoth87 + 0.1175 * cenfah87 + 0.0315 * cenfmb87 + 0.1006 * cencas87 + 0.1286 * cenene87 + 0.1076 * cenoth87 + 0.0314 * ceshou87 + 0.1346 * ceshho87 + 0.0673 * cestrn87 + 0.0337 * cesmao87

[641] XIOMIN287 (ID, Blk 2) Final Demand, Mining, Part Two

xiomin287 =
0.1490 * ipeinf87 + 0.1903 * ipetrn87 + 0.1660 * (ipeind87 + ipeoas87)+ 0.1054 * ipsmap87 + 0.1136 * ipscom87 + 0.1113 * ipsind87 + 0.1097 * (ipsbldgoth87 + ipsutl87 + ipsoaf87) + 0.1129 * irsone87 + 0.1130 * irstom87 + 0.1260 * iroth87 + 0.0585 * iifrmaccc87 + 0.1699 * iinfm87+ 0.0896 * (gpfdpayciv87 + gpfdpaymil87) + 0.1437 * gpfdxpay87 + 0.0896 * gpfnpay87 + 0.0731 * gpfnoth87 + 0.0896 * gpnpay87 + 0.1057 * gpnxpay87

[642] XIOMIN387 (ID, Blk 2) Final Demand, Mining, Part Three

xiomin387 =
0.0936 * exffb87 + 0.2530 * exism87 + 0.1584 * (excapoth87 + excompequ87) + 0.1584 * exmvp87 + 0.1584 * exconxmvp87 + 0.2130 * exoth87 + 0.0329 * exser87 − 0.8204 * imoil87 − 0.1562 * imffb87 − 0.2855 * imismxoil87 − 0.1732 * (imcapoth87 + imcompequ87) − 0.1732 * immvp87 − 0.1732 * imconxmvp87 − 0.1198 * imoth87 − 0.0149 * imser87

[643] XIOMIN87 (ID, Blk 2) Final Demand, Mining, Total

xiomin87 =
xiomin187 + xiomin287 + xiomin387

[644] XIOTPU187 (ID, Blk 2) Final Demand, Transportation & Utilities, Part One

xiotpu187 =
0.1624 * cedmnc87 + 0.0553 * cedmuc87 + 0.1533 * cedmtr87 + 0.1689 * cedmtp87 + 0.1390 * cedfhe87 + 0.1356 * cedoth87 + 0.1569 * cenfah87 + 0.0941 * cenfmb87 + 0.1326 * cencas87 + 0.1616 * cenene87 + 0.1429 * cenoth87 + 0.0926 * ceshou87 + 1.0731 * ceshho87 + 0.4354 * cestrn87 + 0.1185 * cesmao87

[645] XIOTPU287 (ID, Blk 2) Final Demand, Transportation & Utilities, Part Two

xiotpu287 =
0.1439 * ipeinf87 + 0.2039 * ipetrn87 + 0.1901 * (ipeind87 + ipeoas87)+ 0.1831 * ipsmap87 + 0.1507 * ipscom87 + 0.1499 * ipsind87 + 0.1482 * (ipsbldgoth87 + ipsutl87 + ipsoaf87) + 0.1561 * irsone87 + 0.1563 * irstom87 + 0.1570 * iroth87 + 0.1064 * iifrmaccc87 + 0.1426 * iinfm87+ 0.2857 * ((gpfdpayciv8 + gpfdpaymil87) + 0.1844 * gpfdxpay87 + 0.2857 * gpfnpay87 + 0.2219 * gpfnoth87 + 0.2857 * gpnpay87 + 0.2072 * gpnxpay87

[646] XIOTPU387
(ID, Blk 2) Final Demand, Transportation & Utilities, Part Three

xiotpu387 =
0.1712 * exffb87 + 0.1841 * exism87 + 0.1923 * (excapoth87 + excompequ87) + 0.1923 * exmvp87 + 0.1923 * exconxmvp87 +

0.1751 * exoth87 + 0.2095 * exser87 − 0.0984 * imoil87 − 0.1435 * imffb87 − 0.1396 * imismxoil87 − 0.1490 * (imcapoth87 + imcompequ87) − 0.1490 * immvp87 − 0.1490 * imconxmvp87 − 0.1298 * imoth87 − 0.0953 * imser87

[647] XIOTPU87 (ID, Blk 2) Final Demand, Transportation & Utilities, Total

xiotpu87 =
xiotpu187 + xiotpu287 + xiotpu387

[648] XIOWRT187 (ID, Blk 2) Final Demand, Wholesale & Retail Trade, Part One

xiowrt187 =
0.2342 * cedmnc87 + 0.4951 * cedmuc87 + 0.2765 * cedmtr87 + 0.4999 * cedmtp87 + 0.4951 * cedfhe87 + 0.4767 * cedoth87 + 0.3776 * cenfah87 + 0.0315 * cenfmb87 + 0.5345 * cencas87 + 0.3622 * cenene87 + 0.4541 * cenoth87 + 0.0315 * ceshou87 + 0.0362 * ceshho87 + 0.0376 * cestrn87 + 0.0340 * cesmao87

[649] XIOWRT287 (ID, Blk 2) Final Demand, Wholesale & Retail Trade, Part Two

xiowrt287 =
0.2148 * ipeinf87 + 0.2315 * ipetrn87 + 0.2271 * (ipeind87 + ipeoas87) + 0.1165 * ipsmap87 + 0.1480 * ipscom87 + 0.1403 * ipsind87 + 0.1341 * (ipsbldgoth87 + ipsutl87 + ipsoaf87) + 0.1996 * irsone87 + 0.1980 * irstom87 + 0.1795 * iroth87 + 0.0799 * iifrmaccc87 + 0.0747 * iinfm87 + 0.0441 * (gpfdpayciv87 + gpfdpaymil87) + 0.0844 * gpfdxpay87 + 0.0441 * gpfnpay87 + 0.0835 * gpfnoth87 + 0.0441 * gpnpay87 + 0.0939 * gpnxpay

[650] XIOWRT387 (ID, Blk 2) Final Demand, Wholesale & Retail Trade, Part Three

xiowrt387 =
0.1318 * exffb87 + 0.1232 * exism87 + 0.1287 * (excapoth87 + excompequ87) + 0.1287 * exmvp87 + 0.1287 * exconxmvp87 + 0.1155 * exoth87 + 0.1828 * exser87 − 0.0123 * imoil87 − 0.0507 * imffb87 − 0.0434 * imismxoil87 − 0.0499 * (imcapoth87 + imcompequ87) − 0.0499 * immvp87 − 0.0499 * imconxmvp87 − 0.0333 * imoth87 − 0.1687 * imser87

[651] XIOWRT87 (ID, Blk 2) Final Demand, Wholesale & Retail Trade, Total

xiowrt87 =
xiowrt187 + xiowrt287 + xiowrt387

[652] YCEN87 (ID, Blk 2) Income, Intermediate Variable, Nondurable Goods Focus

ycen87 =
(wd+0.1 * (ydvper+yirper+0.4 * (ypr+yf+yr))1.1 * (trp−trpgfhi−trpb)−yipper−txsp−txp)/(pdice/100)

7. Population and Demographics

7.1. *Population*

[653] NP (ID, Blk 1) Population, Total

np =
npt0004 + npt0509 + npt1014 + nptm15a + nptf15a

[654] NP1619 (ID, Blk 1) Population, Noninstitutionalized Civilian, Total, 16–19

np1619 =
npm1619 + npf1619

[655] NP1624 (ID, Blk 1) Population, Noninstitutionalized Civilian, Total, 16–24

np1624 =
np1619 + np2024

[656] NP16A (ID, Blk 1) Population, Noninstitutionalized Civilian, Total, 16 & Over

np16a =
npm16a + npf16a

[657] NP2024 (ID, Blk 1) Population, Noninstitutionalized Civilian, Total, 20–24

np2024 =
    npm2024 + npf2024

[658] NP2534 (ID, Blk 1) Population, Noninstitutionalized Civilian, Total, 25–34

np2534 =
    npm2534 + npf2534

[659] NP2544 (ID, Blk 1) Population, Noninstitutionalized Civilian Total, 25–44

np2544 =
    np2534 + np3544

[660] NP3544 (ID, Blk 1) Population, Noninstitutionalized Civilian, Total, 35–44

np3544 =
    npm3544 + npf3544

[661] NP4554 (ID, Blk 1) Population, Noninstitutionalized Civilian, Total, 45–54

np4554 =
    npm4554 + npf4554

[662] NP5564 (ID, Blk 1) Population, Noninstitutionalized Civilian, Total, 55–64

np5564 =
    npm5564 + npf5564

[663] NP65A (ID, Blk 1) Population, Noninstitutionalized Civilian, Total, 65 & Over

np65a =
    npm65a + npf65a

[664] NPF1619 (ST, Blk 1) Population, Noninstitutionalized Civilian, Femails, 16–19

npf1619 =
    0.9765 * (nptf1617 * (1.0−0.36/100))−(1.0004 * emgfdmil/2326.0)+(nptf1819 * (1.0−0.36/100))−(18.0 * emgfdmil/2326.0)
  − 361.3110

[665] NPF16A (ID, Blk 1) Population, Noninstitutionalized Civilian, Femails, 16 & Over

npf16a =
  npf1619 + npf2024 + npf2534 + npf3544 + npf4554 + npf5564 + npf65a

[666] NPF2024 (ST, Blk 1) Population, Noninstitutionalized Civilian Femails, 20–24

npf2024 =
    0.9861 * (nptf2024 * (1.0−0.26/100))−(88.0 * emgfdmil/2326.0)
  − 349.8940

[667] NPF20A (ID, Blk 1) Population, Noninstitutionalized Civilian, Femails, 20 & Over

npf20a =
  npf2024 + npf2534 + npf3544 + npf4554 + npf5564 + npf65a

[668] NPF2534 (ST, Blk 1) Population, Noninstitutionalized Civilian, Femails, 25–34

npf2534 =
    0.9885 * (nptf2529 * (1.0−0.28/100))−(62.0 * emgfdmil/2326.0)+(nptf3034 * (1.0−0.26/100))−(33.999 * emgfdmil/2326.0)
  − 789.3250

[669] NPF3544 (ST, Blk 1) Population, Noninstitutionalized Civilian Femails, 35–44

npf3544 =
1.0008 * (nptf3539 * (1.0−0.27/100))−(13.0 * emgfdmil/2326.0)+ (nptf4044 * (1.0−0.28/100))−(3.0 * emgfdmil/2326.0)
− 403.5690

[670] NPF4554 (ST, Blk 1) Population, Noninstitutionalized Civilian, Femails, 45–54

npf4554 =
0.9468 * (nptf4549 * (1.0−0.33/100))−(1.0 * emgfdmil/2326.0)+ (nptf5054 * (1.0−0.41/100))−(1.0 * emgfdmil/2326.0)
− 129.1430

[671] NPF5564 (ST, Blk 1) Population, Noninstitutionalized Civilian, Femails, 55–64

npf5564 =
1.0176 * (nptf5559 * (1.0−0.53/100))−(0.0 * emgfdmil/2326.0)+ (nptf6064 * (1.0−0.79/100))−(0.0 * emgfdmil/2326.0)
− 256.7800

[672] NPF65A (ST, Blk 1) Population, Noninstitutionalized Civilian, Femails, 65 & Over

npf65a =
0.9953 * (nptf6569 * (1.0−1.27/100))−(0.0 * emgfdmil/2326.0)+ (nptf70a*(1.0−8.80/100))−(0.0 * emgfdmil/2326.0)
− 389.5360

[673] NPM1619 (ST, Blk 1) Population, Noninstitutionalized Civilian, Males, 16–19

npm1619 =
1.0071 * (nptm1617 * (1.0−1.18/100))−(3.99971 * emgfdmil/ 2326.0)+(nptm1819 * (1.0−1.18/100))−(170.0 * emgfdmil/2326.0)
− 103.6150

[674] NPM16A (ID, Blk 1) Population, Noninstitutionalized Civilian, Males, 16 & Over

npm16a =
npm1619 + npm2024 + npm2534 + npm3544 + npm4554 +
npm5564 + npm65a

[675] NPM2024 (ST, Blk 1) Population, Noninstitutionalized Civilian, Males, 20–24

npm2024 =
1.0429 * (nptm2024 * (1.0−1.58/100))−(722.0 *
emgfdmil/2326.0)
− 107.1460

[676] NPM20A (ID, Blk 1) Population, Noninstitutionalized Civilian, Males, 20 & Over

npm20a =
npm2024 + npm2534 + npm3544 + npm4554 +
npm5564 + npm65a

[677] NPM2534 (ST, Blk 1) Population, Noninstitutionalized Civilian, Males, 25–34

npm2534 =
0.9677 * (nptm2529 * (1.0−1.42/100))−(453.0 *
emgfdmil/2326.0)+(nptm3034 * (1.0−1.13/100))−(287.0 *
emgfdmil/2326.0)
− 401.5310

[678] NPM3544 (ST, Blk 1) Population, Noninstitutionalized Civilian, Males, 35–44

npm3544 =
0.9953 * (nptm3539 * (1.0−0.89/100))−(228.0 *
emgfdmil/2326.0)+(nptm4044 * (1.0−0.77/100))−(106.0 *
emgfdmil/2326.0)
− 328.5300

[679] NPM4554 (ST, Blk 1) Population, Noninstitutionalized Civilian Males, 45–54

npm4554 =
1.0290 * (nptm4549 * (1.0−0.72/100))−(37.001 * emgfdmil/2326.0)+(nptm5054 * (1.0−0.73/100))−(10.0 * emgfdmil/2326.0)
− 158.4850

[680] NPM5564 (ST, Blk 1) Population, Noninstitutionalized Civilian, Males, 55–64

npm5564 =
1.0372 * (nptm5559 * (1.0−0.82/100))−(1.9999 * emgfdmil/2326.0)+(nptm6064 * (1.0−1.00/100))−(0.99945 * emgfdmil/2326.0)
− 307.2620

[681] NPM65A (ST, Blk 1) Population, Noninstitutionalized Civilian, Males, 65 & Over

npm65a =
1.0276 * (nptm6569 * (1.0−1.42/100))−(0.0 * emgfdmil/2326.0)+(nptm70a*(1.0−4.96/100))−(0.0 * emgfdmil/2326.0)
− 213.2580

[682] NPT0004 (ID, Blk 1) Population, Total, 00–04

npt0004 =
npt0004exo*nptpcnt/100

[683] NPT0509 (ID, Blk 1) Population, Total, 05–09

npt0509 =
npt0509exo*nptpcnt/100

[684] NPT1014 (ID, Blk 1) Population, Total, 10–14

npt1014 =
npt1014exo*nptpcnt/100

[685] NPTF15 (ID, Blk 1) Population, Total, 15

nptf15 =
nptf15exo*nptpcnt/100

[686] NPTF15A (ID, Blk 1) Population, Total, 15 & Over

nptf15a =
nptf15 + nptf1617 + nptf1819 + nptf2024 + nptf2529 + nptf3034 +
nptf3539 + nptf4044 + nptf4549 + nptf5054 + nptf5559 +
nptf6064 + nptf6569 + nptf7074 + nptf7579 + nptf8084 + nptf85a

[687] NPTF1617 (ID, Blk 1) Population, Total, Femails, 16–17

nptf1617 =
nptf1617exo*nptpcnt/100

[688] NPTF1819 (ID, Blk 1) Population, Total, Femails, 18–19

nptf1819 =
nptf1819exo*nptpcnt/100

[689] NPTF2024 (ID, Blk 1) Population, Total, Femails, 20–24

nptf2024 =
nptf2024exo*nptpcnt/100

[690] NPTF2529 (ID, Blk 1) Population, Total, Femails, 25–29

nptf2529 =
nptf2529exo*nptpcnt/100

[691] NPTF3034 (ID, Blk 1) Population, Total, Femails, 30–34

nptf3034 =
nptf3034exo*nptpcnt/100

[692] NPTF3539 (ID, Blk 1) Population, Total, Femails, 35–39

nptf3539 =
nptf3539exo*nptpcnt/100

[693] NPTF4044 (ID, Blk 1) Population, Total, Femails, 40–44

nptf4044 =
 nptf4044exo*nptpcnt/100

[694] NPTF4549 (ID, Blk 1) Population, Total, Femails, 45–49

nptf4549 =
 nptf4549exo*nptpcnt/100

[695] NPTF5054 (ID, Blk 1) Population, Total, Femails, 50–54

nptf5054 =
 nptf5054exo*nptpcnt/100

[696] NPTF5559 (ID, Blk 1) Population, Total, Femails, 55–59

nptf5559 =
 nptf5559exo*nptpcnt/100

[697] NPTF6064 (ID, Blk 1) Population, Total, Femails, 60–64

nptf6064 =
 nptf6064exo*nptpcnt/100

[698] NPTF6569 (ID, Blk 1) Population, Total, Femails, 65–69

nptf6569 =
 nptf6569exo*nptpcnt/100

[699] NPTF7074 (ID, Blk 1) Population, Total, Femails, 70–74

nptf7074 =
 nptf7074exo*nptpcnt/100

[700] NPTF70A (ID, Blk 1) Population, Total, Femails, 70 & Over

nptf70a =
 nptf7074 + nptf7579 + nptf8084 + nptf85a

[701] NPTF7579 (ID, Blk 1) Population, Total, Femails, 75–79

nptf7579 =
 nptf7579exo*nptpcnt/100

[702] NPTF8084 (ID, Blk 1) Population, Total, Femails, 80–84

nptf8084 =
    nptf8084exo*nptpcnt/100

[703] NPTF85A (ID, Blk 1) Population, Total, Femails, 85 & Over

nptf85a =
    nptf85aexo*nptpcnt/100

[704] NPTM15 (ID, Blk 1) Population, Total, Males, 15

nptm15 =
    nptm15exo*nptpcnt/100

[705] NPTM15A (ID, Blk 1) Population, Total, Males, 15 & Over

nptm15a =
    nptm15 + nptm1617 + nptm1819 + nptm2024 + nptm2529 +
    nptm3034 + nptm3539 + nptm4044 + nptm4549 + nptm5054 +
    nptm5559 + nptm6064 + nptm6569 + nptm7074 + nptm7579 +
    nptm8084 + nptm85a

[706] NPTM1617 (ID, Blk 1) Population, Total, Males, 16–17

nptm1617 =
    nptm1617exo*nptpcnt/100

[707] NPTM1819 (ID, Blk 1) Population, Total, Males, 18–19

nptm1819 =
    nptm1819exo*nptpcnt/100

[708] NPTM2024 (ID, Blk 1) Population, Total, Males, 20–24

nptm2024 =
    nptm2024exo*nptpcnt/100

[709] NPTM2529 (ID, Blk 1) Population, Total, Males, 25–29

nptm2529 =
    nptm2529exo*nptpcnt/100

[710] NPTM3034 (ID, Blk 1) Population, Total, Males, 30–34

nptm3034 =
 nptm3034exo*nptpcnt/100

[711] NPTM3539 (ID, Blk 1) Population, Total, Males, 35–39

nptm3539 =
 nptm3539exo*nptpcnt/100

[712] NPTM4044 (ID, Blk 1) Population, Total, Males, 40–44

nptm4044 =
 nptm4044exo*nptpcnt/100

[713] NPTM4549 (ID, Blk 1) Population, Total, Males, 45–49

nptm4549 =
 nptm4549exo*nptpcnt/100

[714] NPTM5054 (ID, Blk 1) Population, Total, Males, 50–54

nptm5054 =
 nptm5054exo*nptpcnt/100

[715] NPTM5559 (ID, Blk 1) Population, Total, Males, 55–59

nptm5559 =
 nptm5559exo*nptpcnt/100

[716] NPTM6064 (ID, Blk 1) Population, Total, Males, 60–64

nptm6064 =
 nptm6064exo*nptpcnt/100

[717] NPTM6569 (ID, Blk 1) Population, Total, Males, 65–69

nptm6569 =
 nptm6569exo*nptpcnt/100

[718] NPTM7074 (ID, Blk 1) Population, Total, Males, 70–74

nptm7074 =
 nptm7074exo*nptpcnt/100

[719] NPTM70A (ID, Blk 1) Population, Total, Males, 70 & Over

nptm70a =
nptm7074 + nptm7579 + nptm8084 + nptm85a

[720] NPTM7579 (ID, Blk 1) Population, Total, Males, 75–79

nptm7579 =
nptm7579exo*nptpcnt/100

[721] NPTM8084 (ID, Blk 1) Population, Total, Males, 80–84

nptm8084 =
nptm8084exo*nptpcnt/100

[722] NPTM85A (ID, Blk 1) Population, Total, Males, 85 & Over

nptm85a =
nptm85aexo*nptpcnt/100

[723] RNP2544 (ID, Blk 1) Civilian Population, Total, 25–44, Share of Total Population

rnp2544 =
np2544/np

[724] RNP65A (ID, Blk 1) Civilian Population, Total, 65 & Over, Share of Total Population

rnp65a =
np65a/np

[725] RNPF1619 (ID, Blk 1) Civilian Population, Femails, 16–19, Share of Total Population

rnpf1619 =
npf1619/np

[726] RNPF20A (ID, Blk 1) Civilian Population, Femails, 20 & Over, Share of Total Population

rnpf20a =
(npf16a−npf1619)/np

[727] RNPM1619 (ID, Blk 1) Civilian Population, Males, 16–19, Share of Total Population

rnpm1619 =
    npm1619/np

[728] RNPM20A (ID, Blk 1) Civilian Population, Males, 20 & Over, Share of Total Population

rnpm20a =
    (npm16a−npm1619)/np

7.2. *Household*

[729] NFAMC (ST, Blk 1) Families, Total, Census Definition

nfamc/nhhld =
    12.1903 * 1/ttrend
  + 0.6549

[730] NHHDCSU (ID, Blk 1) Number of Households, Consumer Spending Units

nhhdcsu =
    nfamc + nindivuc

[731] NHHLD (ID, Blk 1) Total Households, Census Definition, Housing Units

nhhld =
    nhhld1624 + nhhld2534 + nhhld3544 + nhhld4554 + nhhld5564 + nhhld65a

[732] NHHLD1624 (ID, Blk 1) Total Households, Head Age 16–24

nhhld1624 =
    rnhhld1624 * np1624

[733] NHHLD2534 (ID, Blk 1) Total Households, Head Age 25–34

nhhld2534 =
    rnhhld2534 * np2534

[734] NHHLD3544 (ID, Blk 1) Total Households, Head Age 35–44

nhhld3544 =
    rnhhld3544 * np3544

[735] NHHLD4554 (ID, Blk 1) Total Households, Head Age 45–54

nhhld4554 =
    rnhhld4554 * np4554

[736] NHHLD5564 (ID, Blk 1) Total Households, Head Age 55–64

nhhld5564 =
    rnhhld5564 * np5564

[737] NHHLD65A (ID, Blk 1) Total Households, Head Age 65 & Older

nhhld65a =
    rnhhld65a*np65a

[738] NINDIVUC (ST, Blk 1) UNRELATED INDIVIDUALS, Total, Census Definition

nindivuc/nhhld =
    − 14.7840 * 1/ttrend
    + 0.4393

[739] RNHHLD1624 (ID, Blk 1) Household Headship Rate, 16–24

rnhhld1624 =
    rnhhld2534exo*nhhldpcnt/100

[740] RNHHLD2534 (ID, Blk 1) Household Headship Rate, 25–34

rnhhld2534 =
    rnhhld2534exo*nhhldpcnt/100

[741] RNHHLD3544 (ID, Blk 1) Household Headship Rate, 35–44

rnhhld3544 =
    rnhhld3544exo*nhhldpcnt/100

[742] RNHHLD4554 (ID, Blk 1) Household Headship Rate, 45–54

rnhhld4554 =
    rnhhld4554exo*nhhldpcnt/100

[743] RNHHLD5564 (ID, Blk 1) Household Headship Rate, 55–64

rnhhld5564 =
    rnhhld5564exo*nhhldpcnt/100

[744] RNHHLD65A (ID, Blk 1) Household Headship Rate, 65 & Over

rnhhld65a =
    rnhhld65aexo*nhhldpcnt/100

8. Money and Finance

The federal funds rate is the key interest rate in Mark10. It is endogenous -as inflation and/or GDP growth rises, so will the Fed funds rate. Monetary policy is determined through the Fed funds rate, which determines the 3-month Treasury bill. The 3-month T-bill, over time, affects the 5-year Treasury note and the 30-year Treasury bond. The yield curve is affected through these three interest rates, the 3-month T-bill, the 5-year note and the 30-year T-bond. They, in turn, affect all other interest rates in the model. The five-year T-note and the 30-year T-bond are also affected by the size of the federal deficit relative to nominal GDP. Excessive federal government borrowing pushes up these interest rates and, consequently, all other long-term interest rates.

8.1. *Interest rate*

[745] RCD3M (ST, Blk 2) Interest Rate, Certificates of Deposit, 3-Month

rcd3m =
    1.1513 * rtbill3m
  – 0.2883

[746] RCD6M (ST, Blk 3) Interest Rate, Certificates of Deposit, 6-Month

rcd6m =
    1.0455 * rcd3m
  – 0.2387

[747] RCORPS_AAA (ST, Blk 2) Interest Rate, Moody's Aaa Corporate Bonds, Seasoned

rcorps_aaa =
1.0005 * rtbond30y
+ 0.6629

[748] RCORPS_BAA (ST, Blk 3) Interest Rate, Moody's Baa Corporate Bonds, Seasoned

rcorps_baa =
1.1693 * rcorps_aaa
− 0.4675

[749] RCP1M (ST, Blk 3) Interest Rate, Commercial Paper, 1-Month

rcp1m =
0.9837 * rcp3m
+ 0.1406

[750] RCP3M (ST, Blk 2) Interest Rate, Commercial Paper, 3-Month

rcp3m =
0.9458 * rcd3m
+ 0.3084

[751] RCP6M (ST, Blk 3) Interest Rate, Commercial Paper, 6-Month

rcp6m =
1.0083 * rcp3m
− 0.0924

[752] RPRIME (ST, Blk 2) Interest Rate, Prime Commercial Bank Loans

rprime =
+ 1.0821 * from0 to3 degree1 far
rff
+ 1.0743

[753] RTBILL3M (ST, Blk 2) Interest Rate, Treasury Bills, 3-Month

rtbill3m =
+ 1.0227 * from0 to3 degree1 far
rff
− 1.0413

[754] RTBILL6M (ST, Blk 3) Interest Rate, Treasury Bills, 6-Month

rtbill6m =
0.9736 * rtbill3m
+ 0.3318

[755] RTBOND10Y (ST, Blk 3) Interest Rate, Treasury Bonds, 10-Year

rtbond10y =
0.6177 * rtbond30y
+ 0.4025 * rtnote5y
− 0.1290

[756] RTBOND30Y (ST, Blk 2) Interest Rate, Treasury Bonds, 30-Year

rtbond30y =
− 0.2442 * runc-runcn
+ 0.8980 * from0 to 10 degree1 far
rtbill3m
− 35.5164 * from0 to 12 degree1 far
netgef/gnp
+ 1.5484

[757] RTNOTE1Y (ST, Blk 3) Interest Rate, Treasury Notes, 1-Year

rtnote1y =
0.7298 * rtbill3m
+ 0.3686 * rtnote5y
− 0.5895

[758] RTNOTE3Y (ST, Blk 3) Interest Rate, Treasury Notes, 3-Year

rtnote3y =
0.1775 * rtbill3m
+ 0.8624 * rtnote5y
− 0.3011

[759] RTNOTE5Y (ST, Blk 2) Interest Rate, Treasury Notes, 5-Year

rtnote5y =
 − 0.2259 * runc-runcn
 + 0.9760 * from0 to6 degree1 far
  rtbill3m
 − 37.8323 * from0 to8 degree1 far
  netgef/gnp
 + 0.7255

[760] RTNOTE7Y (ST, Blk 3) Interest Rate, Treasury Notes, 7-Year

rtnote7y =
 0.6197 * rtnote5y
 + 0.4020 * rtbond30y
 − 0.1562

[761] RDISC (ST, Blk 3) Interest Rate, Discount rate, FRB New York

rdisc =
 0.8694 * rff

[762] REURO3M (ST, Blk 3) Interest Rate, 3-Month EuroDollar

reuro3m =
 0.9942 * rlibor3m
 − 0.0727

[763] RFF (ST, Blk 2) Interest Rate, Federal Funds

rff =
 − 18.7887 * log(m1 * 100/pdigdp)
 + 0.44734 * rpdicehat
 + 9.7391 * from0 to3 degree1 far
  log(gdp87)
 + 46.2973

[764] RLIBOR3M (ST, Blk 2) Interest Rate, 3-Month Libor

rlibor3m =
 0.7809 * rff
 + 0.3211 * rtbill3m
 − 0.1034

[765] RMOREFW (ST, Blk 2) Mortgage Rate, Effective

```
rmorefw =
        0.9625 * rtbond30y
     + 1.7101
```

[766] RMUNIBB20 (ST, Blk 3) Interest Rate, Municipal Bonds, Bond Buyer Index of 20 Bonds

```
rmunibb20 =
        0.8959 * rcorps_aaa
      −1.2554
```

[767] RUTILS_BAA (ST, Blk 3) Interest Rate, Utilitiy Bonds, Moody's BAA, Seasoned

```
rutils_baa =
        1.0546 * rcorps_baa
     − 0.4570
```

8.2. *Loans*

[768] LCBCAI (ST, Blk 2) Business Loans, Commercial & Industrial

```
log(lcbcai) =
        0.4142 * log(kinfm)
     + 0.7064 * log(kpnet87 * pdiip*.01)
     − 0.0170 * from0 to3 degree1 far
           rprime
     − 2.1802
```

[769] LCONI (ST, Blk 2) Consumer Installment Credit, Total

```
log((lconi−lconiauto)/ydp) =
     − 0.0527 * from0 to2 degree1 none
           runc−runcn
     − 0.0104 * from0 to1 degree1 none
           rtbill3m
     − 2.1826
```

[770] LCONIAUTO (ST, Blk 2) Consumer Installment Credit, Auto

```
log(lconiauto) =
    + 1.1437 * from0 to 12 degree2 far
       log((pdicedmnc*cedmnc87+pdicedmtr*cedmtr87 +
       pdicedmuc*cedmuc87)/100)
    - 0.23404
```

8.3. *Money*

[771] VM1 (ID, Blk 2) Money Velocity, M1

```
vm1 =
    m1/gdp
```

[772] VM2 (ID, Blk 2) Money Velocity, M2

```
vm2 =
    gnp/m2
```

[773] M1 (ID, Blk 2) Money Supply, M1

```
m1 =
    mcur + mdd
```

[774] M2 (ID, Blk 2) Money Supply, M2

```
m2 =
    m1 + mtd
```

[775] M3 (ST, Blk 3) Money Supply, M3

```
log(m3) =
    + 1.0856 * from0 to3 degree1 far
        log(m2)
    - 0.434
```

[776] MCUR (ST, Blk 2) Money Supply, Currency and Travelers' Checks

```
log(mcur) =
    - 0.09459 * log(rtbill3m)
    + 1.2784 * log(cen)
    - 3.39414
```

[777] MDD (ST, Blk 2) Money Supply, Demand Deposits and Other Checkable Deposits

log(mdd) =
0.92128 * log(mres)
− 3.43127

[778] MRES (ST, Blk 2) Money Supply, Nonborrowed Reserves

dlog(mres/gdp) =
− 0.0018 * from0 to3 degree1 far rkumfgfrb
− 1.4893 * from0 to3 degree1 far dlog(pdigdp)
+ 0.16309

[779] MTD (ST, Blk 2) Money Supply, Overnight Rp's, MMMF Balances, MMDA'S and Savings and Time Deposits

log(mtd) =
0.76551 * log(mres)
− 0.38264

9. Auto and Petroleum Market

9.1. *Auto production and car sale*

[780] UPCARB (ID, Blk 2) Unit Auto Production, Domestic, BEA

upcarb =
upcardom/upcardom_sf

[781] UPCARDOM (ST, Blk 2) Unit Auto Production, Domestic, WARDS

log(upcardom/upcardom_sf) =
0.9576 * log(uscardom)
+ 0.0387 * log(excar87/puvcar87)
+ 0.0151 * log((gpfnxpay87+gpnxpay87)/puvcar87)
− 0.2342 * spike(75,1)+spike(82,1)+spike(90,1)

− 0.0168 * dqtr1
− 0.0315 * dqtr2
− 0.0663 * dqtr3
+ 0.0728

[782] USCAR (ID, Blk 2) Retail Sales, New Cars, Total

uscar =
uscaran + sduscar

[783] USCARAN (ST, Blk 2) Retail Sales, New Cars, Total

log(uscaran/np16a) =
0.95513 * log(ydpperm87/np16a)
+ 4.04368 * log((ydp87/ydpperm87)/np16a)
+ 0.35208 * log(jcs)
− 0.0158 * rtnote5y
− 0.83838 * log(puvcar87)
+ 0.09558 * spike(85,3)+spike(86,3)+spike(87,3)
− 0.14644 * spike(72,3)+spike(73,4)+spike(75,2)
+ 3.82243 * log(rplcf)
− 0.0158 * from 12 to 20 degree1 far
kucarnew−(np16a*exp(.1953 * log(ttrend)−1.4189))
+ 18.2867

[784] USCARDOM (ID, Blk 2) Retail Sales, New Cars, Domestics

uscardom =
uscar − uscarimp

[785] USCARDOMAN (ID, Blk 3) Retail Sales, New Cars, Domestic, Auto News

uscardoman =
uscaran − uscarimpan

[786] USCARIMP (ID, Blk 2) Retail Sales, New Cars, Imports

uscarimp =
uscarimpan + sduscarimp

[787] USCARIMPAN (ST, Blk 2) Retail Sales, New Cars, Imports

```
log(uscarimpan*puvcar87/np16a) =
        0.7930 * log(uscarimpan*puvcar87/np16a)[-1]
      + 0.2535 * log(ydp87/np16a)
      - 0.0079 * rprime
      - 0.4832 * log(puvcarimp87/pdice)
      + 0.0997 * spike(77,2)
      - 0.2508 * spike(80,2)
      - 0.1461 * spike(87,1)
      - 1.8127
```

[788] UTRKLE3 (ID, Blk 2) Sales, New Light Trucks

```
utrkle3 =
     utrkle3an + sdutrkle3
```

[789] UTRKLE3AN (ST, Blk 2) Sales, New Light Trucks

```
log(utrkle3an/uscaran) =
        0.8355 * log(utrkle3an/uscaran)[-1]
      + 0.5191 * log(np2544/np16a)
      - 0.0271 * log(pdicengas/pdice)
      - 0.0991 * spike(80,1)+spike(81,1)
      + 0.1043 * spike(85,4)
      + 0.3338
```

[790] RIMPCAR (ID, Blk 2) Import Share, New Auto Sales

```
rimpcar =
     uscarimpan/uscaran
```

[791] KUCARNEW (ID, Blk 2) Auto Stock, End Market

```
kucarnew =
     kucarnew[-1]*(1-rscrapauto/4)+uscar/4
```

[792] UKCARDOM (ST, Blk 2) Retail Inventories, New Domestic Autos

ukcardom =
  0.8439 * ukcardom[−1]+(upcarb−uscardom)/4
+ 0.0235 * (imcar87−excar87)/puvcardom87
+ 0.2262

9.2. *Petroleum demand*

[793] QEBLOIL (ST, Blk 2) Petroleum Demand, Domestic

log(qebloil/(gdp87−cestrnxar87−cenene87)) =
  0.9601 * log((cestrnxar87+cenene87)/
    (gdp87−cenene87−cestrnxar87))
+ 54.8727 * 1/ttrend
− 2.6300

[794] QEBLOILDOM (ST, Blk 2) Petroleum Supply, Domestic

log(qebloildom) =
  34.7555 * 1/ttrend
+ 0.0616 * from0 to12 degree2 near far
    log(ppirpp/pdigdp)
+ 2.0693

10. International Sector

10.1. *Exchange rate (international)*

[795] REXMOR15 (ST, Blk 2) Nom Exch Rate Index, Wtd Avg U.S. VS 15 Countries, Morgan Guaranty

log(rexmor15)-(.04 * log(ppirow15/ppixfae)+.06 *
log(ppirow15.1/ppixfae.1)+.07 * log(ppirow15.2/ppixfae.2)+.08 *
log(ppirow15.3/ppixfae.3)+.09 * log(ppirow15.4/ppixfae.4)+.10 *
log(ppirow15.5/ppixfae.5)+.12 * log(ppirow15.6/ppixfae.6)+.10 *
log(ppirow15.7/ppixfae.7)+.09 =
− 0.0678 * log(rrow3m/rtbill3m)
+ 0.2288 * log(ttrend)
− 0.2588 * step(86,1)
+ 3.5840

[796] REXMOR15R (ID, Blk 2) Real Exch Rate Index, Wtd Avg of U.S. VS 15 Countries, Morgan Guaranty

rexmor15r =
    rexmor15 * ppixfae/ppirow15

[797] KNETEXCAB (ID, Blk 2) Foreign Debt Generated by the Cumulative Current Account Balance

knetexcab =
    knetexcab.1 + netexcab/4

[798] INF (ID, Blk 2) Net Foreign Investment

inf =
    netex − trfp − trfg − trfb + ycgn + exrfi − impfi

11. Miscellaneous

11.1. *Residual*

[799] RHAFFI (ST, Blk 3) Housing Affordability Index

rhaffi =
    1.5260 * ydp/nhhdcsu/((1+rmorefw/100) * *120 *
        (rmorefw/1200) * (.8 * puvholdmed_u)/
        ((1+rmorefw/100)**120−1))
    + 12.3338

[800] RATRRIPE (ID, Blk 2) Nominal After-Tax Req'd Return on Investment, Prod Dur Equip

ratrripe =
    (.35 * (1−rmcpt) * rcorps_aaa+.65 * (rcorps_aaa|+3))/100

[801] RATRRIPS (ID, Blk 2) Nominal After-Tax Req'd Return on Investment, Nonres Structures

ratrrips =
    (.5 * (1−rmcpt) * rcorps_aaa+.5 * (rcorps_aaa+3))/100

[802] RATRRIRS (ID, Blk 2) Nominal After-Tax Req'd Return on Investment, Residential Structures

ratrrirs =
(1−((txpf+txpn)/yptax)) * (.01 * rmorefw+.04)

[803] DPVE (ID, Blk 2) Present Value of Tax Depreciation, Producers' Durable Equipment

dpve =
(dmpe/(ratrripe*(.25 * tletrn+.3 * tleinf+.2 * tleoas+.25 * tleind)+dmpe)) * (1−exp(−(ratrripe*(.25 * tletrn+.3 * tleinf+.2 * tleoas+.25 * tleind) * ((dmpe−1)/dmpe)+dmpe−1))) + (dmpe/(ratrripe*(.25 * tletrn+.3 * tleinf+.2 * tleoas+.25 * tleind))) * (exp(−(ratrripe *(.2 * tletrn+.3 * tleinf+.2 * tleoas+.25 * tleind) * ((dmpe−1)/dmpe)+dmpe−1))−exp(−(ratrripe*(.25 * tletrn+.3 * tleinf+.2 * tleoas+.25 * tleind)+dmpe−1)))

[804] DPVS (ID, Blk 2) Present Value of Tax Depreciation, Structures

dpvs =
(dmps/(ratrrips*(.4*tlscom+.15*tlsind+.2*tlsbldgoth+.05*tlsmap+.05*tlsoaf+.15*tlsutl)dmps))*(1−exp(−(ratrrips*(.4*tlscom+.15*tlsind+.2*tlsbldgoth+.05*tlsmap+.05*tlsoaf+.15*tlsutl)*((dmps−1)/dmps)+dmps−1)))+(dmps/(ratrrips*(.4*tlscom+.15*tlsind+.2*tlsbldgoth+.05*tlsmap+.05*tlsoaf+.15*tlsutl)))*(exp(−(ratrrips*(.4*tlscom+.15*tlsind+.2*tlsbldgoth+.05*tlsmap+.05*tlsoaf+.15*tlsutl)*((dmps−1)/dmps)+dmps−1))−exp(−(ratrrips*(.4*tlscom+.15*tlsind+.2*tlsbldgoth+.05*tlsmap+.05*tlsoaf+.15*tlsutl)+dmps−1)))

[805] JCS (ST, Blk 2) Index of Consumer Sentiment, University of Michigan

diff(jcs) =
− 6.3619 * spike(87,4)−spike(88,1)
− 1.4894 * diff(rtbill3m.1)
− 1.1261 * diff(rpdicehat)

```
    – 3.6088 * (((ppirpp/ppirpp.1) * *4)–1)–(((ppirpp.1/
        ppirpp.2) * *4)–1)
    – 3.4002 * diff(runc)
    + 0.9516 * diff(pch(ydp87/np))
```

[806] RSVPER (ID, Blk 3) Personal Saving Rate

```
  rsvper =
    svper/ydp*100
```

III. A Description of Variables in the Wharton Model Mark 10

The variables are listed alphabetically. Table 5.1 gives the abbreviations of ordinary organizations for the data. Table 5.2 gives the information of each variable in the model on its definition, its equation type, units and data source, As for the type of equations, the following conventions are used: (s) estimated stochastic equation, (i) identity, and (e) exogenous.

Table 5.1. Data Sources for the Core Macro Model

BEA.NIPA	Bureau of Econ. Analysis	National Income and Product Account
BEN.UN	Bureau of Econ. Analysis	Unpublished Data
BEA.STK	Bureau of Econ. Analysis	Capital Stock
BLS.EE	Bureau of Labor Statistics	Employment and Earning
BLS.PPI	Bureau of Labor Statistics	Producer Price Index
BLS.CPI	Bureau of Labor Statist.	Consumer Price Index
BLS.PC	Bureau of Labor Statist.	Production & Costs
BLS.ECI	Bureau of Labor Statist.	Employment Cost Index
FRB.MS	Federal Reserve Board	Money Stock
FRB.IP	Federal Reserve Board	Indust. Prod. & Capacity Utilization
FRB.RT	Federal Reserve Board	Selected Interest Rates
FRB.LS	Federal Reserve Board	Loans and Security
BOC.PR	Bureau of CENSUS	Population Report
BOC.HS	Bureau of CENSUS	Housing Survey
DOE	Department of Energy	Petroleum Supply
WEFA	The WEFA Group	

Table 5.2. Variable in the Wharton Model Mark 10

Variable	Definition	T.	Unit	Source
ADJCOR	capital consumption adjustment, corporate business	s	bill. $	BEA.NIPA
CASHFLOW	corporate cashflow	i	bill. $	BEA.NIPA
CCACOR	cap. consumption adjustment, corporate	i	bill. $	BEA.NIPA
CE	consum. expen., total	i	bill. $	BEA.NIPA
CE87	consum. expen., total		bill.87 $	BEA.NIPA
CED	consum. expen., durable goods	i	bill. $	BEA.NIPA
CED87	consum. expen., durable goods	i	bill.87 $	BEA.NIPA
CEDFHE	consum. expen., furniture, house-hold equip.	i	bill. $	BEA.NIPA
CEDFHE87	consum. expen., furniture, house-hold equip.	s	bill.87 $	BEA.NIPA
CEDMNC	consum. expen., new cars	i	bill. $	BEA.NIPA
CEDMNC87	consum. expen., new cars	s	bill. 87 $	BEA.NIPA
CEDMTP	consum. expen., tire, tubes accessories	i	bill. $	BEA.NIPA
CEDMTP87	consum. expen., tire, tubes accessories	s	bill. 87 $	BEA.NIPA
CEDMTR	consum. expen., new, used trucks, recreation vehicle	i	bill. $	BEA.NIPA
CEDMTR87	consum. expen., new, used trucks, recreation vehicle	s	bill. 87 $	BEA.NIPA
CEDMUC	consum. expen., net purchase of used cars	i	bill. $	BEA.NIPA
CEDMUC87	consum. expen., net purchase of used cars	s	bill. 87 $	BEA.NIPA
CEDMVP	consum. expen., motor vehicle & parts	i	bill. $	BEA.NIPA
CEDMVP87	consum. expen., motor vehicle & parts	s	bill. 87 $	BEA.NIPA
CEDOTH	consum. expen., other durable goods	i	bill. $	BEA.NIPA
CEDOTH87	consum. expen., other durable goods, 87	s	bill. 87 $	BEA.NIPA
CEN	consum. expen., nondur, goods	i	bill. $	BEA.NIPA
CEN87	consum. expen., nondur. goods	i	bill. 87 $	BEA.NIPA
CENCAS	consum. expen., clothing & shoes	i	bill. $	BEA.NIPA
CENCAS87	consum. expen., cloth. & shoes	s	bill. 87 $	BEA.NIPA
CENENE	consum. expen., energy	i	bill. $	BEA.NIPA
CENENE87	consum. expen., energy	i	bill. 87 $	BEA.NIPA

(*Continued*)

Table 5.2. (*Continued*)

Variable	Definition	T.	Unit	Source
CENFAB	consum. expen., food, beverages	i	bill. $	BEA.NIPA
CENFAB87	consum. expen., food, bever.	i	bill. 87 $	BEA.NIPA
CENFAH	consum. expen., food & beverages at home	i	bill. $	BEA.NIPA
CENFAH87	cons. exp. food & bev. at home	s	bill. 87 $	BEA.NIPA
CENFMB	cons. ex., purch'd meals & bev	i	bill. $	BEA.NIPA
CENFMB87	cons. expen. purch. M. & bev.	s	bill. 87 $	BEA.NIPA
CENFOC	consum. expen. fuel oil & coal	i	bill. $	BEA.NIPA
CENFOC87	consum. expen., fuel oil & coal	s	bill. 87 $	BEA.NIPA
CENGAS	consum. expen., gas. & oil	i	bill. $	BEA.NIPA
CENGAS87	consum. expen., gas & oil	s	bill. 87 $	BEA.NIPA
CENOTH	consum. expen. other nondurables goods	i	bill. $	BEA.NIPA
CENOTH87	consum. expen., other nondurables goods	s	bill. 87 $	BEA.NIPA
CES	consum. expen., services	i	bill. $	BEA.NIPA
CES87	consum. expen., services	i	bill. 87 $	BEA.NIPA
CESHHO	consum. expen., household operation, total	i	bill. $	BEA.NIPA
CESHHO87	consum. expen., household operation, total	i	bill. 87 $	BEA.NIPA
CESHHOELE	consum. expen., household operation, electricity	i	bill. $	BEA.NIPA
CESHHOELE87	consum. expen., household operation, electricity	s	bill. 87 $	BEA.NIPA
CESHHOGAS	consum. expen., household operation, gas	i	bill. $	BEA.NIPA
CESHHOGAS87	consum. expen., household operation, gas	s	bill. 87 $	BEA.NIPA
CESHHOOTH	consum. expen., household operation, other	i	bill. $	BEA.NIPA
CESHHOOTH87	consum. expen., household operation, other	s	bill. 87 $	BEA.NIPA
CESHOU	consum. expen., housing services	i	bill. $	BEA.NIPA
CESHOU87	consum. expen., housing services	s	bill. 87 $	BEA.NIPA
CESMAO	consum. expen., medical & other services	i	bill. $	BEA.NIPA
CESMAO87	consum. expen., medical & other services	i	bill. 87 $	BEA.NIPA
CESMED	consum. expen., medical care	i	bill. $	BEA.NIPA

(*Continued*)

Table 5.2. (*Continued*)

Variable	Definition	T.	Unit	Source
CESMED87	consum. expen., medical care	s	bill. 87 $	BEA.NIPA
CESOTH	consum. expen., other services	i	bill. $	BEA.NIPA
CESOTH87	consum. expen., other services	s	bill. 87 $	BEA.NIPA
CESTAR	consum. expen., transp. service & auto repair	i	bill. $	BEA.NIPA
CESTAR87	consum. expen., transp. service & auto repair	s	bill. 87 $	BEA.NIPA
CESTRN	consum. expen., transp. service, total	i	bill. $	BEA.NIPA
CESTRN87	consum. expen., transportation service, total	i	bill. 87 $	BEA.NIPA
CESTRNXAR	consum. expen., transportation service, others	i	bill. $	BEA.NIPA
CESTRNXAR87	consum. expen., transportation service, others	s	bill. 87 $	BEA.NIPA
CFX	capital consumption allowance, with CCADJ	i	bill. $	BEA.NIPA
CFX87	capital con. allowance, with CCADJ	s	bill. 87 $	BEA.NIPA
CFXCOR	capital con. allowance, with CCADJ, corporate	s	bill. $	BEA.NIPA
CFXNON	capital con. allowance, with CCADJ, non-corporate	s	bill. $	BEA.NIPA
DPVE	present value of tax deprec. producer's durable equipment	i		
DPVS	present value of tax depreciation, structure	i		
EME	employment, established, total	i	mill. employees	BLS.EE
EMECON	employment, construction	s	*op. cit.*	BLS.EE
EMEFIR	employment, finance, insurance & real estate	s	*op. cit.*	BLS.EE
EMEGF	employment, federal gov. total	i	*op. cit.*	BLS.EE
EMEGGE	employment, gov. & gov. enterprises	i	*op. cit.*	BLS.EE
EMEMFG	employment, MFG, total	s	*op. cit.*	BLS.EE
EMEMIN	employment, Mining	s	*op. cit.*	BLS.EE
EMEPRI	employment, total private	i	*op. cit.*	BLS.EE
EMESER	employment, service, total	s	*op. cit.*	BLS.EE
EMETPU	empl. trans. & pub util, total	s	*op. cit.*	BLS.EE
EMEWRT	emp. whole estate & retail tr.	s	*op. cit.*	BLS.EE
EMHC	emp. household basis, civilian	i	*op. cit.*	BLS.EE

(*Continued*)

Table 5.2. (*Continued*)

Variable	Definition	T.	Unit	Source
EX	export, total	i	bill. $	BEA.NIPA
EX87	export, total	i	bill. 87 $	BEA.NIPA
EXCAPOTH	ex, merchand. other cap. goods	i	bill. $	BEA.NIPA
EXCAPOTH87	ex, merchand. other cap. goods	s	bill. 87 $	BEA.NIPA
EXCAR87	export, merchandise, auto	s	bill. $	BEA.NIPA
EXCOMPEQU	export, merchandise, computer, peripheral and parts	i	bill. 87 $	BEA.NIPA
EXCOMPEQU87	export, merchandise, computer, peripheral and parts	s	bill. $	BEA.NIPA
EXCONXMVP	export, merchandise, consumer goods except MVP	i	bill. 87 $	BEA.NIPA
EXCONXMVP87	export, merchandise, consumer goods except MVP	s	bill. $	BEA.NIPA
EXFFB	export, merchandise, foods, feeds & beverages	i	bill. 87 $	BEA.NIPA
EXFFB87	export, merchandise, foods, feeds & beverages	s	bill. $	BEA.NIPA
EXISM	export, merchandises, industrial supply and materials	i	bill. $	BEA.NIPA
EXISM87	export, merchandises, industrial supply and materials	s	bill. 87 $	BEA.NIPA
EXMER	export, merchandise, total	i	bill. $	BEA.NIPA
EXMER87	export, merchandise, total	s	bill. 87 $	BEA.NIPA
EXMVP	export, merchandise, motor vehicle & parts	i	bill. $	BEA.NIPA
EXMVP87	export, merchandise, motor vehicle & parts	s	bill. 87 $	BEA.NIPA
EXOTH	export, merchandise, other	i	bill. $	BEA.NIPA
EXOTH87	export, merchandise, other	s	bill. 87 $	BEA.NIPA
EXRFI	export, service, factor income	s	bill. $	BEA.NIPA
EXRFI87	export, service, factor income	i	bill. 87 $	BEA.NIPA
EXSER	export, service, total	i	bill. $	BEA.NIPA
EXSER87	export, service, total	s	bill. 87 $	BEA.NIPA
GDP	GDP, total	i	bill. $	BEA.NIPA
GDP87	GDP, total	i	bill. 87 $	BEA.NIPA
GDPPOT87	potential GDP	i	bill. 87 $	BEA.NIPA
GDPXNETEX	gross domestic purchases	i	bill. $	BEA.NIPA
GDPXNETEX87	gross domestic purchases	i	bill. 87 $	BEA.NIPA
GEF	govt. expenditure, federal, total	i	bill. $	BEA.NIPA
GEFUBB	govt. expenditure, federal, total, unified budget basis	i	bill. $	BEA.NIPA

(*Continued*)

Table 5.2. (*Continued*)

Variable	Definition	T.	Unit	Source
GEN	govt. expenditure, state & local, total	i	bill. $	BEA.NIPA
GIA	federal grants in aid, to state & local govt.	i	bill. $	BEA.NIPA
GIA87	federal grants in aid, to state & local govt.	i	bill. 87 $	BEA.NIPA
GIAMEDCAI	federal grands in aid, to state & local govt. MEDICAID	s	bill. $	BEA.NIPA
GNP	GNP	i	bill. $	BEA.NIPA
GNP87	GNP	i	bill. 87 $	BEA.NIPA
GP	govt. purchase, total	i	bill. $	BEA.NIPA
GP87	govt. purchase, total	i	bill. 87 $	BEA.NIPA
GPDUR87	govt. purch, dur. equip., total	i	bill. 87 $	BEA.NIPA
GPF	govt. purchase, federal total	i	bill. $	BEA.NIPA
GPF87	govt. purchase, federal total	i	bill. 87 $	BEA.NIPA
GPFD	govt. purchase, defence, total	i	bill. $	BEA.NIPA
GPFD87	govt. purchase, defence, total	i	bill. 87 $	BEA.NIPA
GPFDPAY	govt. purchase, defence, comp. of employees, total	i	bill. $	BEA.NIPA
GPFDPAY87	govt. purchase, defence, comp. of employees, total	i	bill. 87 $	BEA.NIPA
GPFDPAYCIV	govt. purchase, defence, comp. of employees, civil.	i	bill. $	BEA.NIPA
GPFDPAYCIV87	govt. purchase, defence, comp. of employees, civil.	i	bill. 87 $	BEA.NIPA
GPFDPAYMIL	govt. purchase, federal, defence, comp. of employees, military	i	bill. $	BEA.NIPA
GPFDPAYMIL87	govt. purchase, federal, defence, comp. of employees, military	i	bill. 87 $	BEA.NIPA
GPFDXPAY	govt. purchase, federal, defence, noncompensation	i	bill. $	BEA.NIPA
GPFDXPAY87	govt. purchase, federal, defence, noncompensation	i	bill. 87 $	BEA.NIPA
GPFN	govt. purchase, federal, nondefence, total	i	bill. $	BEA.NIPA
GPFN87	govt. purchase, federal, nondefence, total	i	bill. 87 $	BEA.NIPA
GPFNNONCCC	govt. purchase, federal, nondefence, CCC payments	s	bill. $	BEA.NIPA
GPFNOTH	govt. purchase, federal, nondefence, noncompens., other	i	bill. $	BEA.NIPA

(*Continued*)

Table 5.2. (*Continued*)

Variable	Definition	T.	Unit	Source
GPFNOTH87	govt. purchase, federal, nondefence, noncompens., other	i	bill. 87 $	BEA.NIPA
GPFNPAY	govt. purchase, federal, nondefence, comp. of employees	i	bill. $	BEA.NIPA
GPFNPAY87	govt. purchase, federal, nondefence, comp. of employees	i	bill. 87 $	BEA.NIPA
GPFNXCCC	govt. purchase, federal, nondefence, less CCC payments	i	bill. $	BEA.NIPA
GPFNXCCC87	govt. purchase, federal, nondefence, less CCC payments	i	bill. 87 $	BEA.NIPA
GPFNXPAY	govt. purchase, federal, nondefence, noncompensation	i	bill. $	BEA.NIPA
GPFNXPAY87	govt. purchase, federal, nondefence, noncompensation	i	bill. 87 $	BEA.NIPA
GPFPAY	govt. purchase, federal, compensation of employees	i	bill. $	BEA.NIPA
GPFPAY87	govt. purchase, federal, compensation of employees	i	bill. 87 $	BEA.NIPA
GPN	govt. purch. state & local. total	i	bill. $	BEA.NIPA
GPN87	govt. purch. state & local. total	i	bill. 87 $	BEA.NIPA
GPNPAY	govt. purch. state & local, comp. of employees	i	bill. $	BEA.NIPA
GPNPAY87	govt. purchase, state & local, comp. of employees	i	bill. 87 $	BEA.NIPA
GPNXPAY	govt. purchase, state & local, noncompensation	i	bill. $	BEA.NIPA
GPPAY	govt. purchase, state & local, noncompensation	i	bill. $	BEA.NIPA
GPPAY87	govt. purchase, total, compensation of employees	i	bill. 87 $	BEA.NIPA
GPSTR87	govt. purch. structures, total	i	bill. 87 $	BEA.NIPA
GSLS	subsidies less curr. surplus of govt. enterprises, total	i	ratio	
HRWPCON	average weekly hours, construction	i	hours per week	BLS.EE
HRWPFIR	average weekly hours, finance, insurance & real estate	s	hours per week	BLS.EE

(*Continued*)

Table 5.2. (*Continued*)

Variable	Definition	T.	Unit	Source
HRWPMFG	aver. weekly hours, manuf.	s	hours per week	BLS.EE
HRWPMIN	aver. weekly hours, mining	s	hours per week	BLS.EE
HRWPNFMPRI	average weekly hours, nonfarm private	s	hours per week	BLS.EE
HRWPSER	aver. weekly hours, services	s	hours per week	BLS.EE
HRWPTPU	average weekly hours, transportation & public utilities	s	hours per week	BLS.EE
HRWPWRT	average weekly hours, whole sale & retail trade	s	hours per week	BLS.EE
IFX	fixed investment	i	bill. $as	BEA.NIPA
IFX87	fixed investment	i	bill. 87 $	BEA.NIPA
IGD	gross private domestic investment	i	bill. $as	BEA.NIPA
IGD87	gross private domestic investment	i	bill. $as	BEA.NIPA
II	changes in business inventories, total	i	bill. $as	BEA.NIPA
II87	changes in business inventories, total	i	bill. 87 $	BEA.NIPA
IICAR87	changes in business inventories, automotive	s	bill. 87 $	BEA.NIPA
IIFRM	changes in business inventories, farm + CCC purchases	i	bill. $as	BEA.NIPA
IIFRM87	changes in business inventories, farm + CCC purchases	i	bill. 87 $	BEA.NIPA
IIFRMACCC	changes in business inventories, farm + CCC purchases	s	bill. $as	BEA.NIPA
IIMFG	changes in business inventories, manufacturing	s	bill. $as	BEA.NIPA
IIMFG87	changes in business inventories, manufacturing	i	bill. 87 $	BEA.NIPA
IINFM	Ch. in bus. invent., nonfarm	i	bill. $as	BEA.NIPA
IINFM87	Ch. in bus. invent, nonfarm	i	bill. 87 $	BEA.NIPA
IINFMOTH87	changes in business inven. nonfarm, nonmanufac., other	i	bill. 87 $	BEA.NIPA
IINFMXMFG	changes in business invent., nonfarm, nonmanufac.	i	bill. $as	BEA.NIPA

(*Continued*)

Table 5.2. (*Continued*)

Variable	Definition	T.	Unit	Source
IINFMXMFG87	changes in business invent., nonfarm, nonmanufacturing	i	bill. 87 $	BEA.NIPA
IM	imports, total	i	bill. $as	BEA.NIPA
IM87	imports, total	i	bill. 87 $	BEA.NIPA
IMCAPOTH	merchandise imports, capital goods, other	i	bill. $as	BEA.NIPA
IMCAPOTH87	merchandise imports, other capital goods	s	bill. 87 $	BEA.NIPA
IMCAR87	merchandise imports, auto	s	bill. 87 $	BEA.NIPA
IMCOMPEQU	merchandise imports, computer, peripherals and parts	i	bill. $as	BEA.NIPA
IMCOMPEQU87	merchandise imports, computer, peripherals and parts	s	bill. 87 $	BEA.NIPA
IMCONXMVP	merchandise imports, consumer goods	i	bill. $as	BEA.NIPA
IMCONXMVP87	merchandise imports, consumer goods	s	bill. 87 $	BEA.NIPA
IMFFB	merchandise imports, foods, feeds & beverages	i	bill. $as	BEA.NIPA
IMFFB87	merchandise imports, foods, feeds & beverages	s	bill. 87 $	BEA.NIPA
IMISMXOIL	merchand. imports, indust. supplies & materials, excl. petro.	i	bill. $as	BEA.NIPA
IMISMXOIL87	merchand. imports, indust. supplies &materials, excel. petro.	s	bill. 87 $	BEA.NIPA
IMMER	merchandise imports, total	i	bill. $as	BEA.NIPA
IMMER87	merchandise imports, total	i	bill. 87 $	BEA.NIPA
IMMVP	merch. im. motor v. & parts	i	bill. $as	BEA.NIPA
IMMVP87	merch. im/, motor v. & parts	s	bill. 87 $	BEA.NIPA
IMOIL	merchandise imports, petroleum & products	i	bill. $as	BEA.NIPA
IMOIL87	merchandise imports, petroleum & products	s	bill. 87 $	BEA.NIPA
IMOTH	merchandise imports, other	i	bill. $as	BEA.NIPA
IMOTH87	merchandise imports, other	s	bill. 87 $	BEA.NIPA
IMPFI	service imports, factor income	s	bill. $as	BEA.NIPA
IMPFI87	service imports, factor income	i	bill. 87 $	BEA.NIPA
IMSER	service imports, total	i	bill. $as	BEA.NIPA
IMSER87	service imports, total	s	bill. 87 $	BEA.NIPA

(*Continued*)

Table 5.2. (*Continued*)

Variable	Definition	T.	Unit	Source
IMXOIL	merchandise imports, nonpetroleum products	i	bill. $as	BEA.NIPA
IMXOIL87	merchandise imports, nonpetroleum products	i	ill. 87 $	BEA.NIPA
INF	net foreign investment	i	bill. $as	BEA.NIPA
IP	nonresidential investment, total	i	bill. $as	BEA.NIPA
IP87	nonresidential investment, total	i	bill. 87 $	BEA.NIPA
IPE	nonresidential investment, prod. dur. equip, total	i	bill. $as	BEA.NIPA
IPE87	nonresidential investment, prod. dur. equip, total	i	bill. 87 $	BEA.NIPA
IPEIND	nonresidential investment, prod. dur. equip industrial	i	bill. $as	BEA.NIPA
IPEIND87	nonresid. investment, prod. dur. equip. industrial	s	bill. 87 $	BEA.NIPA
IPEINF	nonresid. investment, prod. dur. equip. info. processing	i	bill. $as	BEA.NIPA
IPEINF87	nonresid. investment, prod. dur. equip. info. processing	s	bill. 87 $	BEA.NIPA
IPEOAS	nonresidential investment, prod. dur. equip. other	i	bill. $as	BEA.NIPA
IPEOAS87	nonresidential investment, prod. dur. equip. other	s	bill. 87 $	BEA.NIPA
IPETRN	nonresid. investment, prod. dur. equip. motor vehicles & parts	i	bill. $as	BEA.NIPA
IPETRN87	nonresid. investment, prod. dur. equip. motor vehicles and parts	s	bill. 87 $	BEA.NIPA
IPS	nonresidential investment, structure total	i	bill. $as	BEA.NIPA
IPS87	nonresidential investment, structure total	i	bill. 87 $	BEA.NIPA
IPSBLDG	nonresidential investment, structure, buildings	i	bill. $as	BEA.NIPA
IPSBLDG87	nonresidential investment, structure, buildings	i	bill. 87 $	BEA.NIPA
IPSBLDGOTH	nonresidential investment, structures other buildings	i	bill. $as	BEA.NIPA
IPSBLDGOTH87	nonresidential investment, structures other buildings	s	bill. 87 $	BEA.NIPA
IPSCOM	nonresidential investment, structures, commercials	i	bill. $as	BEA.NIPA

(*Continued*)

Table 5.2. (*Continued*)

Variable	Definition	T.	Unit	Source
IPSCOM87	nonresidential investment, structures, commercials	s	bill. 87 $	BEA.NIPA
IPSIND	nonresidential investment, structure, industrials	i	bill. $as	BEA.NIPA
IPSIND87	nonresidential investment, structure, industrials	s	bill. 87 $	BEA.NIPA
IPSMAP	nonresid. investment, structures min. exp. shafts wells	i	bill. $as	BEA.NIPA
IPSMAP87	nonresid investment, structures min exp shafts wells	s	bill. 87 $	BEA.NIPA
IPSOAF	nonresidential investment, structures other	i	bill. $as	BEA.NIPA
IPSOAF87	nonresidential investment, structures other	s	bill. 87 $	BEA.NIPA
IPSUTL	nonresidential investment, structures utilities	i	bill. $as	BEA.NIPA
IPSUTL87	nonresidential investment, structures utilities	s	bill. 87 $	BEA.NIPA
IR	residential investment, total	i	bill. $as	BEA.NIPA
IR87	residential investment, total	i	bill. 87 $	BEA.NIPA
IROTH	residential investment, Other	i	bill. $as	BEA.NIPA
IROTH87	residential investment, Other	s	bill. 87 $	BEA.NIPA
IRSONE	residential investment, new housing single-unit structures	i	bill. $as	BEA.NIPA
IRSONE87	residential investment, new housing single-unit structures	s	bill. 87 $	BEA.NIPA
IRSTOM	residential investment, new housing multi-unit structures	i	bill. $as	BEA.NIPA
IRSTOM87	residential investment, new housing multi-unit structures	s	bill. 87 $	BEA.NIPA
IVACOR	inventory valuation adjustment, corporate	s	bill. $as	BEA.NIPA
JCS	index of consumer sentiment, university of Michigan	s	index	Univ. of Michigan
JECWAP	employment cost index, wage & salary, private nonfarm	s	index	BLS.ECI
JIP	IP index, industrial production, total	s	index	FRB.IP
JOMHNFM	output per hour, private business sector	s	index	BLS.PC
JQWRHNFM	compensation per hour, nonfarm business sector	s	index	BLS.PC

(*Continued*)

Table 5.2. (*Continued*)

Variable	Definition	T.	Unit	Source
JULCNFMPRI	unit labor costs, nonfarm business sector	i	index	BLS.PC
JULCNFMPRIAVG	unit labor costs, nonfarm business sector, smoothed	i	index	BLS.PC
KASSTGNNET_U	state and local, net financial assets	s	bill. 87 $	WEFA
KDEBTGFNET	net federal debt, net of agency holding	s	bill. $as	WEFA
KGENET87	net capital stock, public, equipment	i	bill. 87 $	BEA.STK
KGNET87	net capital stock, public, structures	i	bill. 87 $	BEA.STK
KGSNET87	net capital stock, public, total	i	bill. 87 $	BEA.STK
KIMFG87	stock of inventories, manufacturing	s	bill. 87 $	BEA.NIPA
KINFM	stock of inventories, nonfarm	s	bill. $as	BEA.NIPA
KINFM87	stock of inventories, nonfarm	i	bill. 87 $	BEA.NIPA
KINFMOTH87	stock of inventories, other nonfarm	s	bill. 87 $	BEA.NIPA
KNETEXCAB	foreign debt generated by cumulative current account	i	bill. $as	WEFA
KPENET87	nonres net capital stock, prod. dur. equip. total	i	bill. 87 $	BEA.UN
KPENETIND87	nonres net capital stock, prod. dur. equip. industrial	i	bill. 87 $	BEA.UN
KPENETINF87	nonres net capital stock, prod. dur. equip. inform Processing	i	bill. 87 $	BEA.UN
KPENETOAS87	nonres net capital stock, prod. dur. equip. other	i	bill. 87 $	BEA.UN
KPENETTRN87	nonres net capital stock, prod. dur. quip, transportation	i	bill. 87 $	BEA.UN
KPNET87	nonres net capital stock, total	i	bill. 87 $	BEA.UN
KPNETCON87	nonres net capital stock, construction	i	bill. 87 $	BEA.UN
KPNETMFG87	nonres net capital stock, manufacturing	i	bill. 87 $	BEA.UN
KPNETMIN87	nonres. net capital stock, mining	i	bill. 87 $	BEA.UN
KPNETOTH87	nonres net capital stock, other	i	bill. 87 $	BEA.UN
KPNETTPU87	nonres net capital stock, transportation & utilities	i	bill. 87 $	BEA.UN

(*Continued*)

Table 5.2. (*Continued*)

Variable	Definition	T.	Unit	Source
KPNETWRT87	nonres net capital stock, wholesale & retail trade	i	bill. 87 $	BEA.UN
KPOPT87	nonres net capital stock, optimal	s	bill. 87 $	BEA.UN
KPSNET87	nonres net capital stock, structures, total	i	bill. 87 $	BEA.UN
KPSNETBLDG87	nonres net capital stock, buildings	i	bill. 87 $	BEA.UN
KPSNETBLD GOTH87	nonres net capital stock, other building	i	bill. 87 $	BEA.UN
KPSNETCOM87	nonres net capital stock, structures, commercial	i	bill. 87 $	BEA.UN
KPSNETIND87	nonres net capital stock, ind.	i	bill. 87 $	BEA.UN
KPSNETMAP87	nonres net capital stock, mining expl., shafts & wells	i	bill. 87 $	BEA.UN
KPSNETOAF87	nonres net capital stock, structures, other	i	bill. 87 $	BEA.UN
KPSNETUTL87	nonres net cap. stock, utilities	i	bill. 87 $	BEA.UN
KRNET87	net capital stock, residential, total	i	bill. 87 $	BEA.UN
KUCARNEW	auto stock, end market	i	mill.units	WEFA
LCBCAI	business loans, commercial & industrial	s	bill. $as	FRB.LS
LCONI	consumer installment credit, total	s	bill. $as	FRB.LS
LCONIAUTO	consumer installment credit, auto	s	bill. $as	FRB.LS
M1	money supply, M1	i	bill. $as	FRB.MS
M2	money supply, M2	i	bill. $as	FRB.MS
M3	money supply, M3	s	bill. $as	FRB.MS
MCUR	money supply, currency and travelers checks	s	bill. $as	FRB.MS
MDD	money supply, demand deposits & other check. Depos.	s	bill. $	FRB.MS
MRES	money supply, nonborrowed reserves	s	bill. $	FRB.MS
MTD	money supply, overnight rv's, MMMF balances, MMDA'S & sv. & time dep.	s	bill. $	FRB.MS
NETEX	net exports, goods & service, NIPA basis	i	bill. $as	BEA.NIPA

(*Continued*)

Table 5.2. (*Continued*)

Variable	Definition	T.	Unit	Source
NETEX87	net exports, goods & service, NIPA basis	i	bill. 87 $	BEA.NIPA
NETEXCAB	net exports, current account balance	i	bill. $as	BEA.NIPA
NETEXMER	net exports, merchandise, NIPA basis	i	bill. $as	BEA.NIPA
NETEXMER87	net exports, merchandise, NIPA basis	i	bill. 87 $	BEA.NIPA
NETGEF	govt. surplus or deficit, federal, NIPA basis	i	bill. $as	BEA.NIPA
NETGEFUBB	govt. surplus or deficit, federal, unified budget basis	i	bill. $as	BEA.NIPA
NETGEN	govt. surp. or def. state & loc.	i	bill. $as	BEA.NIPA
NETGENOTH	govt. surplus or deficit, state & local, other	i	bill. $as	BEA.NIPA
NETGENSIF	govt. surplus or deficit, state & local, social insurance fund	i	bill. $as	BEA.NIPA
NFAMC	families, total, census definit.	s	mill.	BOC.PR
NHHDCSU	number of households, consumer spending units	i	mill.	BOC.PR
NHHLD	total households, census definition, housing units	i	mill.	BOC.PR
NHHLD1624	total hous'ld head age 16–24	i	mill.	BOC.PR
NHHLD2534	total hous'ld head age 25–34	i	mill.	BOC.PR
NHHLD3544	total hous'ld head age 35–44	i	mill.	BOC.PR
NHHLD4554	total hous'ld head age 45–54	i	mill.	BOC.PR
NHHLD5564	total hous'ld head age 55–64	i	mill.	BOC.PR
NHHLD65A	total hous'lds head age 65 &	i	mill.	BOC.PR
NINDIVUC	unrelated individuals, total, census definition	s	mill.	BOC.PR
NLFC	labor force, civilian, total	i	mill.	BLS.EE
NLFCF	lb force, civilian, female, total	i	mill.	BLS.EE
NLFCF1619	lb force, civil, females, 16–19	i	mill.	BLS.EE
NLFCF2024	lb force, civil, females, 20–24	i	mill.	BLS.EE
NLFCF20A	lb for. civil, females, 20 & over	i	mill.	BLS.EE
NLFCF2534	lb force, civil, females, 25–34	i	mill.	BLS.EE
NLFCF3544	lb force, civil, females, 35–44	i	mill.	BLS.EE
NLFCF4554	lb force, civil, females, 45–54	i	mill.	BLS.EE
NLFCF5564	lb force, civil, females, 55–64	i	mill.	BLS.EE
NLFCF65A	lb force, civil, females, 65 & over	i	mill.	BLS.EE
NLFCM	lb force, civilian, male, total	i	mill.	BLS.EE

(*Continued*)

Table 5.2. (*Continued*)

Variable	Definition	T.	Unit	Source
NLFCM1619	lb force, civil, male, 16–19	i	mill.	BLS.EE
NLFCM2024	lb force, civil, male, 20–24	i	mill.	BLS.EE
NLFCM20A	lb force, civil, male, 20 & over	i	mill.	BLS.EE
NLFCM2534	lb force, civil, male, 25–34	i	mill.	BLS.EE
NLFCM3544	lb force, civil, male, 35–44	i	mill.	BLS.EE
NLFCM4554	lb force, civil, male, 45–54	i	mill.	BLS.EE
NLFCM5564	lb force, civil, male, 55–64	i	mill.	BLS.EE
NLFCM65A	lb force, civil male, 65 & over	i	mill.	BLS.EE
NNP	net national product	i	bill. $	BEA.NIPA
NNP87	net national product	i	bill. 87 $	BEA.NIPA
NP	population, total	i	mill.	BEA.NIPA
NP1619	population, noninstitutional civilian total 16–19	i	mill.	BLS.EE
NP1624	population, noninstitutional civilian total 16–24	i	mill.	BLS.EE
NP16A	population, noninstitut. civilian total 16 & over	i	mill.	BLS.EE
NP2024	population, noninstitutional civilian total 20–24	i	mill.	BLS.EE
NP2534	population, noninstitutional civilian total 25–34	i	mill.	BLS.EE
NP2544	population, noninstitutional civilian total 25–44	i	mill.	BLS.EE
NP3544	population, noninstitutional civilian total 35–44	i	mill.	BLS.EE
NP4554	population, noninstitutional civilian total 45–54	i	mill.	BLS.EE
NP5564	population, noninstitutional civilian total 55–64	i	mill.	BLS.EE
NP65A	population, noninstitutional civilian total 65 & over	i	mill.	BLS.EE
NPF1619	population, females 16–19	s	mill.	BLS.EE
NPF16A	population, females 16 & over	i	mill.	BLS.EE
NPF2024	population, females 20–24	s	mill.	BLS.EE
NPF20A	population, females 20 & over	i	mill.	BLS.EE
NPF2534	population, females 25–34	s	mill.	BLS.EE
NPF3544	population, females 35–44	s	mill.	BLS.EE
NPF4554	population, females 45–55	s	mill.	BLS.EE
NPF5564	population, females 55–64	s	mill.	BLS.EE
NPF65A	popul. females 65 & over	s	mill.	BLS.EE
NPM1619	population, males 16–19	s	mill.	BLS.EE
NPM16A	population, males 16 & over	i	mill.	BLS.EE

(*Continued*)

Table 5.2. (*Continued*)

Variable	Definition	T.	Unit	Source
NPM2024	population, males 20–24	s	mill.	BLS.EE
NPM20A	population, males 20 & over	i	mill.	BLS.EE
NPM2534	population, males 25–34	s	mill.	BLS.EE
NPM3544	population, males 35–44	s	mill.	BLS.EE
NPM4554	population, males 45–54	s	mill.	BLS.EE
NPM5564	population, males 55–64	s	mill.	BLS.EE
NPM65A	population, males 65 & over	s	mill.	BLS.EE
NPT0004	population, total, 00–04	i	mill.	BOC.PR
NPT0509	population, total, 05–09	i	mill.	BOC.PR
NPT1014	population, total, 10–14	i	mill.	BOC.PR
NPTF15	population, total, 15	i	mill.	BOC.PR
NPTF15A	population, total, 15 and over	i	mill.	BOC.PR
NPTF1617	popul., total, females, 16–17	i	mill.	BOC.PR
NPTF1819	popul., total, females, 18–19	i	mill.	BOC.PR
NPTF2024	popul. total, females, 20–24	i	mill.	BOC.PR
NPTF2529	popul. total females, 25–29	i	mill.	BOC.PR
NPTF3034	popul., total, females, 30–34	i	mill.	BOC.PR
NPTF3539	popul., total, females, 35–39	i	mill.	BOC.PR
NPTF4044	popul., total, females, 40–44	i	mill.	BOC.PR
NPTF4549	popul., total, females, 45–49	i	mill.	BOC.PR
NPTF5054	popul., total, females, 50–54	i	mill.	BOC.PR
NPTF5559	popul., total, females, 55–59	i	mill.	BOC.PR
NPTF6064	popul., total, females, 60–64	i	mill.	BOC.PR
NPTF6569	popul., total, females, 65–69	i	mill.	BOC.PR
NPTF7074	popul., total, females, 70–74	i	mill.	BOC.PR
NPTF70A	popul., total, females, 70A	i	mill.	BOC.PR
NPTF7579	popul., total, females, 75–79	i	mill.	BOC.PR
NPTF8084	popul, total, females, 80–84	i	mill.	BOC.PR
NPTF85A	popul., total, females, 85A	i	mill.	BOC.PR
NPTM15	population, total, males, 15	i	mill.	BOC.PR
NPTM15A	popul., total, males, 15 and over	i	mill.	BOC.PR
NPTM1617	popul., total, males, 16–17	i	mill.	BOC.PR
NPTM1819	popul., total males, 18–19	i	mill.	BOC.PR
NPTM2024	popul., total males, 20–24	i	mill.	BOC.PR
NPTM2529	popul., total males, 25–29	i	mill.	BOC.PR
NPTM3034	population, total males, 30–34	i	mill.	BOC.PR
NPTM3539	population, total males, 35–39	i	mill.	BOC.PR
NPTM4044	population, total males, 40–44	i	mill.	BOC.PR
NPTM4549	population, total males, 45–49	i	mill.	BOC.PR
NPTM5054	population, total males, 50–54	i	mill.	BOC.PR
NPTM5559	population, total males, 55–59	i	mill.	BOC.PR
NPTM6064	population, total males, 60–64	i	mill.	BOC.PR

(*Continued*)

Table 5.2. (*Continued*)

Variable	Definition	T.	Unit	Source
NPTM6569	population, total males, 65–69	i	mill.	BOC.PR
NPTM7074	population, total males, 70–74	i	mill.	BOC.PR
NPTM70A	Population, total males, 70A	i	mill.	BOC.PR
NPTM7579	population, total males, 75–79	i	mill.	BOC.PR
NPTM8084	population, total males, 80–84	i	mill.	BOC.PR
NPTM85A	population, total males, 85 and over	i	mill.	BOC.PR
NUN	number of unemployed	i	mill.	BLS.EE
PCIU	CPI, all urban cons. all items	s	82–84=100	BLS.CPI
PCIUAPP	CPI, all ur. cons. appa. & upkp	s	82–84=100	BLS.CPI
PCIUCOM	CPI, all urban cons. commodities	s	82–84=100	BLS.CPI
PCIUENE	CPI, all urban cons., energy	s	82–84=100	BLS.CPI
PCIUENT	CPI, all urban cons. entertainment	s	82–84=100	BLS.CPI
PCIUFAB	CPI, all urban consumers, food & beverages	s	82–84=100	BLS.CPI
PCIUFOO	CPI, all urban consum., food	s	82–84=100	BLS.CPI
PCIUHOU	CPI, all urban consum., housing	s	82–84=100	BLS.CPI
PCIUMED	CPI, all urban consumers, medical care	s	82–84=100	BLS.CPI
PCIUOGS	CPI, all urban consumers, other goods & service	s	82–84=100	BLS.CPI
PCIUREN	CPI, all urban consumers, housing rent residential	s	82–84=100	BLS.CPI
PCIUSER	CPI, all urban consumers, services	s	82–84=100	BLS.CPI
PCIUTRN	CPI, all urban consumers, transportation	s	82–84=100	BLS.CPI
PCIUXENE	CPI, all urban consumers, all items less energy	s	82–84=100	BLS.CPI
PCIUXFAE	CPI, all urban consumers, all items less food & energy	i	82–84=100	BLS.CPI
PCIUXFOO	CPI, all urban consumers, all items less food	i	82–84=100	BLS.CPI
PCIUXMED	CPI, all urban consumers, all items less medical care	s	82–84=100	BLS.CPI
PCIW	CPI, urban wage earners, all items	s	82–84=100	BLS.CPI
PDFGDP	fixed-weight price index, GDP	s	87=100	BEA.NIPA
PDFGNP	fixed-weight price index, GNP	s	87=100	BEA.NIPA

(*Continued*)

Table 5.2. (*Continued*)

Variable	Definition	T.	Unit	Source
PDICE	impl. price deflator cons. expend, total	i	87=100	BEA.NIPA
PDICED	impl. price deflator cons. expend, durable goods	i	87=100	BEA.NIPA
PDICEDFHE	impl. price deflator, cons. expend, furnit & household eq.	s	87=100	BEA.NIPA
PDICEDMNC	impl. price deflator cons. expend, new cars	s	87=100	BEA.NIPA
PDICEDMTP	impl. price deflator, cons. exp tubes accessories & parts	s	87=100	BEA.NIPA
PDICEDMTR	impl. price defl., cons. expend, new & used tracks, rec. vehcl	s	87=100	BEA.NIPA
PDICEDMUC	impl. price defl., cons. expend, net purchase of used cars	s	87=100	BEA.NIPA
PDICEDMVP	impl. price deflator, cons. expend, motor vehicle & parts	i	87=100	BEA.NIPA
PDICEDOTH	impl. price deflator, cons. expend, other dur goods	s	87=100	BEA.NIPA
PDICEN	impl. price deflator, cons. expend, nondurable goods	i	87=100	BEA.NIPA
PDICENCAS	impl. price deflator, cons. expend, clothing & shoes	s	87=100	BEA.NIPA
PDICENENE	impl. price deflator, cons. expend, energy	i	87=100	BEA.NIPA
PDICENFAB	impl. price deflator, cons. expend, foods & beverages	i	87=100	BEA.NIPA
PDICENFAH	impl. price defl., cons. expend, foods & beverages at home	s	87=100	BEA.NIPA
PDICENFMB	impl. price defl., cons. expend, purchased meals & beverages	s	87=100	BEA.NIPA
PDICENFOC	impl. price deflator, cons. expend, fuel oil & coal	s	87=100	BEA.NIPA
PDICENGAS	impl. price deflator, cons. expend, gasoline & oil	s	87=100	BEA.NIPA
PDICENOTH	impl. price deflator, cons. expend, other nondurable goods	s	87=100	BEA.NIPA
PDICES	impl. price deflator, cons. expend, service	i	87=100	BEA.NIPA
PDICESHHO	impl. price defl., cons. expend, household operation total	i	87=100	BEA.NIPA

(*Continued*)

Table 5.2. (*Continued*)

Variable	Definition	T.	Unit	Source
PDICESHHOELE	impl. price defl., cons. expend, household operation, electr	s	87=100	BEA.NIPA
PDICESHHOGAS	impl. price defl cons. expend, household operation gas	s	87=100	BEA.NIPA
PDICESHHOOTH	impl. price defl., cons. expend, household operation, other	s	87=100	BEA.NIPA
PDICESHOU	impl. price deflator, cons. expend, household service	s	87=100	BEA.NIPA
PDICESMAO	impl. price deflator, cons. expend, medical &other service	i	87=100	BEA.NIPA
PDICESMED	impl. price deflator, cons. expend, medical care	s	87=100	BEA.NIPA
PDICESOTH	impl. price deflator, cons. expend, other service	s	87=100	BEA.NIPA
PDICESTAR	impl. price defl., cons. expend, transport, service, auto repair	s	87=100	BEA.NIPA
PDICESTRN	impl. price defl., cons. expend, transportation service, total	i	87=100	BEA.NIPA
PDICESTRNXAR	impl. price defl., cons. expend, transportation service, other	s	87=100	BEA.NIPA
PDIEX	price deflator, export, total	i	87=100	BEA.NIPA
PDIEXCAPOTH	impl. price deflator, export, merch, other capital goods	s	87=100	BEA.NIPA
PDIEXCOMPEQU	impl. price deflator, export, merch, computers	s	87=100	BEA.NIPA
PDIEXCONXMVP	impl. price deflator, export, merch, consumer goods	s	87=100	BEA.NIPA
PDIEXFFB	impl. price deflator, export, merch, foods & beverages	s	87=100	BEA.NIPA
PDIEXISM	impl. price defl., export, merch., indust supplies & materials	s	87=100	BEA.NIPA
PDIEXMER	impl. price deflator, export, merch, total	i	87=100	BEA.NIPA
PDIEXMVP	impl. price deflator, export, merch. motor vehicles & parts	s	87=100	BEA.NIPA
PDIEXOTH	impl. price deflator, export, merch, other	s	87=100	BEA.NIPA
PDIEXRFI	impl. price deflator, export, services, factor income	s	87=100	BEA.NIPA
PDIEXSER	impl. price deflator, export, service, total	s	87=100	BEA.NIPA

(*Continued*)

Table 5.2. (*Continued*)

Variable	Definition	T.	Unit	Source
PDIGDP	impl. price deflator, gross domestic product	i	87=100	BEA.NIPA
PDIGDPNFM	impl. price defl., gross domestic product, nonfarm business	s	87=100	BEA.NIPA
PDIGNP	impl. price deflator, gross national product	i	87=100	BEA.NIPA
PDIGP	impl. price deflator, govt. purchases, total	i	87=100	BEA.NIPA
PDIGPF	impl. price deflator, govt. purchases, federal	i	87=100	BEA.NIPA
PDIGPFD	impl. price defl., govt. purchases, federal defence total	i	87=100	BEA.NIPA
PDIGPFDPAY	impl. price defl., govt. purchases, federal, defence, comp, total	i	87=100	BEA.NIPA
PDIGPFDPAYCIV	impl. price defl. govt. purchases, federal, defence, comp, civilian	s	87=100	BEA.NIPA
PDIGPFDPAYMIL	impl. price defl. govt. purchases, fed defence, comp. military	s	87=100	BEA.NIPA
PDIGPFDXPAY	impl. price defl. govt. purchases, fed defence, noncomp	s	87=100	BEA.NIPA
PDIGPFN	impl. price defl. govt. purchases, federal nondefence, total	i	87=100	BEA.NIPA
PDIGPFNOTH	impl. price defl. govt. purch. fed. nondefence, noncomp., other	s	87=100	BEA.NIPA
PDIGPFNPAY	impl. price defl. govt. purch. fed. nondef., compensation	s	87=100	BEA.NIPA
PDIGPFNXPAY	impl. price defl. govt. purch. fed. nondefence, noncomp.	i	87=100	BEA.NIPA
PDIGPN	impl. price defl. govt. purchases, state & local total	i	87=100	BEA.NIPA
PDIGPNPAY	impl. price defl. govt. purch., state & local compensation	s	87=100	BEA.NIPA
PDIGPNXPAY	impl. price defl. govt. purch. state & local, noncompensation	s	87=100	BEA.NIPA

(*Continued*)

Table 5.2. (*Continued*)

Variable	Definition	T.	Unit	Source
PDIIFX	impl. price deflator, fixed investment, total	i	87=100	BEA.NIPA
PDIIGD	impl. price deflator, gross private domestic investment	i	87=100	BEA.NIPA
PDIIM	impl. price deflator, imports, total	i	87=100	BEA.NIPA
PDIIMCAPOTH	impl. price deflator, imports, merch, other capital goods	s	87=100	BEA.NIPA
PDIIMCOMPEQU	impl. price deflator, imports, merch., computers	s	87=100	BEA.NIPA
PDIIMCONXMVP	impl. price deflator, imports, merch. consumer goods	s	87=100	BEA.NIPA
PDIIMFFB	impl. price defl imports, merch. foods, feeds & bever.	s	87=100	BEA.NIPA
PDIIMISMXOIL	impl. price defl. imports, merch and supply & matls. less petro.	s	87=100	BEA.NIPA
PDIIMMER	impl. price deflator, imports, merch., total	s	87=100	BEA.NIPA
PDIIMMVP	impl. price deflator, imports, merch. motor vehicles & parts	s	87=100	BEA.NIPA
PDIIMOIL	impl. price deflator, imports, merch., petro. & products	s	87=100	BEA.NIPA
PDIIMOTH	impl. price deflator, imports, merch., other	s	87=100	BEA.NIPA
PDIIMPFI	impl. price deflator, imports, services, factor income	s	87=100	BEA.NIPA
PDIIMSER	impl. price deflator, imports, service, total	s	87=100	BEA.NIPA
PDIIMXOIL	impl. price defl. imports, merch nonpetro. Products	i	87=100	BEA.NIPA
PDIIP	impl. price deflator, fixed investment, nonres, total	i	87=100	BEA.NIPA
PDIIPE	impl. price deflator, fixed invest. nonres, prod. dur. eq., total	i	87=100	BEA.NIPA
PDIIPEIND	impl. price defl. fixed invest. nonres. prod. dur. eq., industrial	s	87=100	BEA.NIPA
PDIIPEINF	impl. price defl., fixed invest., nonres, prod. dur. eq. info proc.	s	87=100	BEA.NIPA

(*Continued*)

Table 5.2. (*Continued*)

Variable	Definition	T.	Unit	Source
PDIIPEOAS	impl. price defl., fixed invest., nonres., prod. dur. eq., other	s	87=100	BEA.NIPA
PDIIPETRN	impl. price defl., fixed invest., nonres., prod. dur. eq., transport	s	87=100	BEA.NIPA
PDIIPS	impl. price defl., fixed investment, nonres., str., total	s	87=100	BEA.NIPA
PDIIPSBLDG	impl. price defl. fixed invest, nonres., str., buildings, total	s	87=100	BEA.NIPA
PDIIPSBLDGOTH	impl. price defl., fixed invest, nonres., str., other building	s	87=100	BEA.NIPA
PDIIPSIAC	impl. price defl., fixed invest, nonres. str. commerc. & ind	s	87=100	BEA.NIPA
PDIIPSMAP	impl. price defl., fixed invest, nonres. str. min. expl. shifts, well	s	87=100	BEA.NIPA
PDIIPSOAF	impl. price defl., fixed investment, nonres. str. other	s	87=100	BEA.NIPA
PDIIPSUTL	impl. price defl., fixed investment, nonres. str. utilities	s	87=100	BEA.NIPA
PDIIR	impl. price deflator, fixed investment, res., total	i	87=100	BEA.NIPA
PDIIROTH	impl. price deflator, fixed investment, res., other	s	87=100	BEA.NIPA
PDIIRSONE	impl. price defl., fixed invest. res. new hous., single unit str.	s	87=100	BEA.NIPA
PDIIRSTOM	impl. price defl., fixed invest., res. two or more unit structures	s	87=100	BEA.NIPA
PDIKIMFG	impl. price deflator, inventories, manufacturing	s	87=100	BEA.NIPA
PDIKINFMXMFG	impl. price defl., inventories, nonfarm less manufacturing	s	87=100	BEA.NIPA
PDINNP	implicit deflator, net national product	i	87=100	BEA.NIPA
PICAP	input cost term used, in PPICAP	i	82=100	BLS.PPI BLS.PC BEA.NIPA
PICEQ	input cost term used, in PPICEQ	i	82=100	BLS.PPI BLS.PC BEA.NIPA

(*Continued*)

Table 5.2. (*Continued*)

Variable	Definition	T.	Unit	Source
PIFAP_U	input cost term used, in PPIFAP_U	i	82=100	BLS.PPI BLS.PC BEA.NIPA
PIFCG	input cost term used, in PPIFCG	i	82=100	BLS.PPI BLS.PC BEA.NIPA
PIFHE	input cost term used, in PPIFHE	i	82=100	BLS.PPI BLS.PC BEA.NIPA
PIINT	input cost term used, in PPINT	i	82=100	BLS.PPI BLS.PC BEA.NIPA
PIMAE	input cost term used, in PPIMAE	i	82=100	BLS.PPI BLS.PC BEA.NIPA
PIMMP	input cost term used, in PPIMMP	i	82=100	BLS.PPI BLS.PC BEA.NIPA
PINMP	input cost term used, in PPINMP	i	82=100	BLS.PPI BLS.PC BEA.NIPA
PIPPA	input cost term used, in PPIPPA	i	82=100	BLS.PPI BLS.PC BEA.NIPA
PIRAP	input cost term used, in PPIRAP	i	82=100	BLS.PPI BLS.PC BEA.NIPA
PITEQ	input cost term used, in PPITEQ	i	82=100	BLS.PPI BLS.PC BEA.NIPA
PITPA	input cost term used, in PPITPA	i	82=100	BLS.PPI BLS.PC BEA.NIPA
PPI	PPI, all commodities	s	82=100	BLS.PPI
PPI_U	PPI, all commodities	s	82=100	BLS.PPI
PPICAP	PPI, chemicals	s	82=100	BLS.PPI
PPICAP_U	PPI, chemicals	i	82=100	BLS.PPI
PPICEQ	PPI, finished goods, capital eq.	s	82=100	BLS.PPI
PPICEQ_U	PPI, finished goods, capital eq.	i	82=100	BLS.PPI
PPICMP	PPI, crude materials	s	82=100	BLS.PPI
PPICMP_U	PPI, crude materials	i	82=100	BLS.PPI

(*Continued*)

Table 5.2. (*Continued*)

Variable	Definition	T.	Unit	Source
PPICOL_U	PPI, fuel & related products, coal	s	82=100	BLS.PPI
PPIELP_U	PPI, fuel & related products, electric power	s	82=100	BLS.PPI
PPIFAP	PPI, fuels & related prod. total	s	82=100	BLS.PPI
PPIFAP_U	PPI fuels & related prod. total	i	82=100	BLS.PPI
PPIFCG	PPI, finished, cons/goods	s	82=100	BLS.PPI
PPIFCG_U	PPI, finished, consumgoods	i	82=100	BLS.PPI
PPIFHE	PPI, furnit & household eq.	s	82=100	BLS.PPI
PPIFHE_U	PPI, furn & household eq.	i	82=100	BLS.PPI
PPIFIN	PPI, finished goods, total	s	82=100	BLS.PPI
PPIFIN_U	PPI, finished goods, total	i	82=100	BLS.PPI
PPIFPF	PPI, farm products & processed foods & feeds, total	s	82=100	BLS.PPI
PPIFPF_U	PPI, farm products & processed foods & feeds, total	i	82=100	BLS.PPI
PPIFRM_U	PPI, farm products	i	82=100	BLS.PPI
PPIGAS_U	PPI, fuels & related prod. gas	s	82=100	BLS.PPI
PPIHSL_U	PPI, hides, skins & leather	i	82=100	BLS.PPI
PPIIND	PPI, ind commodities, total	s	82=100	BLS.PPI
PPIIND_U	PPI, ind commodities, total	i	82=100	BLS.PPI
PPIINT	PPI, intermediate materials	s	82=100	BLS.PPI
PPIINT_U	PPI, intermediate materials	i	82=100	BLS.PPI
PPILWP	PPI, lumber & wood products	s	82=100	BLS.PPI
PPILWP_U	PPI, lumber & wood products	i	82=100	BLS.PPI
PPIMAE	PPI, machinery & equipment	s	82=100	BLS.PPI
PPIMAE_U	PPI, machinery & equipment	i	82=100	BLS.PPI
PPIMIS	PPI, miscel. Commodities	s	82=100	BLS.PPI
PPIMIS_U	PPI, miscel commodities	i	82=100	BLS.PPI
PPIMMP	PPI, metals & metal products	s	82=100	BLS.PPI
PPIMMP_U	PPI, metals & metal products	i	82=100	BLS.PPI
PPINMP	PPI, nonmetallic mineral products	s	82=100	BLS.PPI
PPINMP_U	PPI, nonmetal mineral prod.	i	82=100	BLS.PPI
PPIPFF	PPI, processed foods & feeds	s	82=100	BLS.PPI
PPIPFF_U	PPI, processed foods & feeds	i	82=100	BLS.PPI
PPIPPA	PPI, pulp, paper & allied products	s	82=100	BLS.PPI
PPIPPA_U	PPI, pulp, paper & allied products	i	82=100	BLS.PPI
PPIRAP	PPI, rubber & plastics	s	82=100	BLS.PPI
PPIRAP_U	PPI, rubber & plastics	i	82=100	BLS.PPI

(*Continued*)

Table 5.2. (*Continued*)

Variable	Definition	T.	Unit	Source
PPIRPP	PPI, fuels & related products, refine petroleum prod	s	82=100	BLS.PPI
PPIRPP_U	PPI, fuels & related products, refine petroleum prod	i	82=100	BLS.PPI
PPITEQ	PPI, transportation equipment	s	82=100	BLS.PPI
PPITEQ_U	PPI, transportation equip.	i	82=100	BLS.PPI
PPITPA	PPI, Textiles & apparel	s	82=100	BLS.PPI
PPITPA_U	PPI, Textiles & apparel	i	82=100	BLS.PPI
PPIXFAE	PPI, all items less food & energy	s	82=100	BLS.PPI
PPIXFAE_U	PPI, all items less food & energy	i	82=100	BLS.PPI
PUVCAR	unit value, average price, new cars, retail, domestic & imports	s	1000 $	BEA.NIPA
PUVCAR87	unit value, average price, new cars, retail, domestic & imports	s	1000 $	BEA.NIPA
PUVCARDOM87	unit value, average price, new cars, wholesales, domestic	s	1000 $	BEA.NIPA
PUVCARIMP87	unit value, average price, new cars, retail, imports	s	1000 $	BEA.NIPA
PUVHNEW MED_U	unit value, median price, new single unit, homes sold	s	1000 $	BOC.HS
PUVHOLD MED_U	median price, existing single unit homes sold	s	1000 $	Nat. Assoc. of Realtors
QEBLOIL	petroleum demand, domestic	s	mill bbl/day	DOE..PTRO
QEBLOILDOM	petroleum supply, domestic	s	mill bbl/day	DOE..PTRO
RATRRIPE	req'd return on investment, prod. dur. equip	i	decimal	WEFA
RATRRIPS	req'd return on investment	i	decimal	WEFA
RATRRIRS	req'd return on investment, residential	i	decimal	WEFA
RCD3M	interest rate, certificates of deposit, 3-month	s	percent	FRB.RT
RCD6M	interest rate, certificates of deposit, 6-month	s	percent	FRB.RT
RCORPS_AAA	interest rate, MOODY's Ass corporate bond, seasoned	s	percent	MOODY's Investors Service
RCORPS_BAA	interest rate, MOODY's Bss corporate bond, seasoned	s	percent	MOODY's Investors Service

(*Continued*)

Table 5.2. (*Continued*)

Variable	Definition	T.	Unit	Source
RCP1M	interest rate, commercial papers, 1-month	s	percent	FRB.RT
RCP3M	interest rate, commercial papers, 3-month	s	percent	FRB.RT
RCP6M	interest rate, commercial papers, 6-month	s	percent	FRB.RT
RDISC	interest rate, discount rate, FRB New York	s	percent	FRB.RT
REURO3M	interest rate, 3-month euro dollar	s	percent	FRB.RT
REXMOR15	nom. exch. rate, index, wtd. avg. U.S. vs. 15 countries, morgan guaranty	s	index	Morgan Guaranty
REXMOR15R	real exch. rate index, wtd. avg. U.S. vs. 15 countries, morgan guaranty	i	index	Morgan Guaranty
RFF	interest rate, federal funds	s	percent	FRB.RT
RHAFFI	housing affordability index	s	index	Nat. Ass. of Realtors
RIMPCAR	import share, new auto sales	i	per cent	BEA.NIPA
RKUMFGFRB	capacity utilization rate, manufacturing	s	per cent	FRB.IP
RLIBOR3M	interest rate, 3-month libor	s	percent	Chase Manhatten Bank
RMCPT	marginal corporate profit tax rate	i	decimal	BEA.NIPA
RMOREFW	morgge rate, effective	s	percent	FRB.RT
RMUNIBB20	interest rate, municipal bonds, bond buyer index of 20 bonds	s	percent	Bond Bayer
RNHHLD1624	household headship rate, 16–24	i	decimal	WEFA
RNHHLD2534	household headship rate, 25–34	i	decimal	WEFA
RNHHLD3544	household headship rate, 35–44	i	decimal	WEFA
RNHHLD4554	household headship rate, 45–54	i	decimal	WEFA
RNHHLD5564	household headship rate, 55–64	i	decimal	WEFA
RNHHLD65A	household headship rate, 65 & over	i	decimal	WEFA
RNP2544	civilian population, total 25–44, share of total population	i	decimal	BLS.EE
RNP65A	civilian population, total, 65 & over, share of total population	i	decimal	BLS.EE

(*Continued*)

Table 5.2. (*Continued*)

Variable	Definition	T.	Unit	Source
RNPF1619	civilian population, females, 16–19, share of total population	i	decimal	BLS.EE
RNPF20A	civilian population, females, 20 & over, share of total populat.	i	decimal	BLS.EE
RNPM1619	civilian population, males, 16–19, share of total populat	i	decimal	BLS.EE
RNPM20A	civilian population, males, 20 & over, share of total populat.	i	decimal	BLS.EE
RPDICEHAT	anticipated inflation rate, impl. price defl., consump expend.	i	percent	BEA.NIPA
RPDIGNPHAT	anticipated inflation rate, impl. price deflator, GNP	i	percent	BEA.NIPA
RPLC	labor force participat rate, total	i	decimal	BLS.EE
RPLCF	lab. f. partic. rate, female total	i	decimal	BLS.EE
RPLCF1619	lab. f. partic. r, female, 16–19	i	decimal	BLS.EE
RPLCF2024	lab. f. partic. r, female, 20–24	i	decimal	BLS.EE
RPLCF20A	lab. f. part. r, female, 20 & over	i	decimal	BLS.EE
RPLCF2534	lab. f. partic. r, females, 25–34	i	decimal	BLS.EE
RPLCF3544	lab. f. partic. r, female 35–44	i	decimal	BLS.EE
RPLCF4554	lab. f. partic. r, female, 45–54	i	decimal	BLS.EE
RPLCF5564	lab. f. partic. r, female, 55–64	i	decimal	BLS.EE
RPLCF65A	lab. f. parc. r, female, 65 & over	i	decimal	BLS.EE
RPLCM	lab. f. partic. rate, males, total	i	decimal	BLS.EE
RPLCM1619	lab. f. partic. rate, males, 16–19	i	decimal	BLS.EE
RPLCM2024	lab. f. partic. rate, males, 20–24	i	decimal	BLS.EE
RPLCM20A	lab. f. partic. rate, males, 20 & over	i	decimal	BLS.EE
RPLCM2534	lab. f. partic. rate, males, 25–34	i	decimal	BLS.EE
RPLCM3544	lab. f. partic. rate, males, 35–44	i	decimal	BLS.EE
RPLCM4554	lab. f. partic. rate, males, 45–54	i	decimal	BLS.EE
RPLCM5564	lab. f. partic. rate, males, 55–64	i	decimal	BLS.EE
RPLCM65A	lab. f. partic. rate, males, 65 & over	i	decimal	BLS.EE
RPRIME	interest rate, pr. comm. bk loans	s	percent	FRB.RT
RSVPER	personal saving rate	i		
RTBILL3M	interest rate, treas. bills, 3-mon	s	percent	FRB.RT
RTBILL6M	interest rate, treas. bills, 6-mon	s	percent	FRB.RT
RTBOND10Y	interest rate, treas. bds 10-y	s	percent	FRB.RT
RTBOND30Y	interest rate, treas. bds, 30-y.	s	percent	FRB.RT
RTNOTE1Y	interest rate, treas. note, 1-y	s	percent	FRB.RT

(*Continued*)

Table 5.2. (*Continued*)

Variable	Definition	T.	Unit	Source
RTNOTE3Y	interest rate, treas. note, 3-y	s	percent	FRB.RT
RTNOTE5Y	interest rate, treas. note, 5y	s	percent	FRB.RT
RTNOTE7Y	interest rate, treas. note, 7y	s	percent	FRB.RT
RTXCF_ADJ	tax rate, corporate profits tax rate, rate adjustment	s	percent	BEA.NIPA
RTXCF_EFF	tax rate, corporate profits tax, federal, effective rate	i	percent	BEA.NIPA
RUNC	unemployment rate, civilian	i	percent	BLS.EE
RUTILS_BAA	interest rate, utility bonds, moody's BAA, seasoned	s	percent	MOODY's Investor Service
SFXNETEX	final sales to dom. purchase	i	bill. $	BEA.NIPA
SFXNETEX87	final sales to dom. purchase	i	bill. 87 $	BEA.NIPA
SVPER	personal saving	i	bill. $	BEA.NIPA
TRF	transfer pay to foreigners net	i	bill. $	BEA.NIPA
TRGF	transfer pay/total, govt. federal	i	bill. $	BEA.NIPA
TRP	transfer pay. to person, total	i	bill. $	BEA.NIPA
TRP87	transfer pay. to p. real, total	i	bill. $	BEA.NIPA
TRPB	transfer pay. to p. business	s	bill. $	BEA.NIPA
TRPG	transfer payments to person, from govt., total	i	bill. $	BEA.NIPA
TRPGF	transfer payments to person, from govt., federal, total	i	bill. $	BEA.NIPA
TRPGFHI	transfer pay. to person, govt., federal health insurance	s	bill. $	BEA.NIPA
TRPGFOASDI	transfer payments to person, from govt., federal, oasdi	s	bill. $	BEA.NIPA
TRPGFOTH	transfer payments to person, from govt., federal, other	s	bill. $	BEA.NIPA
TRPGFRET	transfer payments to person, from govt., federal, fed. empl.	s	bill. $	BEA.NIPA
TRPGFSSP	transfer payments to person, from govt., federal, oasdhi	i	bill. $	BEA.NIPA
TRPGFUIB	transf. pay. to person, govt., federal, unempl. insurance	s	bill. $	BEA.NIPA
TRPGFVET	transfer pay. to person, from govt., fed., veterans benefits	i	bill. $	BEA.NIPA
TRPGFVETMED	transfer pay. to person, from govt., fed., veter. benef. med.	s	bill. $	BEA.NIPA
TRGFVETOTH	transfer pay. to person, from govt., fed., veter. benef., other	s	bill. $	BEA.NIPA
TRPGN	transfer payments to person, from govt., state & local	i	bill. $	BEA.NIPA

(*Continued*)

Table 5.2. (*Continued*)

Variable	Definition	T.	Unit	Source
TRPGNMEDCAI	transfer payments to person, from govt., state & local	s	bill. $	BEA.NIPA
TRPGNOTH	transfer payments to person, from govt., state & local	s	bill. $	BEA.NIPA
TXC	govt. receipts, profits tax accruals. total	i	bill. $	BEA.NIPA
TXCF	govt. receipts, profits tax accruals. federal	s	bill. $	BEA.NIPA
TXCN	govt. receipts, profits tax accruals, state & local	s	bill. $	BEA.NIPA
TXF	govt. receipts, federal NIPA basis	i	bill. $	BEA.NIPA
TXFUBB	govt. receipts, federal, unified budget basis	i	bill. $	BEA.NIPA
TXI	govt. receipts, ind. bus. tax & nontax accruals, total	i	bill. $	BEA.NIPA
TXIF	govt. receipts, ind. bus. tax & nontax accruals, federal	s	bill. $	BEA.NIPA
TXIN	govt. receipts, ind. bus. tax & nontax accruals, state & local	s	bill. $	BEA.NIPA
TXINPTY	govt. receipts, ind. busi. tax & nontax accruals, prop tax state & local	s	bill. $	BEA.NIPA
TXIXOIL	govt. receipts, ind. bus. tax & nontax accruals, xcl windfall prof., total	i	bill. $	BEA.NIPA
TXN	govt. receipts, state & local	i	bill. $	BEA.NIPA
TXP	govt. receipts, personal tax & nontax receipt total	i	bill. $	BEA.NIPA
TXPAV	govt. receipts, personal tax & nontax receipts, total 4 qtr. mov. avg.	i	bill. $	BEA.NIPA
TXPF	govt. receipts, personal tax & nontax receipts federal	s	bill. $	BEA.NIPA
TXPN	govt. receipts, persona; ltax & nontax, state & local	s	bill. $	BEA.NIPA
TXS	govt. receipts, contribution for social insurance, total	i	bill. $	BEA.NIPA
TXSE	govt. receipts, contribution for social insurance, employer	i	bill. $	BEA.NIPA
TXSF	govt. receipts, contribution for social insurance, federal	s	bill. $	BEA.NIPA

(*Continued*)

Table 5.2. (*Continued*)

Variable	Definition	T.	Unit	Source
TXSN	govt. receipts, contribution for social insurance, state & local	s	bill. $	BEA.NIPA
TXSP	govt. receipts, contribution for social insurance, persons	i	bill. $	BEA.NIPA
UCK	user cost of capital (%), CES equation	i	percent	WEFA
UCKEIND	user cost of capital (%), nonres., pde, industrial equipment	i	percent	WEFA
UCKEINF	user cost of capital (%), nonres., prod dur equip, info processing	i	percent	WEFA
UCKEOAS	user cost of capital (%), nonres., prod. dur. equip., other	i	percent	WEFA
UCKETRN	user cost of capital (%), nonres., prod dur equip, transportation	i	percent	WEFA
UCKIRSGE2	user cost of capital (%), residential, new hous., multi-unit. str.	i	percent	WEFA
UCKIRSONE	user cost of capital (%), residential, new hous., single unit str.	i	percent	WEFA
UCKSBLDGOTH	user cost of capital (%), nonres., structure, building, other	i	percent	WEFA
UCKSCOM	user cost of capital (%), nonres. structures, commercial	i	percent	WEFA
UCKSIND	user cost of capital (%), nonres. structures, industrial	i	percent	WEFA
UCKSMAP	user cost of cap. (%), nonres. str., mining excl. shafts well	i	percent	WEFA
UCKSOAF	user cost of capital (%), nonres., structure, other	i	percent	WEFA
UCKSUTL	user cost of capital (%), nonres., structures, utilities	i	percent	WEFA
UHC	housing unit completed, total	i	mill. units	BOC.HS
UHCGE2	housing unit completed, multi-unit	s	mill. units	BOC.HS
UHCONE	housing unit completed, single unit	s	mill. units	BOC.HS
UHESLD	housing solds, existing single unit	s	mill. units	Nat. assoc. of realtors

(*Continued*)

Table 5.2. (*Continued*)

Variable	Definition	T.	Unit	Source
UHS	housing starts, total	i	mill. units	Nat. assoc. of realtors
UHSGE2	housing starts, multi-unit	s	mill.units	Nat. assoc. of realtors
UHSONE	housing starts, single unit	s	mill.units	Nat. assoc. of realtors
UKCARDOM	retail inventories, new domestic autos	s	mill.units	BEA.UN
UPCARB	unit auto production, domestic, BEA	i	mill.units	BEA.UN
UPCARDOM	unit auto production, domestic, wards	s	mill.units	Auto News
USCAR	retail sales, new cars, total	i	mill.units	BEA.UN
USCARAN	retail sales, new cars total	s	mill.units	Auto News
USCARDOM	retail sales, new cars, domestic	i	mill.units	BEA.UN
USCARDOMAN	retail sales, new cars	i	mill.units	Auto News
USCARIMP	retail sales, new cars, imports	i	mill.units	BEA.UN
USCARIMPAN	retail sales, new cars, imports	s	mill.units	BEA.UN
UTRKLE3	sales, new light trucks	i	mill.units	Auto News
UTRKLE3AN	sales, new light trucks	s	mill.units	Auto News
VM1	money velocity, M1	i	ratio	FRB.MS
VM2	money velocity, M2	i	ratio	FRB.MS
WALD	wage accruals less disbursements, total	i	bill. $	BEA.NIPA
WB	compensation of employees	i	bill. $	BEA.NIPA
WD	wage & salary disbursements, total	s	bill. $	BEA.NIPA
WD_DIFF	wage & salary disburs total, difference calculat internal	i	bill. $	WEFA
WD_SUM	wage & salary disburs., total, bottom up calcul. internal	s	bill. $	BEA.NIPA
WDCPIOTH	wage & salary disburs., other commodity indus. (excl.MFG)	s	bill. $	BEA.NIPA
WDGOV	wage & salary disburs. govt. & govt. industries	s	bill. $	BEA.NIPA
WDMFG	wage & salary disbursements, manufacturing	s	bill. $	BEA.NIPA
WDPSP	wage & salary disbursements, private service producing	s	bill. $	BEA.NIPA
WRGPFDPAYCIV	avg. compens. per manhour, fed. govt., defense civilian	s	current $ per hour	BEA.NIPA

(*Continued*)

Table 5.2. (*Continued*)

Variable	Definition	T.	Unit	Source
WRGPFDPAYMIL	avg. compens. per manhour, federal govt., defence military	s	current $ per hour	BEA.NIPA
WRGPFNPAY	averg. compens. per manhour, federal, govt., nondefence	s	current $ per hour	BEA.NIPA
WRGPFPAY	average compensation per manhour, federal govt	s	current $ per hour	BEA.NIPA
WRGPNPAY	average compensation per manhour, state & local	s	current $ per hour	BEA.NIPA
WRHPCON	average hourly earning, construction	s	current $ per hour	BEA.NIPA
WRHPFIR	average hourly earning, finance, insurance & real estate	s	current $ per hour	BEA.NIPA
WRHPMFG	average hourly earning, manufacturing	s	current $ per hour	BEA.NIPA
WRHPMIN	average hourly earning, mining	s	current $ per hour	BEA.NIPA
WRHPSER	average hourly earning, service	s	current $ per hour	BEA.NIPA
WRHPTPU	average hourly earning, transport & public utilities	s	current $ per hour	BEA.NIPA
WRHPWRT	average hourly earning, wholesale & retail trade	s	current $ per hour	BEA.NIPA
WS	Supplem to wages & salaries	i	bill. $	BEA.NIPA
XIOCON187	final demand, construc. part 1	i	bill. 87 $	BEA.NIPA
XIOCON287	final demand, construc. part 2	i	bill. 87 $	BEA.NIPA
XIOCON387	final demand, construc. part 3	i	bill. 87 $	BEA.NIPA
XIOCON87	final demand, constr. total	i	bill. 87 $	BEA.NIPA
XIOFSR187	final demand, fin. insur. real estate, % other servic. part 1	i	bill. 87 $	BEA.NIPA
XIOFSR287	final demand, fin. insur. real estate & other service, part 2	i	bill. 87 $	BEA.NIPA
XIOFSR387	final demand, fin. insur. real estate, & other service, part 3	i	bill. 87 $	BEA.NIPA
XIOFSR87	final demand, fin. insur. real estate, & other services, total	i	bill. 87 $	BEA.NIPA
XIOMFG187	final demand, manuf. part 1	i	bill. 87 $	BEA.NIPA
XIOMFG287	final demand, manuf., part 2	i	bill. 87 $	BEA.NIPA
XIOMFG387	final demand, manuf. part 3	i	bill. 87 $	BEA.NIPA
XIOMFG87	final demand, manuf. Total	i	bill. 87 $	BEA.NIPA
XIOMIN187	final demand, mining, part 1	i	bill. 87 $	BEA.NIPA
XIOMIN287	final demand, mining, part 2	i	bill. 87 $	BEA.NIPA
XIOMIN387	final demand, mining, part 3	i	bill. 87 $	BEA.NIPA

(*Continued*)

Table 5.2. (*Continued*)

Variable	Definition	T.	Unit	Source
XIOMIN87	final demand, mining, total	i	bill. 87 $	BEA.NIPA
XIOTPU187	final d., transp. utilities, part 1	i	bill. 87 $	BEA.NIPA
XIOTPU287	final d. transp. & util. part 2	i	bill. 87 $	BEA.NIPA
XIOTPU387	final d. transp. & util., part 3	i	bill. 87 $	BEA.NIPA
XIOTPU87	final d. transp.& util., total	i	bill. 87 $	BEA.NIPA
XIOWRT187	final d. wh. & ret., part 1	i	bill. 87 $	BEA.NIPA
XIOWRT287	final d. wh.& ret. trpart 2	i	bill. 87 $	BEA.NIPA
XIOWRT387	final d. wh. & ret. trpart 3	i	bill. 87 $	BEA.NIPA
XIOWRT87	final d., wh. & ret. tr. totl.	i	bill. 87 $	BEA.NIPA
YCEN87	income, intermediate var nondur. goods focus	i	bill. 87 $	BEA.NIPA
YDP	disposable personal income	i	bill. $	BEA.NIPA
YDP87	disposable personal income,	i	bill. 87 $	BEA.NIPA
YDPPERM87	disposable personal income,	i	bill. 87 $	BEA.NIPA
YDVN	profits after tax, dividends	i	bill. $	BEA.NIPA
YDVPER	personal dividend income	s	bill. $	BEA.NIPA
YIN	net interest	i	bill. $	BEA.NIPA
YINGF	net interest paid, federal govt	s	bill. $	BEA.NIPA
YINGN	net int. paid, state & local govt	s	bill. $	BEA.NIPA
YIPPER	Int. paid by consumers to busi.	s	bill. $	BEA.NIPA
YIRPER	personal interest income	s	bill. $	BEA.NIPA
YN	national income	i	bill. $	BEA.NIPA
YOL	other labor income	s	bill. $	BEA.NIPA
YOTH	other income	s	bill. $	BEA.NIPA
YP	personal income	i	bill. $	BEA.NIPA
YPR	proprietors income A & CCADJ, nonfarm	i	bill. $	BEA.NIPA
YPTAX	taxable personal income	i	bill. $	BEA.NIPA
YR	rental income of persons with CCADJ	s	bill. $	BEA.NIPA
Z	corporate profits with IVA & CCADJ	i	bill. $	BEA.NIPA
ZA	profit after tax	i	bill. $	BEA.NIPA
ZB	profits before tax	i	bill. $	BEA.NIPA
ZROW	corporate profits with IVA, rest of world	s	bill. $	BEA.NIPA
ZXADJ	corporate profits with IVA, total	i	bill. $	BEA.NIPA
ZXADJ6011	corporate profits with IVA, federal reserve banks	s	bill. $	BEA.NIPA
ZXADJDOM	corporate profits with IVA, domestic industries	i	bill. $	BEA.NIPA
DCREDIT	dummy var., credit rationing	e		

(*Continued*)

Table 5.2. (*Continued*)

Variable	Definition	T.	Unit	Source
DMPE	depreciation method, for equipment	e		
DMPS	depreciation method, for structure	e		
DQR2	dummy variable, 2nd quarter	e		
DQR3	dummy variable, 3rd quarter	e		
DQR4	dummy variable, 4th quarter	e		
DUMGEF	dummy variable, policy lever, govt. expenditure	e		
EMEGFD	Employ, federal gov. defence	e	mill. empl.	BLS.EE
EMEGFN	employment, federal government, nondefence	e	mill. empl	BLS.EE
EMEGN	employ., state & local govt	e	mill. empl	BLS.EE
EMFDMIL	employment, federal govt. defence, total armed forces	e	mill. employees	BLS.EE
EMHCXE	employment, difference, household vs. established surveys	e	mill. employees	BLS.EE
EXGRAIN	export, grain products	e	bill. 87 $	BEA.NIPA
GDP15W87	Gdp, rest of world	e	bill. 87 $	BEA.NIPA
GEFADJ	govt. expenditure, federal, difference, unified vs NIPA	e	bill. $	BEA.NIPA
GIAOTH87EXO	federal grants in aid, to state & local govt., other,	e	bill. 87 $	BEA.NIPA
GIAOTHEXO	federal grants in aid, to state & local govt., other,	e	bill. $	BEA.NIPA
GNPSDX	GNP, statistical discrepancy	e	bill. $	BEA.NIPA
GNPSDX87	GNP, statistical discrepancy	e	bill. 87 $	BEA.NIPA
GPFDXPAY 87EXO	govt. purchase, federal, defence, noncompensation,	e	bill. 87 $	BEA.NIPA
GPFDXPAYEXO	govt. purchase, federal, defence, noncompensation,	e	bill. $	BEA.NIPA
GPFNNONCCC	govt. purchase, federal, nondefence, CCC payments	e	bill. $	BEA.NIPA
GPFNONCCC87	govt. purchase, federal, nondefence, CCC payments	e	bill. 87 $	BEA.NIPA
GPFNONCCC87	govt. purchase, federal, nondefence, CCC payments	e	bill. 87 $	BEA.NIPA
GPFNOTH87EXO	govt. purchase, federal, nondefence, noncomp other,	e	bill. 87 $	BEA.NIPA
GPFNOTHEXO	govt. purchase, federal, noncomp other	e	bill. $	BEA.NIPA

(*Continued*)

Table 5.2. (*Continued*)

Variable	Definition	T.	Unit	Source
GPNXPAY87	govt. purchase, state & local, noncompensation	e	bill. 87 $	BEA.NIPA
GSLSF	subsidies less curr. surplus, federal govt. enterprise	e	ratio	
GSLSN	subsidies less curr. surplus, state & local govt. enterprise	e	ratio	
IIFRMACCC87	changes in business inventories, farm + CCC purchases	e	bill. 87 $	BEA.NIPA
ITCEIND	investment tax credit, equipment, industrial	e	ratio	WEFA
ITCEINF	investment tax credit, equip., information processing	e	ratio	WEFA
ITCEOAS	investment tax credit, equipment, other	e	ratio	WEFA
ITCETRN	investment tax credit, equipment, transportation equip.	e	ratio	WEFA
ITCSBLDGOTH	investment tax credit, structure, other buildings	e	ratio	WEFA
ITCSCOM	investment tax credit, structure, commercial	e	ratio	WEFA
ITCSIND	investment tax credit, structures, industrial	e	ratio	WEFA
ITCSMAP	investment tax credit, structures, mining, exploration	e	ratio	WEFA
ITCSOAF	inv. tax credit, struct., other	e	ratio	WEFA
ITCSUTL	inv. tax credit, struct. utilities	e	ratio	WEFA
NETCADIF	net export, conceptual diff., NIPA vs. balance of payments	e	bill. $as	BEA.NIPA
NPT0004EXO	popul., total, 00–14, exog. lever	e	mill.	WEFA
NPT0509EXO	pop., total, 05–09, exog. lever	e	mill.	WEFA
NPT1014EXO	pop., total, 10–14, exog. lever	e	mill.	WEFA
NPT15EEXO	pop. total, 15, exog lever	e	mill.	WEFA
NPTCNT	lever to control population	e	index	WEFA
NPTF1617EXO	pop. females, 16–17, exog. lev.	e	mill.	WEFA
NPTF1819EXO	pop. females, 18–19, exo. lev.	e	mill.	WEFA
NPTF2024EXO	pop. females, 20–24, exo. lev.	e	mill.	WEFA
NPTF2529EXO	pop. females, 25–29, exo. lev.	e	mill.	WEFA
NPTF3034EXO	pop. females, 30–34, exo. lev.	e	mill.	WEFA
NPTF3539EXO	pop. females, 35–39	e	mill.	BOC.PR
NPTF4044EXO	pop. females, 40–44	e	mill.	BOC.PR
NPTF4549EXO	pop. females, 45–49	e	mill.	BOC.PR

(*Continued*)

Table 5.2. (*Continued*)

Variable	Definition	T.	Unit	Source
NPTF5054EXO	pop. females, 50–54	e	mill.	BOC.PR
NPTF5559EXO	pop. females, 55–59	e	mill.	BOC.PR
NPTF6064EXO	pop. females, 60–64	e	mill.	BOC.PR
NPTF6569EXO	pop. females, 65–69	e	mill.	BOC.PR
NPTF7074EXO	pop. females, 70–74	e	mill.	BOC.PR
NPTF70AEXO	pop. females, 70A	e	mill.	BOC.PR
NPTF7579EXO	pop. females, 75–79	e	mill.	BOC.PR
NPTF8084EXO	pop. females, 80–84	e	mill.	BOC.PR
NPTF85AEXO	pop. females, 85A	e	mill.	BOC.PR
NPTM15EXO	pop. males, 15, exo. lever	e	mill.	WEFA
NPTM1617EXO	pop. males, 16–17, exo. lever	e	mill.	WEFA
NPTM1819EXO	pop. males, 18–19, exo. lever	e	mill.	WEFA
NPTM2024EXO	pop. males, 20–24, exo. lever	e	mill.	WEFA
NPTM2529EXO	Pop. males, 25–29, exo. lever	e	mill.	WEFA
NPTM3034EXO	pop. males, 30–34, exo. lever	e	mill.	WEFA
NPTM3539EXO	pop. males, 35–39, exo. lever	e	mill.	WEFA
NPTM4044EXO	pop. males, 40–44, exo. lever	e	mill.	WEFA
NPTM4549EXO	pop. males, 45–49, exo. lever	e	mill.	WEFA
NPTM5054EXO	pop. males, 50–54, exo.	e	mill.	WEFA
NPTM5559EXO	pop. males, 55–59, exo.	e	mill.	WEFA
NPTM6064EXO	pop. males, 60–64, exo.	e	mill.	WEFA
NPTM6569EXO	pop. males, 65–69, exo.	e	mill.	WEFA
NPTM7074EXO	pop. males, 70–74, exo.	e	mill.	WEFA
NPTM7579EXO	pop. males, 75–79, exo.	e	mill.	WEFA
NPTM8084EXO	pop. males, 80–84, exo	e	mill	WEFA
NPTM85AEXO	pop. males, 85 and over, exo/	e	mill.	WEFA
PPATPA_SF	PPI, seasonal factor, textiles & apparel	e	82=100	BLS.PPI
PPICAP_SF	PPI, seasonal factor, chemicals	e	82=100	BLS.PPI
PPICEQ_SF	PPI, seasonal factor, finished goods, capital equipment	e	82=100	BLS.PPI
PPICMP_SF	PPI, seasonal factor, crude materials	e	82=100	BLS.PPI
PPIFAP_SF	PPI, seasonal factor, fuels & related products, total	e	82=100	BLS.PPI
PPIFCG_SF	PPI, seasonal factor, finished goods, consumer goods	e	82=100	BLS.PPI
PPIFHE_SF	PPI, seasonal factor, furniture & household equip.	e	82=100	BLS.PPI
PPIFIN_SF	PPI, s.f. finished goods.total	e	82=100	BLS.PPI
PPIFPF_SF	PPI, seasonfactor, farm pr. & processed foods & feeds, total	e	82=100	BLS.PPI

(*Continued*)

Table 5.2. (*Continued*)

Variable	Definition	T.	Unit	Source
PPIFRM	PPI, farm products	e	82=100	BLS.PPI
PPIFRM_SF	PPI, s. f., farm products,	e	82=100	BLS.PPI
PPIHSL	PPI, hides, skin & leather	e	82=100	BLS.PPI
PPIHSL_SF	PPI, seasonal factor, hides, skins & leather	e	82=100	BLS.PPI
PPIIND_SF	PPI, seasonal factor, industrial commodities, total,	e	82=100	BLS.PPI
PPIINT_SF	PPI, seasonal factor, intermediate materials	e	82=100	BLS.PPI
PPILWP_SF	PPI, seasonal factor, lumber & wood products	e	82=100	BLS.PPI
PPIMAE_SF	PPI, seasonal factor, machinery & equipment	e	82=100	BLS.PPI
PPIMIS_SF	PPI, seasonal factor, miscellaneous commodities	e	82=100	BLS.PPI
PPIMMP_SF	PPI, seasonal factor, metals & metal products	e	82=100	BLS.PPI
PPINMP_SF	PPI, seasonal factor, nonmetallic mineral products	e	82=100	BLS.PPI
PPIPFF_SF	PPI, seasonal factor, processed foods & feeds	e	82=100	BLS.PPI
PPIPPA_SF	PPI, seasonal factor, pulp, paper & allied products	e	82=100	BLS.PPI
PPIRAP_SF	PPI, seasonal factor, rubber & plastics	e	82=100	BLS.PPI
PPIROW15	PPI, seasonal factor, rest of world, less foods & energy	e	82=100	BLS.PPI
PPIRPP_SF	PPI, seasonal factor, fuels & related pro., refine petroprod,	e	82=100	BLS.PPI
PPITEQ_SF	PPI, seasonal factor, transportation equipment	e	82=100	BLS.PPI
PPIXFAE_SF	PPI, seasonal factor, all items less food & energy	e	82=100	BLS.PPI
PUVHNEW MED_SF	unit value, median price, new single unit, homes	e	percent	BEA.NIPA
PUVHNEW MED_SF	median price, new single unit home sold	e	percent	BOC.HS
PUVHOLD MED_SF	median price, existing single unit homes sold	e	percent	Nat. Assoc. of Realtors
PUVOILRAC	unit value, average refiner's acquisition cost, composite	e	$ / barrel	DOE..PTRO

(*Continued*)

Table 5.2. (*Continued*)

Variable	Definition	T.	Unit	Source
PUVOILRAC	unit value, average refiner's acquition cost, composite	e	$/barrel	DOE..PTRO
QTR1	dummy variable, 1st quarter	e		
RDEPEIND87	annual depreciate rate, nonres, prod dur equip, indust. equip	e	decimal	BEA.UN
RDEPEINF87	ann dep.r, pr. dur. eq., inf. pr.	e	decimal	BEA.UN
RDEPEOAS87	annual depreciation rate, prod. dur. equip., other	e	decimal	BEA.UN
RDEPETRN87	ann. dep. r, prd dur eq, trans.	e	decimal	BEA.UN
RDEPGE87	annual depreciation rate, nonres., govt. equipment	e	decimal	BEA.UN
RDEPGS87	ann. depr. rate, nonres., gvt. str.	e	decimal	BEA.UN
RDEPSBLDGOTH87	annual depreciate rate, nonres., str. buildings, other	e	decimal	BEA.UN
RDEPSCOM87	ann. depr. rate, nonres., comm.	e	decimal	BEA.UN
RDEPSIND87	ann. depr. rate, nonres., ind.	e	decimal	BEA.UN
RDEPSMAP87	annual depreciate rate, nonres. str., non-mining excl., shifts.	e	decimal	BEA.UN
RDEPSOAF87	ann. depr. rate, nonres, other	e	decimal	BEA.UN
RDEPSUTL87	ann. depr. rate, nonres., utility	e	decimal	BEA.UN
RGDPNSTR	ratio of structures purchase, nondefense	e	percent	BEA.NIPA
RGPFDDUR	ratio of durable equip. purchase, defense	e	percent	BEA.NIPA
RGPFDSTR	ratio of structures purchase, defense	e	percent	BEA.NIPA
RGPFNDUR	ratio of durable equip purchase, nondefense	e	percent	BEA.NIPA
RGPNDUR	ratio of durable equip purchase, state and local	e	percent	BEA.NIPA
RGPNSTR	ratio of structures purchase, state and local	e	percent	BEA.NIPA
RPLCF1619EXO	labor force participation rate, female, 16–19	e	decimal	BLS.EE
RPLCF2024EXO	lb f. partic. r. female, 20–24	e	decimal	BLS.EE
RPLCF20AEXO	lb f. partic. r. female, 20 & over	e	decimal	BLS.EE
RPLCF2534EXO	lb f. partic. r. female, 25–34	e	decimal	BLS.EE
RPLCF3544EXO	lb f. partic. r. female, 35–44	e	decimal	BLS.EE
RPLCF4554EXO	lb f. partic. r. female, 45–54	e	decimal	BLS.EE
RPLCF5564EX	lb f. partic. r. female, 55–64	e	decimal	BLS.EE
RPLCF65AEXO	lb f. partic. r. female, 65 & over	e	decimal	BLS.EE
RPLCM1619EXO	lb f. partic. r. males, 16–19	e	decimal	BLS.EE

(*Continued*)

Table 5.2. (*Continued*)

Variable	Definition	T.	Unit	Source
RPLCM2024EXO	lb f. partic. r. males, 20–24	e	decimal	BLS.EE
RPLCM20AEXO	lb f. partic. r. males, 20 & over	e	decimal	BLS.EE
RPLCM2534EXO	lb f. partic. r. males, 25–34	e	decimal	BLS.EE
RPLCM3544EXO	lb f. partic. r. males, 35–44	e	decimal	BLS.EE
RPLCM4554EXO	lb f. partic. r. males, 45–54	e	decimal	BLS.EE
RPLCM5564EXO	lb f. partic. r. males, 55–64	e	decimal	BLS.EE
RPLCM65AEXO	lb f. partic. r. males, 65 & over	e	decimal	BLS.EE
RROW3M	interest rate, weighted average, for Eurodollars, 3-mon	e	percent	FRB.RT
RSCRAPAUTO	scrappage rate, auto	e		
RTECHCHG	rate of technical change	e		
RTXCF_STAT	corporate profit tax rate, federal, statutory maximum rate	e	percent	BEA.NIPA
RTXCN_EFF	corporate profit tax rate, state & local, effective rate	e	percent	BEA.NIPA
RTXPF_EFF	personal tax rate, federal, effective rate	e	percent	BEA.NIPA
RTXPN_EFF	personal tax rate, state & local, effective rate	e	percent	BEA.NIPA
RTXSE	contribution to social security, pct, paid by employers	e	percent	BEA.NIPA
RTXSSP	soc. sec. tax rate, employees	e	decimal	Statute
RUNCN	unemployment rate, civilian, full employment	e	percent	BLS.EE
SDUSCAR	statist. discrep. U.S. domestic auto sale, BEA vs. AUTO news	e	mill.	WEFA
SDUSCARIMP	statist. discrep., U.S. import auto sales, BEA vs. AUTO news	e	mill.	WEFA
SDUTRKLE3	statist. discrep., light domestic truck, BEA vs. AUTO news	e	mill.	WEFA
TDVRGN	state & local govt. dividends rec'ved.	e	bill. $	BEA.NIPA
TLEBLDGOTH	tax life, nonres., structures, buildings, other	e	years	WEFA
TLEIND	tax life, producers durable equipment, industrial equip.	e	years	WEFA
TLEINF	tax life, equipment, information processing	e	years	WEFA
TLEOAS	tax life, equipment, others	e	years	WEFA
TLETRN	tax life, equip, transportat.	e	years	WEFA

(*Continued*)

Table 5.2. (*Continued*)

Variable	Definition	T.	Unit	Source
TLSCOM	tax life, struc, commercial	e	years	WEFA
TLSIND	tax life, structure, industrial	e	years	WEFA
TLSMAP	tax life, str, mining excl., shafts, wells	e	years	WEFA
TLSOAF	tax life, structure, other	e	years	WEFA
TLSUTL	tax life, nonres., str. utilities	e	years	WEFA
TRFB	transfer payments, to foreigners (net), from business	e	bill. $	BEA.NIPA
TRFG	transfer pay. to foreig(net) govt.	e	bill. $	BEA.NIPA
TRFP	transfer pay. to for.(net), person	e	bill. $	BEA.NIPA
TRPGFHEA	transfer pay'ts, to persons, from govt., fed. health subsidies	e	bill. $	BEA.NIPA
TTREND	time trend	e		
TXIFOIL	govt. rev. windf. prof. t, fed	e	bill. $	BEA.NIPA
TXOSECOVR	soc. security tax, proport. of wage & salaried workers covered	e	bill. $	BEA.NIPA
VRFR	Housing, rental vacancy rate	e	percent	BOC.HS
WALDGF	wage accruals less disbursements, federal govt.	e	bill. $	BEA.NIPA
WALDGN	wage accruals less disbursements, state & local	e	bill. $	BEA.NIPA
WALDPRI	wage accruals less disbursements, private	e	bill. $	BEA.NIPA
WRHMNM	wage rate, statutory minimum	e	current $ $ per hour	BEA.NIPA
XTFADJ	govt. receipts, federal, difference, unified vs. NIPA	e	bill. $	BEA.NIPA
YBASSSP	income, maximum base, social security	e	bill. $	Statute
YCGN	Capital, grants received by the U.S. (net)	e	bill. $	BEA.NIPA
YF	proprietors income with IVA & CCADJ, farm	e	bill. $	BEA.NIPA

Chapter 6

Multiplier Analysis of Wharton Model

1. Introduction

It is customary for practical econometricians to expose the estimated model to a variety of simultaneous equation tests. The purpose of these tests is to see if the whole system can exhibit plausible responses to alternative monetary and fiscal policy shocks. Naturally, the so-called dynamic multiplier analysis must have been made with Mark 10 before making forecast and policy analysis. Unfortunately, however, no document has been available to us so far. Hence, in the following, the results based on Mark 9 model, instead of Mark 10, are summarized as a reference, because fortunately Prof. Klein himself with Prof. F. G. Adams left a detailed study of comparative performance of many econometric models in the United States [1]. This study relied on Mark 9. The names of 11 models chosen and their characteristics are shown in Table 6.1.

2. Some Characteristics of the Mark 9 Model

Its size is almost the same as Mark 10. It contains about 750 variables, of which 280 variables are stochastic, 130 variables are exogenous, and the remaining 340 are definitions in identities. It follows the post- or neo-Keynesian tradition and takes into consideration the important supply-side and financial influences in the economy. Short-run movements in output are, however, primarily determined by changes in aggregate demands. The components of aggregate demand are modeled from the bottom up by using the standard approach. Industry-specific I/O is applied, and output by each of one-digit industries is derived from

Table 6.1. 11 U.S. Econometric Models for Comparative Performance

Name	Model* Size	Remarks
BEA	195	Detailed fiscal sectors
DRI	354	Sectoral detail, long-run consistency
FAIR	30	Emphasizes optimization by agents
FRB	128	Emphasis on financial flows
IND	100	Business cycle model
LM&A	90	Neoclassical synthesis
MICH	86	Short-run, partial adjustment
St.L.	10	Emphasis on money
TAYLOR	20	Rational expectation model
WEFA	281	Ninth version of the Wharton model
SINAI	210	Considerable financial system

Note: *Shows the number of behavioral equations.

the components of final demand spending. It also features important linkages between the financial and real sectors. However, key fiscal policy variables, demographics, oil price, inflation, and growth in the rest of the world are exogenous. Dollar exchange rate is made endogenous as is in Mark 10.

3. Impacts on GNP of Changes in Policy and Exogenous Variables

Four types of multiplier analysis are presented here. The multipliers are based on the simulation results given in the Adams–Klein article previously quoted. Figures 6.1–6.5 are drawn by two editors S. Kinoshita and M. Yamada. They compare the results of WEFA (Wharton model) with those of DRI model and the average of 11 models surveyed and chosen in the model comparison project organized by L. R. Klein and F. G. Adams. The shocks in the studies here are the following four cases with two variations in the first case.

(i) *Spending shock*: It involves an increase in real defense spending by 1% of historical GNP for each period either without monetary accommodation (1A); namely, with M1 held at its base path, or the same shock with interest rates set at historical values (1B).

(1A): In the case of 1A, it is seen from Figure 6.1, the GNP multiplier records its peak of around 1.5 after a period of four

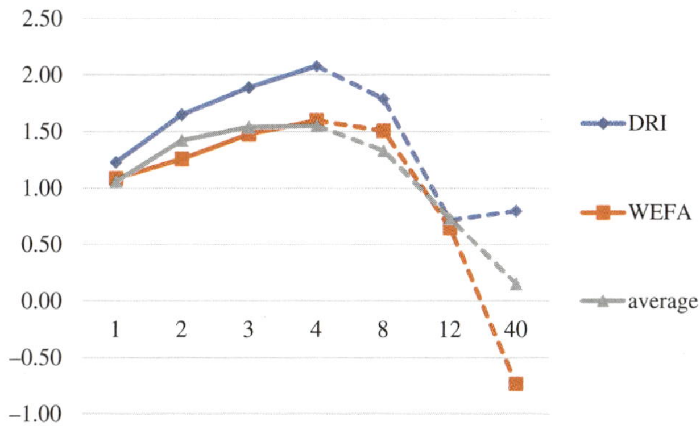

Figure 6.1. (1A) GNP Multiplier of Defense Increase (%)

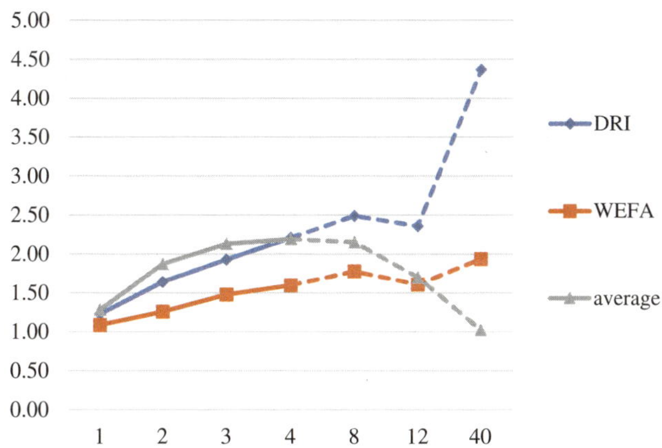

Figure 6.2. (1B) GNP Multiplier of Government Expenditure Increase (%)

quarters, and then drops to a very low or negative level for both the Mark 9 and the average of 11 models.

(1B): The same shock as in A, but with short-run interest rate held at its base path. In contrast, in the case of 1B with monetary accommodation to keep interest rate at the historical level, the multiplier of the Mark 9 shows an increasing trend until 40 quarters with a swing, and reach to around 2.0 in the long-run.

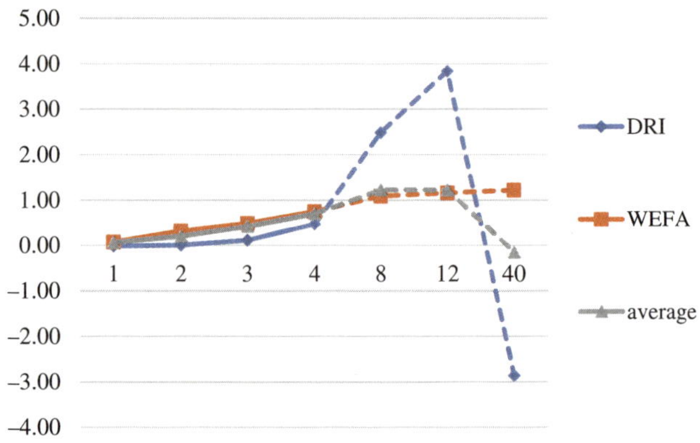

Figure 6.3. (2A) GNP Multiplier of Monetary Shock

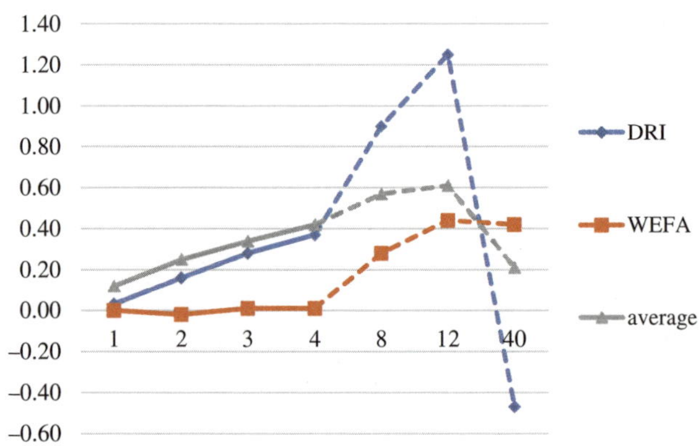

Figure 6.4. (3A) GNP Multiplier of Supply Shock

(ii) *Monetary shock* — (2A): M1 is increased by the amounts 0.14, 0.73, 1.88, and 2.8% in the first four quarters, respectively. From the fifth quarter onwards, M1 is 3% above the base path.

Money supply simulation (2A) shows a gradual upward movement, an impact of around 1.1% of GNP, and stabilizes after 12 quarters. On the other hand, the average of 11 models follows the same path with Mark 9 until 12 quarters, but afterward decreases to almost zero.

(iii) *Supply shock* — (3A): The world oil price is lowered by 20% below the base path. There are no other exogenous changes.

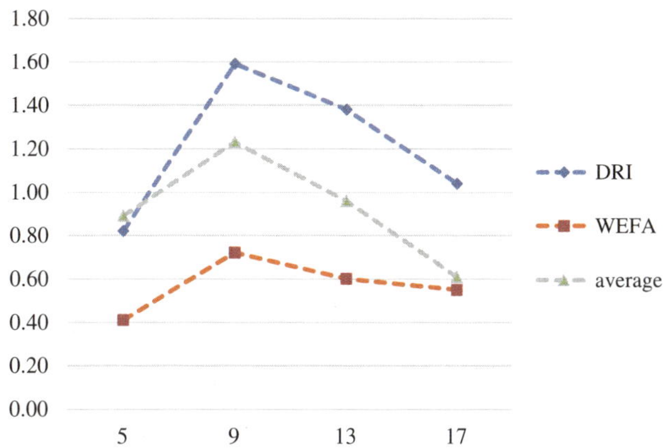

Figure 6.5. (4A) GNP Multiplier of Dollar Depreciation

The supply-side simulation (3A) involves a downward movement in costs. A reduction of world oil price by 20% yields a maximum increase of GNP of 0.54% in the long run. The impact on GNP of Mark 9 is smaller by 0.1%–0.3% than that of the average of 11 models until 12 quarters.

(iv) *External shock* — (4A): Exchange rate of dollar is depreciated by 10% from the baseline with pass-through as specified in the model.

The exchange rate simulation (4A) has a positive impact on GNP, through increased real exports minus decreased real imports. The positive impact peaks around 0.72% of GNP in the second year and then tends to diminish afterward. Although the multipliers among the three models show similar trend pattern Mark 9 is the smallest among them.[1]

[1]The simulation periods for (1A), (1B), (2A), and (3A) are 40 quarters from 1975.1 to 1984.4. We can obtain seven simulated values for 75.1, 75.2, 75.3, 75.4, 76.4, 77.4, and 84.4 in the appendix tables of the original Adams–Klein paper. The numbers, 1, 2, 3, 4, 8, 12, and 40 on the horizontal access in Figs. 6.1–6.4 show the corresponding periods starting at 1. The simulation periods for (4A) are 20 quarters from 1983.1 to 1987.4. In this case, we obtain only four values for 84.1, 85.1, 86.1, and 87.1. We set 5, 9, 13, and 17 for the corresponding periods in Fig. 6.5. For each graph, the solid lines connect the continuous periods, and the broken lines connect the discontinuous periods. Different interpretation must be applied to each portion of the curves.

Reference

[1] Adams, F. G. and L. R. Klein (1991). Performance of Quarterly Econometric Models of the United States: A New Round of Model Comparisons, in L.R. Klein (eds.) *Comparative Performance of U.S. Econometric Models*. Oxford University Press, New York.

Appendices

Later Versions of WEFA Model and Some Observations on Forecasting*

This introduction and Appendices A and B briefly tells the story of the model and its use for forecasting after Mark 10. I came to WEFA in 1993 and left in 1999. In Appendix A, I have reproduced my essay that explained how I came to understand and support Dr. Klein's structural approach in econometric modeling. This essay was prepared for WEFA's 30th anniversary, which occurred about one year after I started working at the company. My graduate training in econometrics was very far from Dr. Klein's works. I was trained in the 1980s at the height of the profession's interest in rational expectations. During the period, the major insight seemed to be a policy ineffectiveness proposition. That approach did not value the Klein type of model. Not surprisingly, I experienced some cognitive dissonance as I learned to use and appreciate the model, and the essay is a defense of the models and forecasting system developed by Dr. Klein.

This book's version is a later version of Mark 10. Many participating economists and students contributed to the model during the 1980s and 1990s. Thus, Mark 10 not only reflected Professor Klein's earlier models but also various contributions of modelers like Robert Westcott, Alan Shaw, Kurt Karl, B. Nariman, and M. Papaioannou, among others.

*The author of this introduction and Appendix A is Daniel Bachman. He is PhD (Brown U) in 1987, and now Senior Manager for US Economics at Deloitte Services, LP (United States). Earlier, he served as the Director of the Center for Forecasting and Modeling at IHS and previously (93–99) a key member of the forecasting team at WEFA. He worked at the US Department of Commerce when he represented it in the Troika forecasting committee.

Appendix B reproduces a previously published article that describes how the Mark 11 version of the WEFA model was adapted for the changes in National Income and Product Accounts (NIPA) introduced by BEA in 1996, known as "chain-weighting."

In 1996, the BEA adopted a new method of calculating aggregate prices and quantities in the National Accounts. This was a direct result of challenges raised by the growing importance of the information technology sector and the experience of falling prices in that sector. This method of "chain-weighting" required a complete respecification of many of the NIPA identities in the model. The immediate problem for modelers was that identities for both prices and aggregate quantities were no longer additive. In fact, the initial method BEA adopted was quite complex, involved average annual weights for historical periods and a "tail" of fixed weights for the most recent quarters. It was impossible to precisely follow BEA's methods in the model. The last essay in this chapter describes how our modeling team solved this problem.

In addition to respecifying the identities, I as team leader chose to adopt error correction model (ECM) techniques in place of polynomial lags for estimating most of the equations. Here, I followed what my training taught me; namely, polynomial lag methods were "arbitrary" and ECMs are better in handling the problems presented by unit roots and cointegration. As of now, major commercial models of the US and global economy like the Fed's FRB/US[1] use versions of ECM techniques for estimation.

[1]After the release of Mark 11, an e-mail from a members of the Fed evaluation team noted that the model's performance appeared to be much "improved". I would interpret it now to mean that the model's simulation properties matched with the prior beliefs of the Fed staff more closely than Mark 10's simulation properties.

A. What Economic Forecasters Really Do*

1 Introduction

In my first months at WEFA, I spent some time thinking about the difference between my academic training and my job. In 1993, WEFA celebrated its 30th anniversary with an academic conference. I presented the following paper.

One of the most confusing features of econometric forecasting is the gap between how outsiders, especially academic economists, view forecasting, and how it is actually done. Econometric forecasting uses tools of statistics and engineering extensively. Forecasters regularly employ apparatus including large models of the economy, advanced statistical techniques and lots of numbers. We appear to be engaged in a statistical exercise with a "scientific" and objective procedure. This view is misleading. Econometric forecasters use judgment as well as engineering techniques. Although this may appear unscientific, we can strongly argue for combining our judgment with models. Actual forecasting practice is not only efficient, it sheds light on some important problems in economic forecasting, and how they might be solved.

2 The Lucas Critique

Robert Lucas [1976] gave a typical view of how forecasting should proceed, and contrasted it with the "dirty" method actually used. Lucas describes econometric forecasting as an entirely statistical exercise: "For purposes

*It has never been published but available on the Web and cited a few times. It provides a support for Klein's works from an unusual viewpoint. I was told afterwards that Professor Klein liked the paper.

of ex ante forecasting, or the unconditional prediction of the vector y_{t+1}, y_{t+2} given observation of y_s and x_s, $s \leq t$, the estimated reduced form, together with a vector autoregression of x_t, the exogenous variables is sufficient." This is simply an exercise in a sophisticated extrapolation, requiring no understanding of the structural parameters, that is, the *economics* of the model [Lucas and Sargent, page 298].

Experienced economic forecasters may wonder just what Lucas and Sargent are talking about. The processes of determining exogenous variables alone are far more complex than estimating a vector autoregression. Lucas and Sargent later dismiss the judgmental elements of forecasting: "the model builders themselves routinely employ an elaborate system of addfactors in forecasting, in an attempt to offset the continuing drift of the model away from the actual series" [page 303].

This is typical of the economic outsider's view of addfactors, the process by which we build judgment into our model-based forecasts. It is also misleading. The addfactors are used in a variety of ways, and the problem of "drift" is relatively minor in this regard. By characterizing forecasting in purely engineering terms, Lucas and Sargent ignored the extent to which successful forecasting requires interaction between a mathematical model and the reasoned judgment of an educated observer. This second element in the mix, the ability of an individual to assimilate information more efficiently than a model, is vital to understanding what forecasters actually do.

3 Not All Economic Behavior Can be Measured

In his famous critique of econometric models, Lucas proposed changing the direction of econometrics to estimate the underlying "structural" parameters of the economic agents involved. The search for these structures (closely related to the search for microfoundations of macroeconomics) has been an important element in rational expectations research since the late 1970s. If we could discover these invariant parameters, we could presumably forecast without the use of the addfactors and re-estimation that Lucas condemned so strongly.

In the last 15 years, a large number of researchers have attempted to carry out Lucas' suggested strategy. The result has been the voluminous literature on "real business cycles" with many clever attempts to surmount a basic problem not noted in the rational expectations literature. Lucas essentially suggested that we need to estimate not reduced form price and quantity equations, but the parameters of the underlying functions. One line of research following Lucas typically begins by postulating a specific utility function, chosen generally for ease of computation. The research immediately becomes unconvincing because the hypothesis tests in the paper are always joint tests of the model and the specific form of the utility function.

In this, the failure of the real business cycle approach to yield usable forecasting models reflects a deep error about economic behavior and analysis. The fundamental behavior of economic actors, the structural parameters Lucas believes matter, is determined in a non-numerical setting. We simply don't have, and could never obtain, a true estimate of a representative utility function. The underlying beliefs that shape behavior, including beliefs about monetary policy, political risk, *etc.* that cannot be measured or described numerically. An important part of economic behavior consists of the mapping of these non-numerical beliefs and values to the numerical world of prices and quantities. No statistical technique can simulate, imitate, or estimate this mapping.

4 How Forecasting Solves the Mapping Problem

Model-based forecasting continues to be useful to our clients, and profitable for us, because current forecasting methodology recognizes the existence of this mapping problem. We use models and numbers in conjunction with our judgment to solve the mapping problem that has defeated academic economists. Addfactors allow us to alter model-based forecasts to allow for the use of judgment. To a surprising degree, it is this judgment, as much as the forecast itself, that we sell to our clients.

The WEFA group provides its clients with a remarkable document called *WEFA Group Forecasting Methodology*. The report describes the steps involved in producing our short-term forecast. Its emphasis is not on solving models, but rather on meetings and the back-and-forth process by which WEFA economists agree on a forecast. It includes sections on "What Happens if Disagreement About the Forecast Arises?" and "What is the Client's Role?", topics which are hardly obvious according to the Lucas and Sargent description. In their world, the forecast is a simple extrapolation about which there can be no disagreement, and the client, or user of the forecast, is ignored. Even a cursory reading of this document indicates clearly that the stress is on the people, not the model.

Rather than selling a model, WEFA sells the judgment and experience of its staff, as the *conclusion* states:

"To produce the highest quality set of forecasts, the WEFA Group professionals must perform like members of an orchestra, staying within the discipline of the common score while making full use of their individual expertise. The combination of seasoned forecasters and a process which has been continually refined during the past 20 years is a tough combination to beat."

An orchestra is not what most academic economists have in mind when thinking about forecasting. But this is what businesses look for when shopping for economic forecasts: not an assurance that we can invert matrices, but that we have a process (including meetings, discussions, and "seasoned forecasters") which is successful. Neither our clients nor our marketing staff would recognize Lucas' description of forecasting, and for good reason. pure engineering-based models of necessity embody less information than the combination of models and judgment that we actually use.

5 Kurt Karl's Two Rules of Forecasting

As an example of how forecasting actually works, I would like to introduce two rules of practical forecasting. Kurt Karl with many years' experience in forecasting for WEFA has explained these to me as I was learning how to run a WEFA forecast. The rules are driven by client needs rather than econometric methodology and indicate some important features of the actual methodology economic forecasters use.

#1: *Don't change the outlook radically in any one month.* Large changes in GDP forecasts drive clients crazy, so we try to avoid them. If we want to change our views, we do it gradually, often by no more than 0.2–0.3 percentage points of GDP each month. One reason clients hate large changes is because their corporate planning mechanisms can't assimilate them. Radical changes are unpopular with our clients for another reason, however. There is enough noise in high-frequency data that almost no announcement or set of announcements in any given month provides enough real information to really change a forecast radically. If a mathematical model changes the outlook radically from one or two bits of data, business economists correctly suspect the model, and not their intuition. This rule tends to make forecasting turning points more difficult. It warns, however, that monthly data can be misleading and require confirmation of new trends from many different data sources before changing our forecast.

#2: *Don't forecast radical changes in GDP growth from one quarter to another*. Early in our forecast we often find radical changes in GDP growth rates because of Auto Service assumptions about cars, or Regional Service assumptions about housing starts. Our clients, however, do not believe that we can forecast which quarter will be 5% and which will be 1% — and they are right. We, therefore, attempt to forecast a steady growth rate consistent with the annual rates we aim for. Clients don't expect or want us to attempt to determine the exact quarterly pattern of growth. What they want to know is the average growth rate for the economy over the next few years. They won't believe that we can forecast quarterly growth rates accurately, and probably we shouldn't.

These are client-generated rules and seem to reflect a profound understanding of what we do and don't know about the economy. The clients want our forecast of the underlying growth rate (which we do know something about), and they know that we are unlikely to learn a great deal from one month's data.

These rules suggest how important our judgment is. Left to its own devices, the model will not generate smooth growth patterns, and may well give radically different answers each month, as data are revised. Our confidence in these changes is low, so we eliminate them. Our forecast then reflects our basic, overall view of the economy, which is what our clients want to know and pay us for.

6 How Judgment Enters the Forecast

Judgment is, therefore, vital to the forecasting process. Judgment is necessary to create forecasts that reflect all the information at hand, including information that can't be easily summarized numerically, and judgment is necessary to provide forecasts that reflect clients' needs for a clear view of the economic future. We impose our judgment on the model by adjusting the value of any variable about which we have more confidence in our own ideas than the model results. The deviation from the model-predicted value is the addfactor, a source of some embarrassment among economic forecasters. In fact, addfactors are not only an embarrassment, they are an important link in the forecasting process, and provide an important solution to the Lucas critique. Lucas's description of the use of addfactors shows a typical misunderstanding of how and why we make these adjustments:

"Finally and most suggestively, the practice of using patterns in recent residuals is to revise intercept estimates for forecasting purposes. For example, if a "run of positive residuals (predicted less actual) arises in an equation in recent periods, one revises the estimated intercept downward by their average amount." [1976, p. 23]. Lucas is apparently unaware of the description of forecast adjustment in Klein's [1970] review of forecasting methodology.

Klein discusses two reasons for adjustment of forecast values: "first, the existence of non-random residuals (as described by Lucas)" and, second, "Other structural changes for known legislative or institutional reasons." [p. 50]. Klein goes on to note that "In addition there are 'inside information' and 'latest news'." Klein discusses the method used to include this information in some detail. "After the preparation of preliminary predictions from the most recently adjusted Wharton-EFU Model, there is a discussion of the assumptions and properties of the prediction with business and government specialists. A priori information on impending labor disputes, hedge purchasing, production bottlenecks, major economic decisions and similar phenomena are then suggested for further modification of parameter or residual values, and a revised forecast is prepared." [pp. 50–51].

Addfactors are, therefore, much more than simple adjustments for the tendency of equation-based predictions to "drift" off over time. If this were the case, we would now simply reestimate the model every month, an operation possible with modern computers. Even the reestimated model would require addfactors, however, because we simply know more than can be expressed mathematically or contained in the equations. The forecaster's judgment counts, too.

Addfactors have a great virtue which is ignored both within and outside of the business economics community. We publish the addfactors in our monthly book and provide a record of where the forecasting team's judgment overrode the model. We not only use our judgment, we actually put it on record. Carl Christ [1993, p. 79] quoted Paul Samuelson as saying that econometric forecasts are a black box inside of which we find only Larry Klein. But it's not a black box! Klein's judgments, and ours, are published for the world to see. That students of forecasting do not take addfactors seriously is sad. It suggests that a fascination with the engineering model of forecasting has blinded academic researchers to the most interesting and exciting part of the forecasting process.

Why, 15 years after the Lucas critique was published, do economic forecasting firms continue to use large-scale macroeconometric models? Addfactors provide the clue. Large-scale econometric models are employed not to complete the forecast, but to provide the discipline necessary in light of the complicated relationships involved in the real economy. The model handles those that can be statistically or mathematically modeled for us. But, as I mentioned earlier, many key relationships are mappings from the non-numerate to the numerate domain: the election of new president changes consumers' views of their permanent income, for example. These relationships cannot be modeled statistically, but they are vital for the economic outlook. Economic forecasters mimic the mapping from non-numerate to numerate domain by using addfactors when necessary.

Addfactors are a simple, convenient, and reliable solution to the problem of the Lucas critique. Unlike the research agenda Lucas suggested, they are not sterile. In fact, they are significantly more convincing to non-economists precisely because non-economists understand this "mapping problem". Purely mathematical models of any type will never appear as appealing to non-economists as the current process. Even if Lucas and Sargent could estimate a correct model with deep structural parameters, they couldn't sell it! Economic actors know that there is more to analyzing the economy than doing math. They are unlikely to ever be convinced that econometric methodology, useful though it may be, can substitute for reasoned judgment.

7 Economic Forecasting is Story-telling, not Engineering

The array of statistical modeling techniques has fooled some people into believing that forecasting the economy should be a statistical exercise which could, in principle, be automated and left to computers and research assistants. The new numbers could then be transmitted automatically every month to our clients. Economic analysis is not, at its heart, similar to engineering or mathematics. It is about telling our clients stories which help them understand the business environment in which they operate. The numbers tell an important part of the story, but it is not surprising that mathematical techniques sometimes fail, and that we must use other forms of knowledge to supplement econometric model building.

The idea that economics should use storytelling in concert with our other tools has recently been discussed by Donald McCloskey [1985, 1990]. Forecasting practice supports the view that economic analysis consists of more than logic and facts. We deliver to our clients a coherent story of where the economy will go using the best economic tools available. We do so while supplying sufficient detail that our clients can determine the moral of our story for their industry or company.

Econometric models insure that each month's installment fits the same parameters and has the same characters as the previous month's story. Our model also determines when we need to bring our judgment to play, and forces us to consider all of the consequences of our opinions. Thus, when our forecast team decides that we want a story of a 3% growth rate next year, and the model doesn't support it, I bring the problem back to the team. We then try to think more carefully about the story's details: do we want more growth in exports, or investment or consumption? Why are we overriding the model? The model creates a framework in which to operate, forcing us to state our judgment explicitly.

8 Conclusion: Constrained Storytelling Remains Valuable

The Lucas Critique was a very potent criticism of forecasting with macroeconometric models. Lucas and Sargent's wild claims about the uselessness of econometric forecasting and simulation are clearly wrong, however. The continued use of macroeconometric models itself contradicts their view. We use these models because, when used correctly, they are effective tools for understanding how the economy works. Lucas and Sargent were unable or unwilling to understand how forecasters actually use the models, insisting on substituting their own methodology for the one described by Larry Klein in his 1970 essay. Economists and business planners continue to find our combination of model and judgment of great value in understanding and interpreting the world in which we live.

References

[1] WEFA (1992). *The WEFA Group Forecasting Methodology*, Bala Cynwyd, Pennsylvania (1992).

[2] Christ, C. F. (1993). Assessing applied econometric results, *Federal Reserve Bank of St. Louis Review* **75**(2), pp. 71–94.

[3] Klein, L. (1971). *An Essay on the Theory of Economic Prediction*. Chicago: Markham Publishing Co.

[4] Lucas, R. E. (1980). Methods and problems in business cycle theory, *Journal of Money Credit and Banking* **12**(2), pp. 696–713.

[5] Lucas, R. E. and T. Sargent (1978). After the Phillips Curve, in *Rational Expectations and Econometric Practice*, (ed.) Robert E. Lucas and Thomas Sargent. Minneapolis, University of Minnesota Press.

[6] Lucas, R. E. (1976). Econometric Policy Evaluation: A Critique, in *The Phillips Curve and Labor Markets*, in Karl Brunner and Alan Meltzer (ed.) Carnegie-Rochester Conference Series on Public Policy, Vol. 1. Amsterdam: North Holland.

[7] Mankiw, N. G. (1990). A quick refresher course in macroeconomics, *Journal of Economic Literature* **28**(4), pp. 1645–1660.

[8] McCloskey, D. (1990). *If You're So Smart: The Narrative of Economic Expertise*. Chicago: University of Chicago Press.

[9] McCloskey, D. (1985). *The Rhetoric of Economics*. Madison: University of Wisconsin Press.

B. The WEFA: Macro Model with Chain-Weighted GDP*

Abstract

We describe the impact of the new GDP methodology on WEFA's Quarterly model. First we briefly describe WEFA's Mark 11 Quarterly model and its uses, which create certain restrictions on the model specification. We then discuss the question of the possible impact of the new methodology on estimated elasticities and model multipliers. Since we adopted a new econometric methodology with the new model, the elasticities cannot be usefully compared. Finally, we describe our solution to the "adding up" problem created by BEA's complex Fisher Index number approximation. The new WEFA model uses a chained Laysperes index formula to approximate BEA's complete formula.

1 Introduction

In 1996 the BEA introduced a number of changes into the methodology for calculating the National Income and Product Accounts (NIPAs). The NIPAs have traditionally been the core of large-scale macroeconometric models used by industry and government for economic forecasting and analysis. WEFA is the oldest company to use this methodology in commercial applications, and, like other industry and government forecasters, was forced to respecify much of our model. We found little to suggest that the new data provide a substantially different view of the past, or that the new data would force us to rethink our view of the multipliers in our model. In our view, the major problem is that the components of GDP do not add up easily. Since our model has a very detailed breakdown of GDP, and since we use the model for long-term

*The authors of the original article of this section, quoted in Foreword, are D. Bachman, Peter Jaquette, Kurt Karl and Pasquale Rocco; all staffs of WEFA Inc then. (Baldwin Tower, Eddy stone PA 19022) At present, Peter Jacquette: Senior Director, Global Oil at PIRA Energy Group Pasquale; Kurt Karl Chief Economist, Swiss re; Pasquale Rocco: Director of Research at TWIN Capital Management, Inc.

forecasting and analysis, we were forced to adopt an approximation of BEA's complex methodology for adding up GDP components. No approximation can solve all of the problems BEA has created with the new methodology. Our approximation is a chained Laspeyeres index, which is a useful compromise between short-run and long-run accuracy.

2 The Quarterly Model

WEFA's Quarterly model has changed substantially from the early version described by Vijaya Duggal, Lawrence Klein, and Michael McCarthy [1, 2]. The current version of the model uses many of the advances in macroeconomics that have occurred over the past thirty years. The model includes a detailed monetary sector, and has monetarist properties in the medium term. It also includes a long-run supply constraint in the form of a potential GDP equation. Expectations are explicitly modeled using survey data, and expected inflation appears in both labor cost and capital cost equations.

The model includes the following sectors (see Appendix and its subsequent subsections for details):

- Aggregate demand, by detailed category
- Price sector, including an expectations-augmented Phillips curve
- Aggregate supply
- Many specialized sectors such as a detailed auto sales
- Production sector, a housing sector,
- Producer price sector.

3 Estimation Techniques

As is usual for large-scale macroeconometric models, we use single equation techniques to estimate most equations. In our experience, simultaneous estimation does not add sufficient benefit to justify the cost and complexity added to the process. MARK 11 differs from its predecessors in making extensive use of error correction models (ECM). These functional forms are used in most final demand equations in place of the traditional Almon lags. Many other key equations are also specified using these techniques.

Error correction models assume that two series move, or "drift" together. Although the series are not "mean reverting" a linear combination of the two series is "mean reverting". (A series is said to be mean reverting if the mean of one subset of the series is the same as the mean in a different subset). This suggests that, when one series is shocked, or moves in such a way that the error from the linear combination is large, the other series will move to preserve the combination. When two series drift together in this way, they are said to be cointegrated. In general, we did not carry out formal cointegration tests in building the model. Instead, we assumed that one equation — the "cointegration equation" — described the long-run relationship. For example, consumer spending in each category was assumed to depend, in the long run, on the level of income and the relative price of that consumer category. This yields the long-run equation below (Eq. (1)):

$$Y_t = \beta_0 + \beta_1 X_{1t} + \beta_2 X_{2t} + \varepsilon_t \tag{1}$$

where Y is the dependent variable, the X's are the independent variables, and ε is the error or deviation from the long-run in period t. The variables are typically in log terms. We then estimated a full equation by including the deviation in an equation in percent changes (log differences), as shown in Eq. 2.

$$\begin{aligned}\%\Delta Y_t = \alpha_0 + \alpha_1 \%\Delta Y_{t-1} + \alpha_2 \%\Delta X_{1t} \\ + \alpha_3 \%\Delta X_{2t} + \alpha_4 \varepsilon_{t-1} + \eta_t\end{aligned} \tag{2}$$

The elasticities can now be easily identified. The β terms are the long-run elasticities of the respective variables, and the terms α_1, α_2, and α_3 are the short-run elasticities. α_4 is the speed of adjustment parameter to deviations from the long-term trend (ε). It must be between zero and negative one if the equation is stable (returns to the long-run equilibrium), and the variable adjusts more quickly, the closer is this parameter to -1. We normally substitute $\mathrm{Y}_{\mathrm{t}-1} - \beta_0 - \beta_1 \mathrm{X}_{\mathrm{t}-1} - \beta_2 \mathrm{X}_{\mathrm{t}-2}$ for the $\varepsilon_{\mathrm{t}-1}$ term.

As an example, Table 1 shows the equation for real exports of consumer goods less automobiles (EXCONXMVP92). The bold-faced part of the equation is the long-run relationship. Relative prices have a long-run elasticity of -1.35, and foreign GDP has an elasticity of 2.1. The short-run elasticities for prices and foreign GDP are, respectively, 0.45 and 2.58.

Table 1. Estimated Equation for Exports of Consumer Goods *less* Automobiles

dlog(exconxmvp92)=
0.02872 * dlog(exconxmvp92)[−1]
−0.10076 * [log(exconxmvp92.1)
−(−1.3513)*log(pdcexconxmvp.1*rexmor18.1/ppirow18.1)
−(2.0975)*log(gdp18w92.1)
−(0.0291)
+ 2.58291 * dlog(gdp18w92)
− 0.44851 * dlog(pdcexconxmvp*rexmor18/ppirow18)
− 0.00048

Notes: EXCONXMVP92 is real exports of consumer goods less automobiles: PDCEXCONXMVP is the chained price index for exports of consumer goods less automobiles: REXMOR18 is the Morgan Guaranty Trade-Weighted exchange rate: GDP18W92 is a trade-weighted foreign GDP measure: and PPIROW is the rest of world PPI used to construct the Morgan Guaranty exchange rate.

4 Simulation Characteristics

The U.S. Economic Model has Keynesian characteristics in the short run (0 to 2 years), monetarist characteristics in the medium run (5 to 10 years) and neoclassical growth properties in the long run (15+ years).

4.1A Short-Run Keynesian characteristics:

An IS-LM framework dominates short-run behavior. Consumption depends on permanent income less health care transfers, but can be affected in the short run by consumer confidence as well. The investment equations include both accelerator and cost-of-capital components. Exports and imports depend on world and U.S. demand and relative prices, including the exchange rate. Government purchases are generally exogenous in the model.

4.2B Medium-Run Monetarist Characteristics:

Wage demands are determined through an expectations-augmented wage equation of the Lucas type. Unemployment relative to the exogenous natural rate affects real wage inflation (deflating by a measure of inflationary expectations). As a result, a positive aggregate demand shock will push up wages. Employment then falls back toward the full employment level, but at a permanently higher level of inflation.

4.3C Long-Run Neoclassical Growth Characteristics:

Output is constrained through the price sector to grow at the combined rate of labor, productivity, and an exogenous technical change parameter. If it grows too fast, capacity utilization rises, and inflation accelerates, reducing demand and growth.

WEFA's model was originally developed for forecasting. Although this remains one of its main purposes, it has also proven to have great value as the core of a set of detailed models of the economy. The models allow users to analyze the impact of a given macroeconomic shock on different industries and regions. The ability to carry out risk analysis in this manner has proven very valuable to those interested in the differential impacts of shocks, and especially for financial institutions, who can use the set of integrated models to judge the vulnerability of a given portfolio to macroeconomic events.

There are three separate model systems that must be used to obtain such results. First, the core macroeconomic model (the model under discussion in this paper) creates the basic simulation of the overall economy. Second, the impact on the elements of final demand is translated into impact by industry and employment by industry via an input-output based industry model. Finally, the impact by industry determines (through the differential importance of industries in regional economies) regional impacts through a linked set of state and metro area models.

An important feature of this system is the need for considerable detail at the final demand level in the core model. By building up GDP from detailed categories of final demand, we are in a better position to translate the GDP impact into industry impacts. Section 7 shows the substantial level of detail in the core model. Because of the importance of this use of the model, we needed to maintain the current level of complexity in the model, despite the "adding-up" problem described below.

5 BEA's new GDP methodology

BEA's new methodology has been documented elsewhere (see Alan Young [5], and J. Steven Landefeld and Robert Parker [3] for a detailed discussion of the new methodology). The Bureau adopted a number of important changes in the 1992 benchmark revision. These include:

a) dividing government purchases into investment and consumption components, and adding an estimate of public capital consumption to the NIPAs.
b) new method of depreciation for the capital stocks.
c) the new method of chain-weighting to obtain GDP aggregate quan tity and price measures.

The last change was the most important and controversial change, and has had the biggest impact on model building and forecasting. We will therefore concentrate on the issues raised by the new method of chain weighting to calculate real GDP and the GDP deflator.

5.1 Data changes

Each benchmark revision has created a changed set of data for judging economic history (although one of the purposes of the new methodology is to reduce the changes in historical data from adopting a new base year). This revision was no exception, and some observers believe that the new methodology might have a larger impact on our historical view of the economy.

Our analysis does not suggest that the new data tells us anything substantially different about the past business cycles. The short-run story of the economy is not substantially changed. The long-run view, however, may be somewhat different, particularly in the past ten years. The following comparison uses the old 1987 fixed-weighted data and the new 1992 chain-weighted data.

Short-run changes in GDP are not very different using the two measures over the period 1960–1995. In only 25 of 143 quarters (from 1960Q1 to 1995Q3) is the difference between the percentage change in a given quarter greater than 0.3 percentage points. The new data show the same high and low points in recessions (See Michael R. Pakko [4] for a detailed discussion of this issue).

The implications for long-run growth measures are different, however. Table 2 compares average growth rates by decade for GDP and its components. For most of the decades GDP growth is slightly higher, but the difference is not great. In the period 1990 to 1995 GDP growth is definitely lower, as expected since the fixed-weighted methodology

Table 2. Average Growth Rates for Real Quarterly GDP and Components

	1950–59	1960–69	1970–79	1980–89	1990–95*
GDP					
New	4.4	4.3	3.3	2.8	1.9
Old	4.2	4.1	3.0	2.5	2.4
Cons. Expenditure					
New	3.8	4.4	3.5	3.1	2.1
Old	3.7	4.2	3.3	2.8	2.4
Fixed Investment					
New	4.7	5.4	5.4	2.3	3.1
Old	4.6	4.6	5.0	1.9	5.8
Exports					
New	6.0	10.5	9.1	5.8	7.6
Old	6.0	10.3	8.5	5.1	7.7
Imports					
New	10.2	9.2	6.3	6.8	7.1
Old	11.1	9.0	6.2	6.9	8.2
Gov't Purchases					
New	7.1	3.7	0.7	2.9	0.4
Old	6.7	3.9	0.2	2.8	0.4

exaggerated growth beyond the old base year. The only components to show important differences are fixed investment, because of the importance of computers in this category, and imports. Lower imports in the 1990s probably reflect the increasing importance of increasingly cheaper computer equipment imports. In both the investment and computer cases, the rising nominal share of computer equipment combined with falling prices created a relatively large distortion in the fixed-weighted data, which the chain-weighted data largely corrects.

The numbers shown here are not large enough to change our view of long-run historical productivity growth in the United States, or, at first glance, to strongly affect any other knowledge we have of how the economy operates in the long run. Most of the changes are important mainly for our view of what happened over the past five or ten years.

5.2 Elasticity changes

One of the important and interesting questions that often arises is whether the new data affected our estimates of various elasticities in the model. Unfortunately, we cannot answer this question directly because we changed our estimation techniques in Mark 11 to use many more of the error correction models described above. Early experiments with our older Almon-lag structure did not reveal any major differences in the multipliers or simulation characteristics of the model, so we are inclined to believe that the revised data would have little affect on most individual elasticities. Only those areas (primarily in investment of information processing equipment, for examples) where the new methodology had a direct impact would be likely to see any changes in elasticities.

5.3 The adding-up problem

The major problem we faced with the new data was the technical question of how to define identities in the model. Additive identities have traditionally been important in this model because they track the traditional C+I+G framework for macroeconomics taught in the US, and which our clients expect to see in their analysis. Prior to the revision, we simply estimated equations for individual components of real GDP and added them up to get total real GDP. The new methodology does not allow this, as the real components do not add up to the real total. This issue was the most contentious in the aftermath of the publication of the new methodology. (See the comments of Evelina Tainer in the NABE news of November 1995, p. 29 for an example of how a working business economist approached the revision). The remainder of this paper will concentrate on our solution to this specific modeling problem.)

Because of the complexity of BEA's methodology, forecasters can no longer expect to mimic BEA precisely in building up real GDP from its components. All models will be forced to approximate, in some form, the annual-weighted Fisher Ideal chained numbers. Any choice will require a tradeoff between accuracy and simplicity. For example, the simplest method is to simply add the components and ignore the residual or forecast it separately. For short-term forecasting this may work well, but for long-term forecasting, it is likely to be inaccurate. It is precisely in comparisons of GDP levels and in growth measures of long periods of time that the new methodology is most valuable, because nominal shares and relative prices will change by large amounts over such periods. Thus, either the forecasted residual will become unacceptably large in the long-run forecast, or the forecast error risks being very large, if the components are simply added together. WEFA's model approximates the

BEA methodology with a chained Laspeyeres calculation. Real GDP is built up from components according to Eq. 3 below:

$$\Delta\% Y92_t = \frac{X_{1,t-1}}{Y_{t-1}} \times \Delta\% X_1 92_t + \frac{X_{2,t-1}}{Y_{t-1}} \times \Delta\% X_2 92_t \qquad (3)$$

where Y is the aggregate measure (here with two components, X_1 and X_2), 92 indicates a real (chained) 1992 dollar value, and Δ% indicates percentage change (calculated by log differences). The current real percentage change in Y is therefore a weighted average of the percentage change of the components, where the weights are the previous period's nominal shares of the total. We add a statistical discrepancy to the equation to correct for the approximation over history. This discrepancy will always be set to zero during the forecast period. Thus, the final form for the identity that determines real fixed business investment (IP92) from its components, equipment investment (IPE92) and structures investment (IPS92) is illustrated in Eq. 4:

$$\begin{aligned} IP92_t = {} & \exp\left(\Delta\% IPS92 \times \frac{IPS_{t-1}}{IP_{t-1}} + \Delta\% IPE92 \frac{IPE_{t-1}}{IP_{t-1}}\right) \\ & \times IP92_{t-1} + SDIP92_t \qquad (4) \end{aligned}$$

Note that the statistical discrepancies have no relationship to the published "residuals" in the NIPA table. We can, and do, publish forecasts of these residuals, but only by simply calculating them after the forecast. The published residual may be non-zero even when the forecast values of the discrepancies are all set to zero. An additional set of statistical discrepancies exists for the nominal values of the lowest level of detail forecast. In each case, the formula, (Eq. 5 below),

$$\text{Nominal} = \frac{\text{Price} \times \text{Real}}{100} \qquad (5)$$

holds only approximately. (If BEA used pure Fisher index calculations, the identity would hold exactly.) A set of residuals therefore exists for the equations that bridge from the real to the nominal level of the detail forecasted in the model. These discrepancies are set equal to the latest value over the entire forecast period to avoid leap-off problems.

One additional set of approximations is required to complete the set of identities. Since the nominal detail must add to the nominal aggregates in the usual manner, the model will produce forecasts of implicit aggregate deflators by simple division. However, these deflators will not be exactly equal to the actual chain-weighted deflators during history for the reasons mentioned above. Thus, a third set of residuals is required for the aggregate price identities. These will be set to equal the last historical value in the forecast.

The new BEA methodology thus requires three new types of identities: real, nominal detail, and nominal aggregates. Each set has its own set of residuals, as well. In the WEFA model, the residuals are exogenous variables. It would also be possible to add the residuals as addfactors: the difference is merely one of housekeeping and has no impact on how the model works. We chose to use exogenous residuals to simplify the use of the model for our subscribers.

WEFA's approximation is not the only method of approximating the identities. In the tail (basically, that period over which the BEA lacks full current and past annual weights), BEA uses a fixed-weighted methodology. Forecasters interested in accurate forecasts over the very short-term (e.g., in current quarter models) may wish to use identities that incorporate the current fixed weights. These will presumably be more accurate for initial announcements of GDP. Each year, however, BEA will change the weights (by switching to the most recent available year). At that time, one past year's worth of data will be revised to use chain-weights.

Because of the change in methodology, no one approximation will be completely correct. Forecasters that use the fixed weights will sacrifice the long-run properties of the Fisher identities for short-run accuracy. Forecasters that use an approximation of chain-weighting may have somewhat lower short-run accuracy, but forecasts in the medium and long term will accurately reflect the impact of the new methodology, and provide users with a truer picture of the evolution of the economy over time.

We at WEFA have chosen to use the chain-weights for all forecasting for the following reasons:

1) The difference between the two measures is small over short horizons. The difference between fixed weights (where the weights are recent) and chain weights is small when the fixed weights are close to the forecast period. This, of course, will always be the case with the published data, since the fixed weights in the tail are from a recent period.

2) *Holding weights fixed at a given time will be extremely misleading for longrun horizons*. WEFA's longest forecast has a 25 year horizon. The difference between a chain-weighted and fixed-weighted forecast over this period would be very large, and create many problems of interpretation. Of course, a forecast based on fixed-weighted GDP over such a period would lose precisely the best features of the new methodology.
3) Mixed forecasting would be confusing to forecast and model users. A forecast that uses fixed weights in the short run and chain weights in the long run mixes data concepts in a confusing way. Suppose, for example, we want to compare forecasts from last year and this year for next year to see how the outlook has changed. If forecasts out one year use fixed-weights, and beyond one year chain weights, last year's forecast will have used a different weighting scheme than this year's. The forecasts will then be impossible to compare with any accuracy.

Using the chain-weighted approximations for short-term forecast leaves us violating an unwritten rule of forecasting. Our model now forecasts revised data, because the approximation is closer to the formulas BEA will use in its annual revision, when it applies the chain-weighted methodology, than the formulas it will use in the initial news releases. This is an unfortunate side effect of the new methodology. Users who wish to compare forecasts may need to be aware of such issues.

Appendix: The WEFA model in detail

The following describes some of the essential details of WEFA's Mark 11 quarterly model. This discussion is not exhaustive, and interested readers should contact WEFA for more information and complete documentation of our model.

1 Aggregate demand

The components of demand are modeled from the bottom up using standard approaches that employ various measures of permanent income/output and relative prices. This is the heart of the model, and is most important for short-run analysis. Each individual component of aggregate demand has its own stochastic equation for the real, 1992 chained dollar quantity, although equations in broad follow similar specifications. A separate price (deflator) equation is also estimated for each detailed component and used to create the nominal value for each detailed component. Components of aggregate demand are modeled as follows (see Table A1 for details.):

Consumption (25 detailed categories) is generally assumed to depend on permanent income and relative prices. Certain categories depend on sector-specific variables. Automobile purchases, for example, depend largely on unit sales of automobiles, which are modeled in a stock-flow framework in a separate section of the model.

Gross domestic investment (22 detailed categories) generally depends on the user cost of capital relative to overall prices. The investment equations also contain short-term accelerator terms, so that a rise in aggregate demand will initially call forth a rise in investment spending. If interest rates, and the user cost of capital, rises along with aggregate demand, investment spending will eventually be displaced, however.

Government purchases (9 detailed categories) are generally assumed to be exogenous, with the exception of pay variables. The government's wage bill depends on an employment assumption and a wage, which is strongly influenced by private wages. Otherwise both Federal and State and Local purchases are determined exogenously.

Exports (10 detailed categories) are estimated as functions of the relative price of home and foreign goods (including the exchange rate) and foreign GDP. The relationships are fairly aggregate: foreign prices are represented by a trade-weighted foreign PPI, and foreign demand by a trade-weighted foreign GDP.

Imports (11 detailed categories) mirror the export equations, with the exception that the relative price terms and demand terms can be more specific. Demand for imports of motor vehicles and parts is determined in the auto sector, for example, where unit light vehicle sales are divided into domestic and imported sales based on relative prices and income (the portion of imports tends to rise with higher income levels).

In addition, two sectors (housing and light vehicles) include detailed estimates unit sales and other variables of interest. Light vehicle sales, for example, are depend on the driving age population, per capita income, and (in the short-run) consumer confidence. Sales are divided between cars and light trucks depending on relative price and demographics, and total consumer expenditure on cars and on other motor vehicles then follows the unit purchases closely.

Table A1. Detailed Components of Aggregate Demand in WEFA Mark 11

Consumption Expenditure	
New Autos	Housing
Used Autos, Net	Household Operation, Electricity
Other Motor Vehicles	Household Operation, Gas
Tires, Acces, and Parts	Hous. Oper., Water & Sanitary Services
Furniture & Household Equip	Hous. Oper., Telephone & Telegraph
Other Durables	Household Operation, Domestic Service
Clothing and Shoes	Household Operation, Other
Off Premises Food Consumption	User Operated Transportation
Purchased Meals	Local Transportation
Other Food	Intercity Transportation
Gasoline and Oil	Medical Care Services
Fuel Oil and Coal	Other Services
Other Nondurables	
Gross Domestic Investment	
Residential Invest., Single Family Str.	Nonresidential Structures, Other
Residential Inves.t, Mult-Family Str.	Producers' Durable Equip., Industrial
Residential Investment, Other Str.	Prod.' Dur. Eq., Information Processing
Residential Investment, Equipment	Prod. Dur. Equipment, Transp.
Nonresid. Str., Commercial Buildings	Producers' Dur. Equipment, Other
Nonresid. Str., Industrial Buildings	Inventories, Farm
Nonresidential Structures, Farm B.	Inventories, Manufacturing
Nonresidential Structures, Other B.	Inventories, Auto Dealers
Nonresidential Structures, Utilities	Inventories, Other Nonmanufacturing
Nonresid. Str., Mining and Petroleum	
Exports	
Foods, Feeds, and Beverages	Motor Vehicles and Parts
Industrial Supplies and Materials	Consumer Goods, Less Motor Vehicles and Parts
Computer Equipment	Other Goods
Civilian Aircraft	Services
Other Capital Goods	
Imports	
Foods, Feeds, and Beverages	Other Capital Goods
Oil and Petroleum Products	Motor Vehicles and Parts
Other Ind. Supplies and Materials	Cons. Goods, Less Motor V. and Parts
Computer Equipment	Other Goods
Civilian Aircraft	Services

(*Continued*)

Table A1. (*Continued*)

Government Purchases	
Federal Def. Consumption, Nonpay*	Federal Nondefense Investment*
Federal Defense Consumption, Pay	State and Local Consumption, Nonpay
Federal Defense Investment*	State and Local Consumption, Pay
Federal Nondef. Consumpt. Nonpay*	State and Local Investment
Federal Nondefense Consumpt. Pay	

*Intermediate categories (consumption of durable goods, e.g.) not shown in table. Stochastic equations exist for all except when indicated by $*$, which are exogenous.

2 The monetary sector and interest rates

Mark 11 uses two key interest rates to forecast financial conditions. The Fed funds rate is the main proxy for short-term interest rates, and mainly reflects Federal Reserve monetary policy. Long-term interest rates follow the 30-year bond rate, which is determined by economic conditions, the size of the Federal debt, and short-term rates. The model determines interest rate spreads for most intermediate Treasury rates and yields (eight), eight additional private short-term interest rates, and six private long-term bond yields using the two key rates and other economic variables. The wide variety of interest rates primarily help users who wish to examine the risk implications of a macro shock for various types of securities.

Monetary policy and short-term interest rates are determined together. The key equations are the reserves equation, which summarizes Federal reserve behavior, and the Fed funds rate, which is an inverted money demand function. The Fed sets reserve growth depending on present and past inflation and capacity utilization. Higher inflation or capacity utilization will reduce reserve growth; lower inflation or capacity utilization will raise reserve growth. The level of demand deposits follows the level of reserves closely, and is the main determinant of the crucial monetary aggregate in the model, M1. The Fed Funds rate equation is an inverted money demand function of the standard form shown in Eq. A1.

$$m - p = \phi y - \lambda r, \tag{A1}$$

where m is the nominal stock of money, p is the price level, y is the level of real output, and r is an inflation-adjusted interest rate. All variables are in logs, so ϕ is the income elasticity of money, and λ is the interest elasticity of money. The income elasticity of money in the model equals 0.57, with an income elasticity close to one.

3 Prices and aggregate supply

Prices adjust in the medium term when aggregate demand is not equal to aggregate supply. The price adjustment serves to force aggregate demand toward aggregate supply over the five- to ten-year horizon. The model's price response works through two equations which allow for cost-pushwage inflation as well as the effect of capacity constraints and bottlenecks. The result is an expectations adjusted Phillips curve in which workers attempt to maintain real wages, but which allows for traditional Keynesian demand-pull inflation as well. Inflationary shocks can become embedded in the model through the wage process, unless aggregate demand falls sufficiently to create slack labor markets. Labor market conditions, energy prices, and capacity utilization then determine final demand deflators through a mark-up equation.

Inflationary expectations are measured by the Philadelphia Fed's Survey of Professional Forecasters. Expected inflation appears in both the labor side of the economy: in the expectations-augmented Phillips curve, and in the capital side of the economy: in the user cost of capital (as well as in the formation of long-term interest rates). As a result, an inflationary shock can build a permanently higher level of inflationary expectations, labor cost growth, and a permanently higher level of long-term interest rates, even when unemployment returns to the exogenous "natural rate". The model therefore encapsulates the view that the Phillips curve is only operational in the short run, consistent with rational expectations research.

4 Aggregate supply

Potential GDP, the main proxy for aggregate supply, is determined through a Cobb–Douglas production function, based on WEFA estimates of the non-accelerating inflation rate of unemployment (NAIRU) and official capital stock data. WEFA assumes that labor supply is exogenous to the model, not because we believe this to be the case, but because there is no firm guide or consensus on the feedback effects from the economy to the labor force. We therefore prefer to make explicit assumptions about labor force changes in forecasting and scenario building.

References

[1] Duggal, V., L. Klein, and M. McCarthy (1974). The Wharton Model Mark III: A modern IS-LM construct, *International Economic Review* **15**(3), pp. 572–594.

[2] Duggal, V., L. Klein, and M. McCarthy (1995). *Economic Statistics, NABE News*, No. 114, pp. 24–45.

[3] Landefeld, J. S. and R. Parker (1995). Preview of the comprehensive revision of the national income and product accounts: BEA's new featured measures of output and prices, *Survey of Current Business* **75**(7), pp. 31–38.

[4] Pakko, M. R. (1997). The business cycle and chain-weighted GDP: Has our perspective changed? *Federal Reserve Bank of St. Louis Review* **79**(5), pp. 39–49.

[5] Young, A. (1992). Alternative measures of change in real output and prices, *Survey of Current Business* **72**(4), pp. 32–41.

Author Index

N

P

R

S

T

W

Y

Subject Index